THE OTHER SIDE OF FEAR

WHAT OTHERS ARE SAYING ABOUT *THE OTHER SIDE OF FEAR*

"I remember the first time I read a chapter from this book, I thought two things: One, this is brilliant and beautiful; two, Brock Heasley is an important storyteller I want to work with."

—Dallas Jenkins, creator, *The Chosen*

"Told with wit and humor, this is an emotional, raw story about how tragedy can shape you and faith can lead you through."

—Kasie West, author, *The Distance Between Us*

"While most of us can't relate to a Hollywood worthy personal history, Heasley approaches retelling his and his father's story with an honesty that surfaced some vivid memories from my own teenage life. During our family dinner yesterday, in response to their mother's inquiry about what our family's mission should be, our teenage daughter responded, 'to have empathy.' She doesn't know it yet, but, for her father, this memoir helped answer my daughter's wish in a way that neither she nor I could have imagined. I remember (and I didn't know I had forgotten) what youth was like."

—Neal Harmon, CEO, VidAngel

THE OTHER SIDE OF FEAR

a true story of murder, forgiveness, and the peace only faith can bring

BROCK HEASLEY

PLAIN SIGHT PUBLISHING
AN IMPRINT OF CEDAR FORT, INC.
SPRINGVILLE, UTAH

ISBN 13: 978-1-4621-3851-7

Published by Plain Sight Publishing, an imprint of Cedar Fort, Inc.
2373 W. 700 S., Springville, UT, 84663
Distributed by Cedar Fort, Inc., www.cedarfort.com

LIBRARY OF CONGRESS CONTROL NUMBER: 2020945596

Cover design by Wes Wheeler

Printed in the United States of America

10 9 8 7 6 5 4 3 2 1

Printed on acid-free paper

For Dad, who is remembered.

CONTENTS

PROLOGUE

To avoid the news cameras out front, my family was ushered down the long hallway and out through the back of the church. For a while, we stood silently at the edge of the parking lot, huddled close together less for warmth than for comfort. Mom, in her best black skirt and bright red top, looked down and dried her tears. She smiled faintly and appeared almost relieved. This day had been coming for a long time.

Grandma, a proud and forever smoker, could barely breathe. She leaned on Grandpa for support, her bad knees knocking together high above her heels. There was a bitterness to her mourning that choked out sentiment, leaving nothing but the sharp anger she displayed on her face. She muttered the same refrain she'd been repeating over and over again since Saturday night: "Parents shouldn't have to bury their children." No one disagreed with her.

It was one of those oddly cold, bright days where if you weren't standing directly in the path of the white and warming sun, you'd freeze. I wrapped one arm tightly around Mom and the other around two of my younger brothers, who stuck close to me. My third brother, also younger, stood as an island unto himself, shivering slightly, arms draped at his sides with as much stillness as he could manage.

The hearse pulled up. We moved to the nearby trees along the sidewalk surrounding the church to allow room for the casket to be rolled out, watching as the long, ornate box and the body inside it were loaded in carefully by the strangers from the funeral home. They were so solemn and so precise in the way they went about it, but it seemed a performance. Routine and impersonal in its efficiency. They weren't thinking about Dad's legendary ghost stories or his belly laugh at the Peeping Tom scene in *Back to the Future* or the loud pop he could make pulling his finger out of his mouth. They didn't know him at all. Were they thinking about the game later that night? Hatching dinner plans? Digesting the day's political news? How dare they.

The back door to the hearse lowered and clicked into place. The signal given, we all piled into cars to start the long journey to the cemetery way beyond the edge of town. The news cameras followed but only until we were out of sight. Mom, in the front seat, wiped her tears. She turned around to tell me how much the talk I gave during the funeral meant to her, and how impressed she and everyone else had been with the power of my delivery and composure on the stand. Embarrassed and flattered, I thanked my dedicated, proud, and delusional mother. She dismissed my modesty as false and said the talk reminded her of a moment she'd had with Dad just a week earlier.

They were sitting together on the couch in the living room, talking. It was one of those conversations that meandered from the inane to the consequential, a web of familiar concerns and topics. Dad, who was not sick, spoke, as he often did, of his impending death and how much he looked forward to the afterlife. It would be wonderful. Glorious. So much to learn and to see.

Mom hit her absolute limit. After years of Dad's supposed premonitions and irritating fatalism, she'd had enough and finally asked him the one question she had wanted to ask for years but had never before dared:

"Bill, do you *want* to die?"

Dad fell silent. He took a moment to consider his words carefully. Mom could see by the look on his face he was desperately trying to craft the correct answer to her very direct question. He didn't want to hurt her. Finally, he gave his measured response.

"If it weren't for you . . . and the boys . . . yes, I'm ready to go now."

I

THE FATHER

1

THE SHOOTING

The guns fed us. No one, after all, makes a living retailing junk food. Not one good enough to support a wife and four sons, anyway. The bullets and the barrels sold right alongside the soda bottles and the Slim Jims put food on the table and gave us a home. Us, and Dad's employees—both of whom had gone home early that night from the dirty little store on the outskirts of Fresno, California.

Once home, Dad could look forward to adding receipts and counting money long into the night. It might take even longer if his sons bristled again at helping or, even better, tempted him into a rubber band war. Closing time, especially by himself, was a chore, but it didn't require him to be a husband or a handyman or a father or a disciplinarian. All he had to do between the flipping of the "closed" sign and the pulling of the car into his driveway—which probably needed to be cleared of bikes and toys—was to perform the routine: Close out the register. Lock the freezer. Put away the inventory. Shut off the lights and secure the door with the deadbolt and lock on the way out.

It took Dad a good fifteen minutes to pack up the dozens of guns by himself. During business hours, they rested in two display cases doubling as the store's front counters; Now and Laters and trucker hats made a pit stop on top of the .45s and Thirty Ought Sixes on their way out the door. Dangling yellow tags attached to the guns on tiny white strings shouted the sale price from behind the clean, always clear glass.

At around 5:30 PM, Dad removed the guns quickly, one by one, and placed them with great care into two long, black clamshell cases for storage during the night. Without markers or leftover impressions on the foam pads lining the inside, he still knew the precise placement of each handgun and rifle inside their carriages. Once packed, he'd transport them into the iron safe in the storage room just behind the freezers.

Dad performed this routine night after night with little incident—with the exception of that night. On that night, he never made it to the safe.

Neither did the guns.

The two masked men kicked in the front door with a shout. "YOU'RE DEAD, SUCKER!"

Their semi-automatics lit up only fifteen feet away from the fat man behind the counter, ejecting bullet after bullet directly at him. The first sailed toward Dad's chest. It missed. The next rocketed into his stomach, forcing him to double over from the impact. But not from the pain. That hadn't registered yet.

Dad made a grab for his own gun stuck between the waistband of his pants and his hip. He got the weapon up and out but didn't have enough time to do anything productive with it as more bullets tore with great speed through his muscle and flesh, his body jerking with the impact of each one as it burst into him. His gun fell to the floor as he did, with a thud behind the display cases still filled with all the firearms he hadn't had a chance to pack up yet.

The see-through glass fronts of the cases exploded into twinkling shards as the two men fired into them. Quickly, one of them collected the store's most valuable merchandise into a bag while the other shooter fired even more bullets, this time at point-blank range, up and down my father's body as he lay on the floor. Satisfied the store's owner could not survive such a barrage, the men then worked together to gather up the rest of the spoils. When they were done, the only thing left on the carpeted shelves lining the now-broken cases was the broken glass.

With his pants and shirt already soaked red, Dad had just enough of his wits remaining to grab his gun off the floor to fight back. On his back and without much mobility, his mind ignored the quickly rising swells of enormous torment in his lower body while his hand searched, doing its best to find his metal piece before the shooters saw what he was doing. Frantic and fading, he grabbed one of the display guns that had fallen to the floor. The yellow tag dangled.

Click.

Display guns are never loaded.

The shooters gave Dad's body one last sweep of bullets. He jerked up and down on the hard, uncaring floor of the store, blood exiting from fresh wounds on his legs to make room for hot new guests. Some of those guests exited just as quickly as they entered, leaving behind two holes of searing pain in their wake. Others dug into Dad's flesh and took residence.

Finally, the shooting stopped. Dad went still.

The two masked men, bags full of black, shiny treasures, turned around and left in a hurry, slamming the door behind them.

2

THE CALL

Bill's Bait & Tackle was the last stop going west off the highway. It was a tiny little shop on a dusty piece of land so far outside the city limits I was never sure if it was still even *in* Fresno. As he lay barely breathing and bleeding out on the floor, Dad was truly alone. It was early evening. The only other business for miles, the bar next door, hadn't even opened up for the night yet. He shouted for help anyway.

No response.

He shouted again.

Nothing.

He could either lay there and die or try to beat the clock and call 911.

The phone may as well have been across the street. It had made sense to mount it high on the wall near eye level for taking calls and servicing customers simultaneously, but bullet-ridden legs had shifted priorities downward. There was no way to tell the full extent of the damage, but with the pain settling in and grinding against his will, Dad knew the movement upwards was going to be a punishing chore, if not impossible. The newly crimson floor beneath him argued against giving too much air to such impossibilities.

Relying mostly on his undamaged arms, Dad propped himself up from the floor to a stool to lean against the wall on which hung the phone. He grabbed the phone, dialed what he thought was 911 on the keypad at the base, and, somehow, laid himself back down on the floor with the corded receiver in hand.

411 OPERATOR: Information, what city, please?
DAD: I've been shot. My n-name is Bill Heasley, I'm at—
411 OPERATOR: Sir? I'm sorry, sir, this is information, not emergency services.
DAD: This . . . ungh . . . this isn't 911?
411 OPERATOR: No, sir.
DAD: Can you, unnh . . . connect me to 911?
411 OPERATOR: I'm sorry sir, I can't do that. I am not able to do that from my station. Now, is there something else I can help you with? Is there another number you're looking for?
DAD: You can't connect me? I've been shot.
411 OPERATOR: Sir, I have no way to do that from my station. You're going to have to hang up and try calling 911 again.
DAD: Please, ungh . . .
411 OPERATOR: Sir.
DAD: Do you—could you go somewhere where you can make a call for me?
411 OPERATOR: Sir, I'm sorry, sir, but we're not allowed to leave our stations. I could get into trouble with my supervisor. You're going to need to redial.
DAD: Please . . .

With a concerning degree of added agony, Dad got back up off the floor to go to the stool to lean on the wall to hang up the phone on the 411 employee of the month. He picked the receiver up—again—and punched the numbers on the keypad one more time, being sure to now do it with accuracy. Finally, as the phone rang the correct number, he carefully laid himself back down onto the floor.

911 OPERATOR: 911, what is the emergency?
DAD: I've been shot. This is Bill's Bait & Tackle. My name is Bill Heasley. I'm at 40—
911 OPERATOR: Okay, sir, wait, wait, wait. Shh shh shh. I know where you are, sir. Now, you've been shot by a robber or what?
DAD: Multiple times. Five or six times.

911 OPERATOR: Okay. Now, Bill, where were you hit?
DAD: In the lower . . . in . . . in the stomach and in the legs. Quickly.
911 OPERATOR: Okay, sir. We are going to get the ambulance and paramedics out there. We are sending them out there as I am talking to you. I need to know if you know of the suspects.
DAD: No, they wore masks. Hurry.
911 OPERATOR: Okay, how many of them were there?
DAD: Oh, I don't know. Two, I think.
911 OPERATOR: Are you the only one that's there, Bill?
DAD: Yes.
911 OPERATOR: Okay. Now, we're gonna get officers there right away. Okay? Okay, now you rest. Is there anybody there with you?
DAD: No.
911 OPERATOR: Okay, Bill, now how are you feeling?
DAD: Bad. Wintery.
911 OPERATOR: O-okay. Now, we-we've got paramedics on the way also. Is there anybody you can get to be with you before we get there?
DAD: No, I'm all alone.
911 OPERATOR: Okay, Bill, we're gonna get right there, okay? Go ahead and just set the phone down. Set the phone down, please.
DAD: [Heavy breathing.]
911 OPERATOR: Now, I'm gonna sit on the phone with you. You don't have to talk if you don't feel like it, okay?
DAD: [Heavy breathing.]
911 OPERATOR: Just try to take it real easy, okay?
DAD: I'm not gonna make it.
911 OPERATOR: Yes, you are, sir. You are going to make it.
DAD: [Grunting.] I've been shot about six times.
911 OPERATOR: Okay.
DAD: One badly. I think my kidney's bleedin'.
911 OPERATOR: Okay. Now, do you have anything around you? Do you have a blanket or coat you could stick on you?

DAD: No.
911 OPERATOR: Okay.
DAD: Oh . . . [Heavy breathing.] In my stomach. It went clean through, I think.
911 OPERATOR: Okay, now that's a good sign. That's a good sign.
DAD: [Heavy sigh.]
911 OPERATOR: Now I'm just gonna transfer you to the paramedics as I'm talking to you, so hang on the line with me, sir.

Another phone rang on the line, and another woman picked up the call. The 911 operator and the woman shared a brief bit of confusion as at first neither one was sure the other one could hear them. Dad fell silent.

911 OPERATOR: This is the FSO. I've got a man who's been shot. He's been shot in his stomach and in several other places. I want you to talk to him.
EMERGENCY SERVICE: Okay. Sir? . . . Sir?
911 OPERATOR: Bill?
EMERGENCY SERVICE: Bill?
DAD: Yes.
EMERGENCY SERVICE: Okay. I want you to stay on the line with me, okay? Okay, what I'm gonna do is switch you over to EMS, but I'm gonna stay on the line with you, okay?

There was a click and then static as the line switched again, this time to a man in a room with a lot of activity full of whirring machinery.

PARAMEDIC DISPATCH: EMS Dispatch.
EMERGENCY SERVICE: Go ahead, sir.
DAD: Yeah?
Emergency Service: Bill, talk to him.
PARAMEDIC DISPATCH: Okay, sir, you're at Forty Twelve West Whitesbridge?
EMERGENCY SERVICE: Yeah, he's the shooting victim. I'm sending medical right now.

PARAMEDIC DISPATCH: Okay, all right. And this is Bill's Bait & Tackle?

DAD: I'm on—

EMERGENCY SERVICE: Yes. That's him. You need to talk to him.

DAD: I can't hardly talk.

PARAMEDIC DISPATCH: Sir? Sir, what is your name?

DAD: Bill Heasley.

PARAMEDIC DISPATCH: Okay, Bill. You're from Bill's Bait & Tackle?

DAD: Yes.

PARAMEDIC DISPATCH: You're the one—where is your gunshot wound at?

DAD: In the . . . in the stomach.

PARAMEDIC DISPATCH: In the stomach?

DAD: Lower right side. About five or six times in the legs.

PARAMEDIC DISPATCH: Okay, are you laying down right now?

DAD: Yeah.

PARAMEDIC DISPATCH: Is anybody there with you?

DAD: Nobody came in. I called for help.

PARAMEDIC DISPATCH: Okay, that's right. You need to—you need to lay down. Lay down and you need to calm down. We've got ambulances that are just a few minutes out, all right? So you're shot in the abdomen, in the stomach area?

DAD: Yeah, and a bunch of times in the legs.

PARAMEDIC DISPATCH: Okay. How many shots are—do you have?

DAD: Probably six times, I don't know.

PARAMEDIC DISPATCH: I just want you to rest, try to slow your breathing down. I'll stay on the phone with you, all right?

PARAMEDIC DISPATCH: You have to hurry.

PARAMEDIC DISPATCH: Okay, we're on our way. Are you laying down?

DAD: Yes.

PARAMEDIC DISPATCH: Okay, flat on your back.
DAD: No, on the side.
PARAMEDIC DISPATCH: I want you to lay flat on your back.
DAD: Oh . . . unh . . . .
PARAMEDIC DISPATCH: It'll help with the—
DAD: Unh . . .
PARAMEDIC DISPATCH: —the blood, okay?
DAD: Aah . . . You've gotta hurry, mister.
PARAMEDIC DISPATCH: Okay, put your legs up. Put your legs up in the air.
DAD: Unh . . .
PARAMEDIC DISPATCH: Put something under your legs.
DAD: Aah . . . the left leg I can hardly move, that's the one that's shot.
PARAMEDIC DISPATCH: Okay, put something under your legs.
DAD: I can't.
PARAMEDIC DISPATCH: Okay. We're on our way so—
DAD: It's hard for me to breathe on my back.
PARAMEDIC DISPATCH: Okay, then, get comfortable on your side.
DAD: Okay.
PARAMEDIC DISPATCH: Okay, no one's there, right? That guy left, with the gun? Did the guy leave with the gun?
DAD: There was a couple . . .
PARAMEDIC DISPATCH: Okay, they're gone, right?
DAD: Yeah.
PARAMEDIC DISPATCH (to someone else in the room): They're gone. The scene's secure. I'm talkin' to the guy on the phone. [Back to Dad]: All right, they're right outside your door. They're coming in. All right, sir?
DAD: What?
PARAMEDIC DISPATCH: They're right outside the door. They're on their way in.

DAD: Who is?
PARAMEDIC DISPATCH: The paramedics.
DAD: [Heavy sigh.] Aah, man. My legs hurt. [Long heavy breathing.] I'm starting to feel cold.
PARAMEDIC DISPATCH: Okay.
DAD: [Long, heavy breathing.]
PARAMEDIC DISPATCH(to someone else in the room): I am talking to the gentleman on the phone. The scene is secure. Call North Central and tell them to stick it up their butt. [Back to Dad]: Sir, they're right outside the door. They're coming in, all right?
DAD: [Heavy breathing.]
PARAMEDIC DISPATCH: Bill, can you hear me?
DAD: Yeah, I can hear you.

Dad's breathing continued to get louder and heavier, almost overwhelming what the tiny speakers on his phone could handle.

PARAMEDIC DISPATCH: Slow your breathing down a little bit.
DAD: I can't.

The heavy breathing got faster.

DAD: Listen . . .
PARAMEDIC DISPATCH: Yes?
DAD: My home phone is 226-7036.
PARAMEDIC DISPATCH: Okay, they'll get hold of—the sheriff's office will get hold of them right away, cuz they're right outside too.
DAD: Okay, listen to me.
PARAMEDIC DISPATCH: Okay.
DAD: I don't know if I'm gonna make it.
PARAMEDIC DISPATCH: Yes, you will.
DAD: Okay, okay, okay—
PARAMEDIC DISPATCH: Go ahead.
Dad: Okay.
PARAMEDIC DISPATCH: All right.

DAD: Tell my wife that I love her.
PARAMEDIC DISPATCH: 226?
DAD: Yes. 7036.
PARAMEDIC DISPATCH: Okay.
DAD: Tell my . . . my boys I love them too.
PARAMEDIC DISPATCH: All right.
DAD: [Heavy breathing.] And that . . . to be good.
PARAMEDIC DISPATCH: Okay.
DAD: [Heavy breathing.] Oh . . .
PARAMEDIC DISPATCH: Okay, Bill, just take it easy. Keep your breathing down a little bit.
DAD: [Heavy breathing.]
PARAMEDIC DISPATCH: Okay, we're—they're right outside your door. They should be comin'. I'll stay on the phone with you, okay?
DAD: Also . . . call my wife.
PARAMEDIC DISPATCH: Uh huh?
DAD: Tell her to get the El—

The line went dead.

With the pain getting worse, there was no way for Dad to get back up and call again. The message had been delivered and help would be there any minute now. They were right outside, after all. Dad's only job was to not pass out from the blood loss and the shock before they entered. Any fall into the dark would almost certainly be fatal.

A big soda drinker, Dad always kept one of the flat boxes they came in on the floor underneath the phone to toss the empty cans into for recycling later. To keep his mind off the increasing pain and to keep himself awake, he grabbed the cans and crushed them in his hands, letting the cold metal dig into his palm to cause sensation somewhere—*anywhere*—else on his body. He had gone through a fair amount of the cans by the time a police officer finally came through the door, gun drawn.

After making sure the shooters had indeed taken off and that Dad was in fact still alive, the cop waved the paramedics over and they entered the building. With Dad barely breathing, their job was to get him in good enough shape to make the trip to the hospital.

They started by cutting off his clothes to access the wounds. Dad's pants and shirt were shredded, along with his undergarments. To the more dramatic wounds they applied a staple gun to close them up fast. The rest they bandaged. Anything to stop the blood from running out.

In a matter of minutes, Dad was on the stretcher and into the ambulance. Certain of his fate that night, he had only one thing on his mind as they made the fifteen-minute trip to Valley Medical Center. He pleaded with one of the paramedics to call my mom and tell her he loved her. "Please," he gasped. He said it over and over and over again, like a mantra: "Tell my wife I love her. Please, tell her. Tell my wife I love her." He felt like he was already dead, but she had to know.

Finally, the paramedic agreed.

Dad knew all the efforts to save him were pointless. They were welcome to try, but it wasn't going to happen. Not with the amount of blood he'd lost and at his age. Not on that night. And, with the message safely delivered, he was okay with that. He calmed down and stayed that way, willing to let what needed to happen, happen.

3

BULLETS

Mom read a magazine at the dining room table and counted the minutes that had passed since the time he should have been home. It was dark outside, and that meant he was half an hour late. The later it got, the more alone and more nervous she felt. In the living room, their four boys danced.

We twirled, stomped, and leapt off the couch, crashing to the living room floor and popping back up again to do pirouettes until we toppled over and slapped the floor like clumsy sea lions against the shore. Little obedience was offered to the beat of the bubblegum pop music blasting out from the stereo; we much preferred our anti-rhythmic lurching to whatever the thumping bass told us to do.

It was my duty to lead my brothers in all things masculine when Dad wasn't around, but I wasn't great at it. I couldn't figure it out. Nothing I understood about being a man appealed to me. Sports weren't my thing, and my humor was more of the triple-syllable words variety than the fart brand. Wrestling? Stupid. Wrestling on television? Stupider. I aspired to something higher, such as not knocking over the lamp on the coffee table as I flew through the air.

The ringing telephone could hardly be heard over all the noise. Because Mom cherished her time to watch us frolic about the house, a call from anyone other than Dad would not be tolerated. She wanted daughters desperately but never got any. When she finally did hear the phone, she picked it up with both hope and irritation.

In between jumping over my younger brothers and putting dents in the walls, I caught half glimpses of Mom in the chair just below the phone mount in the kitchen. The cord had been tangled so badly from overuse and children underfoot it couldn't stretch far enough away from the wall to allow her to sit back down comfortably at the table. She spoke in that sing-song voice she reserved only for the phone, but there was an edge to her tone that served as a clear signal to whoever was on the other end that their conversation would be short. Judging by how annoyed she looked, it wasn't Dad.

MOM: Hello?
WOMAN: Hi. Is this Jill Heasley?
MOM: Yes. Who is this?
WOMAN: I'm . . . a paramedic. I just brought your husband, Bill, to the emergency room at Valley Medical Center.
MOM: Did he have a car accident?
WOMAN: Oh no, no. Not a car accident.
MOM: W-was he shot?
WOMAN: Bill wants me to tell you that he loves you and to tell the kids that he loves them too. I have to go now. I'm sorry.
MOM: Wait—wait a minute. Could you please just tell me what happened?
WOMAN: No, I'm sorry. I can't. I just needed to tell you that Bill loves you. And the kids. And that they should be good.
MOM: O-oh. All right. Uh . . . thank you.

The stereo blared. By the time Mom hung up the phone the edge in her voice was gone. I wandered over to see what was going on. The concern that washed over her face changed the temperature in the room.

* * *

My family's life navigated and revolved around firearms. Guns, and lots of them. Black, shiny, sculpted metal death that when held feels oh so good, like shaking a thick, cold hand that doesn't crush your fingers but instead gives them security and comfort, paradoxically creating a very different kind of warmth. Three of my tiny fingers could wrap perfectly around the hilt, with the thumb going around the back and the index finger sliding forward to its place hovering just over the trigger. Even just giving an empty gun a light squeeze and pretending at the power that could come from such little effort had an accompanying intoxication. They haven't invented a joystick yet that lets you feel that kind of control.

A lot of my friends had never seen a gun, much less touched one. An undercover cop lived in our neighborhood. He was my friend's dad and he had a gun. But my dad had *guns.* They were cool, powerful, and you could kill people with them.

Or yourself.

One Halloween night Dad came home late. My brothers and I dealt with the stress of the elongated anticipation as best we could by putting on and patching up our homemade cardboard robot costumes while keeping at least one of our eyes on the driveway. At any minute, Dad would pull up with the candy. We never had to worry about whether or not we would be handing out the good stuff. Dad owned his own mini-mart/gun store—we called it The Shop. He guaranteed our unadorned, otherwise unremarkable neighborhood door was the most popular one on the block each and every year.

Nothing else mattered on Halloween but the candy and how much of it my brothers and I could collectively obtain. Mom and Dad always inspected the haul first, tossing out any pieces that were obviously housing needles and, therefore, the HIV virus. Then we were given a choice.

"Okay, boys," Dad would say by way of ritual. "You can go ahead and eat all that candy if you want. You dressed up and you earned it and your mother and I won't stop you. Or, if you'd like, you could sell it to me."

The value of candy was never undersold in my father's house, if not my mother's. He loved it as much as we did. Each November, a big, brown paper bag full of our sold off wares was a prominent fixture on top of the refrigerator. That way, Dad could retrieve his purchases at any moment of the day for his own personal consumption. At least, that was the idea. More often than not, as we'd sit together entranced by *Star Trek: The Next Generation* or watching (enduring, in my case) the game on TV, a piece of the candy would come flying and smack my brothers and me in the backs of our heads. After scrambling frantically to scoop it up from wherever it had bounced to, we would quickly shout back an enthusiastic "Thanks, Dad!" and unwrap and munch and wait for the next one to come sailing through the air.

On that Halloween night, when I saw the familiar silver Toyota minivan pull into the driveway, I couldn't help myself. I burst out of the house and ran as fast as I could to see what sugary spoils Dad had brought. Sure, we'd have our own bags full of the stuff later that night, but a quick snack before heading out wasn't out of the question.

Two of my little brothers, Logan and McKay, were right behind me. From the front door of the house to the side door of the van, they stayed hot on my trail. Only the speed and distance afforded by my longer legs prevented them from pushing me into the van as I came to a dead stop and reached for the handle to slide the big door back. With thoughts of darkened streets, grotesque figures, and a heavy bag of processed sugar in my hand commanding me, I was oblivious to all else in the world.

"Brock!" Dad shouted. "Wait, son! Stop! DON'T OPEN THE—"

I threw open the door. I had barely a split-second to register one of Dad's .45s falling out and onto the ground. The L-shaped hunk of metal met the concrete right at the point of the handle.

BAM!

The shot rang out and for a brief moment all other sounds were sucked into it. My mother gasped, afraid of what might happen next. The barrel of the gun joined the handle on the concrete with a small, tinny rattle. I fell next, down and backwards.

A bullet-sized hole had formed in the roof of the van. A hair dryer that had been inexplicably left on the floor under the backseat had been shot clean through. Miraculously, I was completely unharmed. My brothers standing right behind me stared in amazement. Everyone was fine. We were all rushed inside quickly.

"Son, you need to listen!" Dad said after making sure the door to the house was closed. "When I tell you to not open the door—YOU DON'T OPEN THE DOOR. If that gun had landed pointed any other way . . . "

"Sorry! I'm sorry, Dad! I'm sorry!"

I shook hard with fear and regret. *If that gun had landed pointed any other way . . .*

My parents threw away the hair dryer and made us all promise never to speak of the incident again. We were all lucky—so very *lucky*—that it was just before sundown and no one with fast fingers and Child Protective Services on speed-dial had been outside to notice what happened.

Thankfully (for me anyway), I wasn't the one in trouble. Mom really let Dad have it. Guns were the friends of my father she disapproved of but had to let in the door anyway. So long as they stayed away from the children, she could begrudgingly accept them as the foundation for whatever meager fortune we had. Now, Dad was pushing right up against the upper limits of her tolerance.

"I can't—I'm trying to imagine why you had a loaded gun in the van in the first place, Bill! Why would you need it to be loaded?"

"It slid into the back as I was coming down the off ramp," Dad explained. "I didn't—I knew it was loaded but I didn't mean for Brock to—it's not going to happen again. The boys know to respect the weapon. This was my fault. It won't happen again, I promise you."

Dad's reassurances meant little. Now, there was a new rule—no loaded guns in the house or in the cars. It was a change Dad was reluctant to make. Despite whatever else could happen accidentally with a loaded gun around, he was quite certain that *not* having one would be far worse should someone decide our modest home housed things far more valuable than its orange-stucco'ed exterior otherwise suggested. He didn't need my mother to remind him of how dangerous guns were and how dangerous it was to sell them. That was precisely the reason he needed one.

The Shop, you see, was under constant threat of burglary. There were many mornings I would wake up to find Dad had left during the middle of the night because the silent alarm had gone off and someone was helping themselves to the inventory. Whether it happened at bedtime or at three in the morning, Dad had to go secure the store and scare away anyone who might still be there.

But nothing like that had ever happened while he was actually inside.

* * *

"Brock," Mom said as she searched for her keys. "Get your shoes on. We're going to the hospital."

4

M&M's

Mom, her eyes glassy like two freshly scrubbed crystal balls about to tell a truth I was pretty sure I did not want to hear, turned off the music in the living room. Tyler, my youngest brother, was two years old. He was the only one who didn't stop dancing.

"What?" I asked. "Mom, what's going on?"

"It's your father." She was far away, hatching and rejecting plans for what to do next with such speed I could practically see them fly by as her vacant stare darted back and forth. "Something's happened and he's—they've taken him to the hospital. I'm going to call my parents, and I want you to come with us. To the hospital. Your brothers . . . they'll stay here, but I want you with me."

"Is he all right?"

"I don't know."

"But something happened to him?"

"I don't know."

My grandparents lived just a few blocks away. Even so, the wait for them to arrive was excruciating. Within that space of time bred a million possibilities, some of them pretty terrible and most of them involving a gun. *Has to be a gun*, I thought. What else could it be?

Mom called a couple women from church to come over to be with my brothers. She only wanted me with her. Just me. There were times when being the oldest had its perks, and going to the hospital and drinking chocolate milk when something important was going down was one of them. I eagerly searched for my shoes.

My four-year-old brother, McKay, was a spoiled brat—an unfortunate and irritating affliction of personality brought on by a defect in his heart that sped it up into a dangerous double rhythm whenever he got too worked up. Crying would do it. So would swimming, oddly enough. If you took his teddy bear and he cried, you had to give it back and then buy him one that talked or sang or pooped its pants. Anything to make him happy or else he would have an attack. The upside? When McKay had to be rushed to the hospital, I usually went too and got to pick something out from the vending machines in the cafeteria. I always chose chocolate milk. It was the closest thing to candy Mom would allow us to have outside of Halloween. Cool, creamy *chocolate* milk in that little paper carton. Once again, it would be mine. As a bonus, and given the hour, I knew I might even get to stay up late that night. There really was a lot to get excited about.

As we drove downtown in my grandparents' car, I was so grateful telepaths existed strictly within the confines of *X-Men* comic books. A telepath would see through me right away. They'd see that while my father was potentially hurt, shot, suffering and/or dead (no, not dead), all I could think about was how to manipulate the situation into a sugar rush. Was there something wrong with me? Or was I just trying to make the best of a bad situation?

No way I'd be going to school in the morning. When I eventually did go back in a couple days or even a week (!) later, I'd say my dad had been shot. That was kind of cool. And if he was already dead or was going to die? Well, he wasn't—of course he wasn't—so I was free to do some guilt-free fantasizing about what it would be like if he did. I'd be that kid, that kid whose dad had died. I'd get to play with that for a while, and it could only work in my favor when it came time to choose teams for kickball.

It wasn't that whatever was going on with Dad didn't feel real. The whole situation actually felt inevitable, which is just about the best, most comforting version of real. He sold guns. That's a dangerous profession, and it was only sensible to think he might be hurt at some point. That was logical. My family didn't watch the nightly news and think, "Well, at least that horrible thing on screen is not happening to us." Instead, we thought, "Gee, I wonder *when* that will happen to us?" Dad taught us to accept that inevitable reality, to live our lives on the other side of fear.

He was tough like that. The other kids in the neighborhood felt like their dads could handle anything, but with my dad it was actually true.

My dad was built like a tank and could probably take one down if it dared mess with him. Yes, the bad things would happen, but he could never die from them.

It was January 17, 1989, three days before my twelfth birthday (a cool part of the eventual story I'd be able to tell). When we arrived at the hospital, Grandpa helped my still shaking mother out of the car. Both he and Grandma were good about always being there when we needed them, but also hanging back to allow my mother to do what she needed to do according to how she understood to do it. They gave counsel, not lectures or opinions that were not to be argued with.

We all followed Mom's lead to the emergency room. I'd never been to an adult ER before. I was expecting something noisier. Where were the people screaming about their severed fingers and the doctors rushing about wildly, arms flailing as they waved off the impossible-to-meet demands of put-upon nurses and bleeding patients? What about the gurney (that's what it's called, right?) with the dying man being rushed to an operating room while his frantic wife ran alongside him weeping until the nurses pulled her away? Where this picture of what the emergency room was supposed to look like came from, I didn't know, but the eerily quiet scene in front of me was the last thing I expected. It creeped me out.

The voices that could be heard were few and hushed, many of them interrupted by bass-heavy fits of coughing. The low-ceilinged room was full but not to capacity. Most of the frightened people huddled together in groups around campfires of germs and bacteria, seated in chairs that looked like something straight out of *Star Trek* (the original series) with their bowl-like shape and many bright, garish colors. No one had any loose appendages they were trying to support or a barely bandaged head bleeding down the side of their face. They all just looked really sick. Most of them were Hispanic. I knew we were on that side of town, but I wondered why that was.

Once through the emergency room, a nurse led us to a secondary waiting room for, I assumed, family members of victims of awesome crimes. Inside the softly lit room were a small couch and a few padded chairs. In the corner between them sat a tiny table with a lamp and a phone. (Maybe to order pizza?) My grandparents and I were ushered in, but a doctor took Mom away immediately. Whatever secret knowledge awaited her, the rest of us weren't allowed to hear it. Instead, we waited quietly.

In the silence, I thought more about chocolate milk, school, and telepaths. I couldn't wait for my friends to find out what was going on.

When Mom finally came back, she didn't have much to tell. She seemed calm, but it was the kind of calm people adopt to convince themselves that they're all right and that their home isn't really burning. That it's not cancer in those X-rays. That the car wasn't just hit by an oncoming truck.

That your husband wasn't just fatally wounded.

The blankness that returned to Mom's eyes was a sign that the calm was just a precursor for what would come next. She sat down next to me after closing the door behind her and began to speak, the tremor in her left hand slight but visible as she used it to lean on her chair.

"There was a robbery and . . . Bill has been shot. Many times. They've got him stabilized right now. He's in critical condition and th-they'll start working on him soon."

"How many times?" I asked.

"T-they don't know yet, Brock. It's too hard to tell. Some of his wounds are where the bullets came . . . went in . . . and some of them are where they went out."

"Can we see him?"

"Not right now." She turned to Grandpa and Grandma. "They let me see him for a little bit . . . I talked to him . . . but it's hard for him to say anything right now. They don't want anyone else to come back just yet. There's a chance we could see him later . . . when they're transporting him to surgery, but we'll have to wait and see."

Great! It was almost eight 'clock and in another hour I normally would have been going to bed. My brothers were probably already getting ready and putting on their PJs. Suckers.

"Jill," Grandpa began to ask. "What's . . . "

I found it impossible to focus properly on the conversation. Some confusing medical terms were thrown around, but I got the gist: Dad was in a bad way and the doctors were going to work on him, and it would be awhile before they knew when—or if—he'd survive. Probably not a question we could count on having answered that night.

"Dad," Mom said, "what about the boys? Can you call home and talk to Sister Vance and Sister Pennington for me? Tell them . . . "

I knew Mom was concerned about my brothers, but I also knew her well enough to see she was using them as a distraction from what was going on. She would busy herself as best she could until the doctors came back with some (definitely good) news. Until then: paranoia, worry. That was Mom. I knew Dad was going to be fine. We were in a hospital (at night!), the place that makes everything better. The only real question, the only one worth asking, was, when? When would Dad be okay? And that's when it hit me—what about my birthday party?

"Mom?"

She was still talking to Grandpa.

"Mom?"

"W-what? Brock, what?"

"Mom, do you think we'll still be able to go to the game?"

"What game?"

"The hockey game. For my birthday. Dad is gonna take us on Friday."

Some people think hockey is a sport. It is not a sport. It's a live stunt show. You can almost always guarantee there will be a fight either on the ice or (preferably) in the stands. The games themselves are barely contained madness. The players skate so quickly and turn so sharply and stop so suddenly that the very ground beneath their feet gives way into a quick puff of white. How did they do that? It defied all my understanding of what a person could reasonably do with their bodies without breaking them in half.

And then there was the snack bar. I knew it was a fountain drink and that (supposedly) the same ingredients used in the back rooms of the Selland Arena were also at my local 7-11, but it was only at hockey games that I got to taste the sweet, sweet nectar that was the best Sprite known to man. One sip after a bite of that other delicious staple of any hockey watchin' diet—nachos—and you'd have had a hard time convincing me that heaven didn't have its own ice rink. Nachos and Sprite—that's what was at stake.

"No, Brock," Mom said. "I don't think your father is going to feel up to that."

"Oh." I suspected that might be her answer and didn't try to hide my disappointment. I recovered quickly. "Can I call Matt and Nathan and Wes? To tell them what's going on? They think we're still going, but if we're not then I need to tell them. I could call them right now. I mean, there's a phone here and we're just waiting anyway."

"I don't know."

"Please? Mom, I'll make the calls short. I promise. I'll just tell them what's going on and then I'll get off the phone."

"All right," she said with a sigh. She was far too tired to battle with me that night. "Go ahead and call them."

I excitedly grabbed the receiver from the phone on the table. They were gonna freak. I called Matt first, calming myself down beforehand in order to act appropriately concerned. I didn't want to be thought cold or uncaring.

> **ME:** Hey, Matt, I've got some bad news.
> **MATT:** Okay, what's up, bud?
> **ME:** Um, we have to cancel my birthday party on Friday. My dad was shot and he's in the hospital now.
> **MATT:** You're kidding.
> **ME:** No, it's bad. It doesn't look like he's gonna be well enough to go to the game, if he comes out of it at all. We don't know for sure, but it's probably better to just cancel the party. Maybe we'll go next week.
> **MATT:** Wow. Uh. Uh . . . okay?
> **ME:** Yeah.
> **MATT:** . . .
> **Me:** I gotta call the others. See ya.
> **ME:** Um, see ya.

Matt's reaction was typical. By the time my calls were done I was quite pleased with myself. I knew that immediately after hanging up my friends would dash over to their parents to tell them what had happened and they, in turn, would dash back to the phone to tell everyone they knew. It was a safe bet that within the hour the hospital would be crawling with members of our church.

It was both the natural consequence and the function of belonging to a church that believes all of humanity is a rather large and very real family—so much so that Latter-Day Saints even refer to themselves as brothers and sisters. If one of their brothers or sisters is hurt, all possible services are offered, be it food or babysitting or a shoulder to lean on. It's the responsibility all members of the Church share.

Sure enough, within an hour, thirty people had shown up. It occurred to me that Mom knew what would happen if I made my calls and probably wanted exactly this.

They were all adults; none of my friends came to comfort me. Okay, it was late, but how often does your dad get shot and nearly die? (Nearly, mind you.) I was disappointed. I felt robbed. Mostly, I was bothered by all the hugging.

There was no way the little waiting room was going to hold us all. The hospital staff moved us away from Emergency and toward the elevator leading to surgery. Along the wall in the hallway was a long bench upon which my mother sat at one end and I at the other. Friends of my mother and mothers of my friends sat and stood by us, wherever they could fit.

A part of me liked the attention, but the greater part wasn't exactly sure how to behave. I felt small. Awkward. I didn't know what was expected of me, but I was sure I wasn't coming through. Everyone seemed to be in distress, and none of my reassurances helped. Worse, no matter how hard I tried, I just couldn't feel what they were feeling. Dad, after all, was gonna be okay. I knew he would be.

But what if they're right to be so concerned? What if I'm wrong?

I hadn't given that possibility enough attention. All these people were worried and seemed to think something might actually be not okay at the end of this. But they had to be wrong because I knew they were wrong. I knew it. And I wanted my chocolate milk.

There was one person who got it.

"Brock, I saw a vending machine down the hall over there. Is there something I can get for you?"

Brother Willingham was our home teacher. Once a month he visited my family, taught us a spiritual lesson, and made sure we were doing okay. If we were sick, Brother Willingham was the man Dad would call to come assist him in giving us a blessing. He was a large man with wide shoulders. He reminded me of Dad, just taller and in a suit.

That night, the thing that was of the greatest comfort to me was a pack of M&M's. It was better than chocolate milk. Plus—bonus—Dad was in no position to swindle it away from me.

I wondered why Brother Willingham bought those M&M's for me. He had spent his own money. He had sacrificed for *me*, the one who wasn't shot, the one who wasn't crying at the other end of the bench. Why buy me M&M's at a time when there was so much else to worry about?

This was no solution to Dad's problem or to Mom's worry, but it was a solution to *my* problem. I relaxed. I didn't have to put on a show for anybody. All I had to do was eat my M&M's and wait it out. I felt better knowing someone was on my side and not waiting for the full body shudders and the tears that would prove just how broken up I was by . . . my father . . . dying.

I looked over at Mom. Now, with people to lean on, she fell apart, collapsing into sobs as all her strength left her. Later, her mind would wipe away the memory of the entire night.

I watched her in wonder and agony. Seeing Mom that way twisted my insides into knots. How could I be so sure? How could I be so blindly confident that Dad wasn't in mortal danger when people far more educated and experienced than I had decided it was unknowable?

Because this was not the end of the world.

I assumed it would feel like the end of the world if Dad was going to actually die. All my hope and confidence in life continuing from one moment to the next was in my parents. If one of them were truly going to be taken from me, then there would be an indication. I was convinced God would not allow something of such significant impact without telling me about it first.

Mom's fear easily overwhelmed whatever other feelings might want to enter in. That's why I was there, wasn't it? Because she couldn't help but think of the horribleness of it all, and I couldn't help but think every other way.

I wondered how I might tell her and if she'd believe me. I knew I could convince anyone of anything given enough time and if I spoke persuasively enough. Sure, there was a lot I didn't understand about what was going on, but that didn't mean I was wrong. Would she see it that way? Or would she doubt me?

I moved over and sat beside her. She quickly wrapped her arms around me and buried her head in my shoulder. Softly and quietly, I told her.

"Mom, I think everything's going to be okay. Dad will be all right."

She held me tighter and cried some more.

5

EDUCATED GUESSES

A full-sized *Donkey Kong* video game cabinet sat near the front door. I spent every possible minute jumping barrels and rescuing damsels in distress, my Atomic Fire Ball cooling in a Dixie cup full of water next to the joystick (a low-rent chemistry experiment that made it easier for me to skip the "fire" and get right to the sugar). Meanwhile, just a few feet away, someone would ask Dad if he could see a handgun before purchasing a Coke and a pack of Marlboros.

I knew there wasn't much to it. The entirety of the Shop seemed quite a bit smaller than the three-bedroom house we lived in. It was definitely dustier. Winds from around countryside and farmlands kicked up the dirt surrounding it on the regular, pushing it all inside and casting a thin blanket of wispy grime on the cracked cement floor. A broom behind the counter justified its existence by shooing it all away on at least a quarterly basis. Deep, muddy puddles dressed the Shop on all sides after a rain, with the exception of the side it shared with the bar next door. The front faced out toward the highway, a flat slab of concrete its only accoutrement—if you could see it. The man-made parking surface was usually covered in oil and sludge.

The backrooms—secret places at every grocery store and mini-mart my father didn't own—didn't hide anything special. Just palettes of beer and soda. The walk-in freezer housing the fishing bait Dad distributed throughout the valley, as effective as it was as a refuge during the summer, reeked of worm and earth.

I was Bill's son, the little prince within the Shop that was his kingdom. The *Donkey Kong* games were always free of charge. So were the New York Seltzers (always the vanilla crème) that gave such sweet relief when the temperatures swelled and the swamp cooler wasn't cutting it. Drinks, frozen burritos of questionable nutritional value, and candy (whose nutritional value—or lack thereof—was never in question) were all there for the taking, as long as I asked King Dad first.

One particularly busy day, he bestowed upon me all necessary authority to run the place in his stead while he took a call in the back. For my part, I hated even going up to the attendant to hand him money while Dad pumped the gas outside. Something about dealing with adults in an official setting made me nervous. I didn't want to mess anything up. (It's money! Think of the consequences! [What consequences?] I don't know!) But I did it anyway, atop the stool brought out from the back so I could greet customers at eye level. This is how I ended up, at nine years old, selling my first and only alcohol.

The adults that came into the Shop that day put me at ease. They got a big kick out of my large, bowl-cut brown head peering out from behind the register and ringing up their purchases. Counting back change was beyond me, but no one seemed to mind. I soon eased into a routine and hit the sales tax button with confidence.

Once Dad was done with his call, he came back out to count the money.

"How did you do, son?"

"Good!" I said. "It was fun. I sold some candy bars and some of the shrimp cocktails. And some beer. I sold a lot of beer." I was so proud of myself. "Beer is expensive!"

"You sold beer?"

"Yep."

"Brock, you can't sell alcohol!"

"What? What do you mean? Yes, I did. I sold it."

"Brock, listen to me." Dad was a little panicky. He looked around. No one else was in the store at that point, but still . . . "You can never sell beer or alcohol! I know you didn't know, but I could get in a lot of trouble."

"What about Near Beer?"

Near Beer was Dad's favorite non-alcoholic beer. Even though he had given up drinking long before I was born, he still loved the taste. I tried it a few times and thought it must have been sense memory or something because the taste of feet wrapped in soggy bread seemed an odd thing to want to revisit. I figured the only attraction to beer in the first place must be the alcohol itself. Only a brain turned to mush could actually enjoy that grainy, obscene flavor. Dad decided it was okay for me to sell Near Beer, but never again did I sell the real stuff.

Dad's small wholesale bait distribution empire was run out of the narrow walking space that passed for the main backroom. I made my first million (in nine-year-old dollars) packaging worms at the tall wooden table with years of soil and sweat caked into it. I worked alongside my younger brother Logan (just two years younger) at the high chairs that barely reached the table, removing the worms from flat boxes of black, moist earth and packing them into white, cup-shaped Styrofoam cartons with the Bill's Bait & Tackle logo on them for use as live fish bait. The worm version of death row.

My brother and I did lots of odd jobs. The key to the Shop's presentation was an oft-used bottle of Windex and a roll of paper towels that were never more than arm's reach from the front register. The glass display cases were top priority. What gun unseen in its full splendor could then be sold?

Outside, Logan and I had room to run and play and shoot. We were a deadly two-man, BB-gun-firing squad. No toy army man was safe. Logan was a crack shot, while I saw to it the only true casualty of the war against our green plastic oppressors was the shade tree we lined them up against.

Easier prey were the minnows in the tanks at the back corner of the inside of the Shop. There to keep a particularly squirmy form of fishing bait fresh, the metal tanks were no aquarium. Deep and always green around the edges, they looked more like Cannery Row chum buckets than appropriate housing for live merchandise.

A small, long-handled net for collecting the fish rested nearby, and it was my pleasure and privilege to use it. After scooping the minnows up and bringing them out into the open air, they'd hop and flail in my trap, gasping for the water I denied them. I teased them with death like a bored, merciless god.

Sometimes a particularly slippery one would manage to hop his way out of the net and back into the tank before I had decided his suffering was over. To assert my authority, I'd pull it back out again. It was part of the game. No harm truly done. I always made certain each one made it back into the tank. There was another, later death awaiting them.

* * *

It was nearly eleven at night (!) when I finally saw Dad for the first time since the shooting. He was in mid-transit to the operating room, alive and somewhat responsive, but not in good shape. Six hours had passed since he had been shot, and it would be many hours more before the doctors were through with him.

As Mom and I sat together on the bench in the hallway, they rushed Dad out from between the double doors and prepared to load him into the elevator. The doctors motioned to us to come over and talk to him. I hesitated. What could I say? Whatever it was, everyone would hear it. I cared about that. What did they think I was supposed to say?

Mom went first, leaning in close to Dad's ear. I couldn't hear her. She stroked his face and tears fell. The doctors looked antsy. Was time of the essence? Were we holding them up from saving Dad's life? Maybe we should just step back and get out of the way.

Mom looked back at me, and I went over to Dad quickly. He was broken, painted orange, and ugly. Tubes ran out of him in all sorts of places where they should not. Wires dangled everywhere. He didn't move except to breathe and turn his head. He was my father, supposedly, but he looked so unfamiliar and weak I immediately felt uncomfortable. His appearance frightened me.

With my mother and everyone from church watching, I spoke quietly. No tears dotted my eyes.

"I love you, Dad."

His eyes, bloodshot and the skin around them puffy, rolled up toward me. A small smile crept over his face. He was just lucid enough to whisper back, "I love you, too, son."

And with that he was off to surgery.

As I watched him being loaded into the elevator I took a good long minute to consider the possibility I had just seen Dad for the last time. What would it be like to grow up without him? At almost twelve years old, I was the oldest of four boys. My mother held no outside job. She never had as far back as I could remember, and I was pretty sure money-making was not in her skill set. Who would take care of us? Someone else would have to take care of us; Mom wouldn't be able to handle it. If Dad died, what would we do?

Reality—so-called—tried to settle in. Dad was hurt, badly. He'd lost a lot of blood, and vital parts of his body were severely damaged. He was dying. No one was saying it, but it was obvious that's what was happening.

But that was the present. Heading to a final destination and arriving there are two different things.

For all the knowledge the doctors possessed, even they could only speculate at Dad's fate. Anyone could look at what was happening and extrapolate from that the probable, negative outcome of the night. They could do that and be certain they were right. Or, they could be wrong no matter what their fancy degrees and years of experience told them. Death was the educated guess. But, it was still just a guess.

I didn't have to guess. I knew.

No, I reminded myself. *This isn't it.*

6

PLAYING THE PART

Me Me and Pa, Dad's parents, sat me and my brothers down on the living room couch the next morning to tell us the facts. Me Me was grave in her assessments even in the best of times, but on that morning a dark pall crossed her countenance that I had only seen once before, right after Great-Grandpa Chuck died. Worse was Pa. He was usually so jovial; smiles and agreement came so easily to him. You knew things were bad if he was concerned.

"Boys, your father is not doing well," he began. "He's in critical condition, and it's very likely he will not make it through this. He has been hurt very, very badly. And you need to know that, even if he does make it through this, your father is gone."

"That's right," Me Me continued. "God forbid he doesn't make it out of this, but if he does he's never going to be the same. Not ever again. He will always be damaged, and he won't be able to play with you like he used to. He won't be able to run and maybe not even walk. He's going to need help from you—from all of us—to do simple things like getting dressed and going . . . " She started to tear up. "I'm sorry . . . going from place to place."

"Your mother needs your help, too." Pa picked it back up, turning his attention toward me. "Until your dad comes home, *if* he comes home, Brock, you're the man of the house now. You do what your mother says, be a good boy, and help her and support her. It's time for all of you to grow up. That's the hard thing you have to do now. Your father is broken and you're going to have to get used to the idea that things are never going to be the same."

My brothers listened in silence, not sure what to say. Mom stood nearby, slightly horrified. I understood where Me Me and Pa were coming from, but their prophecies of doom were entirely premature. Dad was a young thirty-nine years old. Things were going to be okay. Why was I so alone in that assurance?

For some reason, God wasn't speaking to anyone else the same way He spoke to me. That meant I had a very real "get out of jail free card" that I didn't necessarily want or need, but it was tempting to take advantage of it anyway. No parent or teacher or blue-haired attendance lady would give me any grief over using it to skip school the day after my father was shot.

Mom practically begged me to stay home. While the circumstances of her petition were unique, this was not a new opportunity. As far as she was concerned, the ability to read came in a distant second to being safe and secure in an environment where one's nausea can be constantly attended to by a large Tupperware bowl. The merest hint of a headache, stomachache, or acute spontaneous combustion was reason enough to spread the sheets over the couch, buy Popsicles in every flavor, and rent a video game or two to make sure I stayed indoors until the angel of death passed us by. My word alone was good enough, no temperature taking necessary.

The temptation was great, but I could never do something so dishonest as to feign a sickness. That was out of the question. Doing such a thing was sure to induce a different kind of nausea in the pit of my stomach, a legitimate illness of the soul given physical manifestation. One could argue that such sickness would, in effect, become its own justification, but that was a kind of paradoxical guilt I dared not attempt. Would the universe even survive such a breach of the guilt/time continuum? I was sure our mortal realm could not possibly afford to find out.

The decision to head back to school the morning after the shooting was easy. If I had honestly felt even an inkling of what Me Me and Pa were telling me, I might have stayed home, but the last thing I wanted to be guilty of was taking advantage of my father's injured state. School was most definitely on the agenda.

Besides, I was terribly, terribly excited about going to school the morning after. The idea of a place full of overly concerned teachers and amazed, admiring peers inspired a little laugh inside me that I tried very hard to not let out. I couldn't wait to see their faces and for them to see how not a big deal it all was. And they would certainly see that. They'd marvel at how I was so okay with everything and wonder at how it was possible. In a way, it would be like a prank. The local news report on the devastating shooting would tell them one thing, but my face and confident, joyful demeanor would prove quite another.

And then I arrived at school and saw their faces.

My attitude was perverse. The pitiful, sad eyes that greeted me as I walked the hallways shamed me, their sympathy an extended gift I could not refuse. I hung my head low and did everything I could to not meet anyone's gaze. Doing the matter-of-fact, the "oh, it's no big deal he'll be all right" seemed like a slap in the face of their concern. I couldn't do it. Sure as I was of Dad's recovery, I could not be so dismissive of the very real feelings everyone had about what my family was going through.

I decided to leave my posturing where it belonged, firmly tucked away with the rest of my beliefs. It wasn't just honest compassion I would betray with my cavalier manner; it was the very Source of my knowledge. If God was speaking to me, then I could lay no claim to its origin and thus had no right to make light or feed my desire for attention with it. It was too sacred for that.

There was a part I was supposed to play at school, just as I had in the hospital. Proclaiming my father was fine when clearly—*clearly*—he wasn't going to be, wasn't going to reassure anyone. It was just going to worry them even more, only now about my emotional stability. I gave in to what was expected and endured who I had to be to help others get through the awkwardness that it was to be around me.

My friends, nervous and not knowing exactly what to say or how I'd react if they said it, didn't ask many questions at first, which was disappointing. But by lunchtime, after they were convinced I wasn't going to curl up into the fetal position and rock back and forth at my desk while the tears fell, they wanted all the details. Finally. A crowd gathered around me in the cafeteria. Kids leaned in from as many as five seats away. I couldn't help it; I liked talking about it. Even the smallest detail of the night before, like the fact that I'd stayed up all the way to midnight was fascinating to them.

Oh, who was I kidding? That was by far the coolest part.

* * *

After school let out, I began what would become a ritual for the next two weeks: visiting Dad to see how he was doing in the intensive care unit at Valley Medical Center. He was "listed in critical condition," which I understood to mean that if he died then the doctors could throw up their hands and say, "Not my fault."

The ICU is a house of horrors. It's a place for people who are shot up to the brim with drugs and have many colored wires and devices hanging out of them. These people are often disturbingly ugly and may suffer from weird, slug-like protrusions from their skin and skin discoloration. They moan, hallucinate, and die. A lot. The only reason you'd ever let a child into an ICU would be to scare and scar them.

I couldn't imagine any other reason Dad would be in a place like that besides what he was there for. A bear of a man, nothing *but* multiple gunshots had the power to drag him in there. He only stood five feet, eight inches, but no one would have thought to call him small. Some of that was cheeseburgers and fries, but most of it was because he had the build of a Mack truck.

He pitched in high school and was even scouted by the major leagues until he blew out his knee. He was a brown belt in karate. A sometime golfer. An all-the-time shooter of clay pigeons and targets. A lot of his athleticism he wasted away on long hours sitting behind the wheel of his delivery van or behind the counter at the Shop, but he was still active when called upon.

He was the only parent on the block who would play football with me and my friends. Dad was our all-time quarterback, sending the ball as high he could throw it so we all had plenty of time to marvel at the brown dot way up in the sky. Only Superman could possibly throw the ball any farther.

He was nearsighted and wore glasses for years until corrective surgery negated the need. His eyes were brown, like his hair, which was kept short and conservative except for an unfortunate giant sideburns period in the 1970s. His hands were more like paws, hairy on top, rough on the underside, and seemingly massive enough to swallow my head whole. Or protect it.

I spent most of my time with Dad in the ICU looking anywhere but in his direction. Death had his way with him and then spit him back out and let him live anyway. His eyes were at once swollen and sunken in, with dark circles surrounding them, pitting them inside their sockets. He was still mostly orange. I was told that this was because of some liquid or other they had to baste onto him for surgery, like a turkey. I didn't get what looking like a diseased Oompa Loompa had to do with surgery. From his neck hung a weird tube with a hose running out of it to who-knows-where. It pulled on him so tightly that his neck skin looked as though it had dislodged from the muscle and bone as it ran halfway down his shoulder.

My understanding of Dad's plight was not helped by the fact that he was hard to understand and hear. Just having the simplest of conversations required getting in very close to his face, which was the last thing I wanted to do. I mean, I loved my dad, but I very much preferred the non-zombie version. From what little I could make out, he seemed pretty upbeat, but was that him putting on a brave face for the rest of us, or was he kind of stoned?

Either way, it was a breach of contract. This was not the man who could outrun speeding big wheels and wrestle giant, closeted beasts. If fathers were supposed to be strong for their sons, my dad was supposed to be the strongest. His forearms were like Popeye's, his hands capable of beating mountains into shape.

Beep.

Beep.

Beep.

Beep.

Beep.

Did the beeping of monitors drive Dad nuts like it did me? An up-to-the-minute record of his heartbeat was kept on a long sheet of paper coiled like a lazy snake on the hospital floor. Did they need the sound as well? If it hadn't been for the steady stream of people with badges coming in and going out and checking and rechecking his status, there might have been a chance for him to forget for a moment about his decrepit state . . . but for that constant beeping.

Dad didn't think like that. That was all me. Of the pain he would only say, "It hurts." There was so much in that simple statement, and so much evidence to back it up.

For the most part, Dad's care was excellent. He had a qualified team of physicians and health care professionals. Except for Nurse Fumbly. If the bullets weren't going to do him in, then Nurse Fumbly aimed to pick up the slack.

Dad's stomach had been sliced open first by a bullet and then again by a surgeon's knife to repair the harm done. When the bullet ripped through, it tore apart the kidney and blew out through Dad's back. It was a clean exit, but it could have been much, much worse. That solitary abdominal hit—likely the first bullet to gain entry and surely the one that brought him down to begin with—missed his spine by only a quarter of an inch. Of the very elite club of individuals who have been shot upwards of twelve times, few can report, "I was lucky." But Dad did it with conviction. Sure, his body wasn't a pretty sight, but the worst of what the bullets could do to him had been felt on the cold floor of the Shop. No, what really hurt was that long cut the surgeons made straight down the middle of his stomach.

Nurse Fumbly liked to call it her tray. Multiple times daily during Dad's hospital stay, tubes needed to be changed, bags of fluid swapped, and wires crossed. It was all very technical. Too technical for Nurse Fumbly. In order to free up her mind and hands, she took her plate of medical goodies and placed it on the nearest available surface—my father's fleshy bed of sensitivity. He would wince and cry out, but you didn't disturb Nurse Fumbly when she was "in the zone."

"Now, let's see. This wire goes here . . . no, that's not right. Wait, I've got it. This tube goes over here and . . . oh, dear."

Finally, my father knew fear. He also knew a good story when he lucked into one, and while he prayed that this woman would not do to him what even two ill-meaning men and their semi-automatic submachine guns could not manage, it was easy to see that he took great delight in telling the tale of the daily, comical threats to his well-being. He especially enjoyed imitating her low mutterings: "I know it's . . . no, that doesn't make sense. Perhaps if I . . . "

Despite Nurse Fumbly's best efforts, Dad made steady progress every day for his two weeks in the ICU before they took him off the critical list, defying all the early predictions of his physicians. For two weeks they were certain he would not be long for this world. For two weeks my family and friends wondered and hoped and prayed. For two weeks I never doubted.

Three weeks after the shooting, Dad was sent home.

I was right. Or God was. Whichever.

7

A SUSPICIOUS PEACE

Dad met his new life with no small amount of vocal displeasure. His complaints were not pitiful bids for attention but rather a compulsive expression of his frustration. He longed to get back to work, run his store, and stop depending on others for his every need. In his mind, he was just fine. The agony was in waiting for his body to catch up.

His wounds were an all-over, spotted ugliness. The multiple sprays of bullets left him well ventilated, and keeping his new, jumbo-sized pores clean and free of contaminants was no small chore. Someone—not Dad—had to swab each wound (a hole, really) with alcohol and pack it with gauze. All eighteen of them. Some were entry wounds and some were exit wounds, and some entry wounds had no corresponding exit wound. Every last one was an open door to infection.

The two wounds on his upper body were made by the one bullet that flew through his abdomen. All the other bullets chewed up his legs. The nastiest mark was carved out by a bullet that neither entered nor exited, but instead merely grazed his left thigh. It left behind a three-inch long gash that was the easiest to clean and, exposed to the open air as it was, also the most painful.

The first time my mother performed the swabbing, cleaning, and bandaging it took her two and a half hours. It was she who most often shouldered the responsibility, but I put in my time as well. Seeing the cotton swab get swallowed up by the sticky, gaping pits was like watching a spoon go into thick pudding. The wounds seemed endlessly full of puss and blood, no matter how much and how often we cleaned them out. Dad did his best to grip the bedposts and endure, but the alcohol on the tips of the pointlessly soft, white sticks had to be spread liberally. When I pulled them back out, they were covered in red. Dad grimaced and so did I. Every single time. After the bullet hole or graze had been thoroughly cleaned out, we packed it with gauze to fill in where chunks of flesh had gone missing so that nothing unclean could take their place. A square of gauze was then placed on top of that gauze to lock everything in. Another stretch of gauze wrapped around the leg and taped securely held the entire concoction together. All of this was done for all eighteen wounds, three-to-five times daily.

This went on for weeks. And all Dad could do was lay there while it happened to him.

Visitors were frequent. The brave ones (chiefly my friends, who I insisted check him out) would sneak a peek at Dad's Swiss-cheesed lower body, a show he was only too willing to put on. "How did he live through it?" they wanted to know. "*How* did he *do* that?"

The family estimate was thirteen. Thirteen different bullets struck Dad that night, we concluded, based purely on the mathematics. We couldn't just count the fresh holes. Nor could we simply divide the eighteen marks by two between entry wounds and exit wounds. Dad's body was a much more complicated word problem of human suffering than that.

There were a few things we did know for sure. We knew the bullet that hit his stomach passed clean through. That was one bullet for two wounds.

We could also account for one other bullet—the grazer—because it never fully entered his body. So that was two for three.

X-rays showed five bullets still remained in Dad's legs. They had no corresponding exit and could each account for exactly one hole. Five more brought our total to eight wounds, leaving ten wounds we couldn't make heads or tails of. An even number. It seemed logical that half of those ten were entries and half were exits, meaning five more bullets.

Thirteen bullets in all. It was unimaginable to most people, including myself. A twice-weekly migraine that I'd had since I was very young was my only reference point for "extremely painful." Certain smells and bright lights, as well as lack of sleep, would trigger the knife-stabbing sensations behind my left eyeball. Mom tried to convince me that eating too much chocolate was also a catalyst, which made her evil. The older I got, the more the intensity of the pain varied. Sometimes, the migraines were mild and I could continue with my schoolwork; other times the pain was so bad I would vomit. If one bullet is like a very intense migraine, then how much worse would thirteen be? What in the world would thirteen migraines hitting you at once even feel like?

Visitors were *horrified* by the fact that five bullets remained inside of Dad, floating around in places they didn't belong, places they *couldn't* belong. Never mind the guys that tried to kill him. It was the irresponsible doctors whose heads they wanted! I half-expected the gawkers to duck, frightened that one of the bullets might regain its momentum and suddenly achieve escape velocity. Dad played it off like it was no big deal, but the look on his face was pure delight at their unhinged reactions.

Leaving the bullets inside the legs *was* the responsible choice. Any surgery to remove them risked hitting an artery. Either the bullets would stay put and not cause any future problems, or they would work their way to the surface of the skin and could be taken out. Four of the bullets chose the more likely scenario and stayed precisely where they were for the rest of his life. One little metallic swimmer was slightly more restless.

Dad had felt it rising, ever so slowly, for many days beforehand. He'd even been able to nudge it around with his finger while it lay just under the surface of his skin. When he woke up that morning and found the small, shiny protrusion on his upper right thigh, he knew just what to do. He'd been waiting for this. Here, finally, after relying on the at times not-so-tender mercies of the medical establishment and his own family, was a challenge he could face down alone.

"Brock! Get in here, son!"

I ran into the bedroom. Dad's volume level indicated tragedy. His face registered nothing but excitement. "What? What happened?"

"Check it out!" Dad said. "It finally came through!"

At first, he tried to remove it with tweezers, but there was no way to get a decent grip on the smooth, rounded tip of the bullet head. He could have used the points on the tweezers to dig in and around the bullet, but that was a task better suited for a sharper instrument.

"Get me a knife," Dad said.

With the knife, he easily dug under the skin and manipulated the bullet, but that led to greater pain. The sucker would not budge without reminding him exactly why it was there in the first place. "You try," he said. I did my best, both of us hoping that it was simply a matter of approaching it from the right angle. The slippery thing mocked us both.

This continued for weeks. Each day the bullet moved just a little more, and each day Dad grew more and more frustrated. In the mornings, he'd work and work at it. In the afternoons, he'd curse it. The bullet wasn't coming out any other way than how it came in—without any desire or design of his. Over a month after it first surfaced, Dad finally made the appointment with his doctor and the bullet was removed with surgical ease.

The rest of the bullets only saw action with metal detectors. It's funny; it was always the first question, but it had the least interesting answer.

"What do you do at airport metal detectors?" people would ask.

"I tell them I was shot," Dad would say.

This made visits to the airport particularly interesting as explanations were needed but little proof could be given. It always turned into a thing. Dad did everything he could to keep the confusion going as long as possible.

> *Sir, please remove all metal—belts, coins, watches—from your person.*
> I did. I was shot.
> *What was that?*
> I said I was shot.
> *Shot?*
> Like, with a gun.
> *You have a gun, sir?*
> No, I don't *have* a gun. I was shot *with* a gun.
> *I can't allow you to bring a gun aboard the plane, sir.*
> I don't have a gun, I only have ammunition. In my legs.
> *I can't allow you to bring ammunition aboard the plane either, sir.*
> *Please, empty your pockets.*
> No, they're in my legs. There are bullets in my legs.
> *Your legs?*
> Yes, inside of them.
> *Like under the—*
> Skin, yes.
> *You say you were shot?*
> Yes.
> *How many rounds?*
> About thirteen, I think.
> *And how many are still inside of you?*

About four.

Okay, this I gotta hear.

His was not a tale told in passing. It was a story that demanded multiple repetitions of "Wait . . . what?" and a full telling. Perhaps it was unfair to the rest of the passengers trying to board, but that made no difference to Dad. He would happily get stuck talking to perfect strangers about his story and be almost entirely, blissfully unaware of anything else going on around him.

This was Dad's way. It was a fact he had been shot. That sort of thing happens occasionally. Guns exist and that means bad, ill-intentioned, and short-on-cash people can use them to do bad things. It's best to just acknowledge the pain and move on and enjoy the story. Life doesn't stop for bullets. (Well, sometimes it does, but not in this case.)

That the two shooters went in with the idea to kill Dad cannot be disputed. With so many rounds fired and so much destruction confined to such a small space, it was the only logical conclusion. As one police officer put it, "It was obvious they weren't gonna leave any witnesses behind." The bullet that sailed into the wall behind the counter testified of this. It went in at exactly the same level as Dad's chest. It was likely the first shot fired and would have been by far the deadliest had it actually hit him.

The shooters didn't know him, but they decided his life held so little meaning they were justified in taking action to terminate it anyway. If they had ever met Dad before, it could only have been as customers, two of the many who streamed in and out of the Shop every day. Maybe they were thirsty one hot afternoon and came in to grab a beer or a Coke. Maybe Dad waited on them and he wished them a nice day. Perhaps they nodded back and it was only afterward they considered what a ripe target the fat, smiling man behind the counter with all those guns would be. He seemed a nice enough person; there would be nothing personal about the attack on his life. The ending of it would just be a means to an end. And their ends were very, very important.

It may have been just that impersonal for them, but it couldn't be for Dad. He was the guy who bled out on the floor. The causes of his pain and suffering had names.

Craig Bush.

Ricky Foster.

Within a week of the shooting they were caught and put in jail, trial pending. The robbery, as pointless and short-term a gain as there ever was, left so much consequence in its wake.

And yet, the most worked up I ever saw Dad get about the shooters was when he clinched his fist tightly, raised it up, shook it a little, and said, "All I want is five minutes alone in a room with those guys. Just five minutes . . . " It was like a joke. There were no crying jags, no lamenting the losses he'd suffered. He didn't ask why it happened to him, and he spoke no ill of the men even while his physical misery waylaid him for weeks. The men were black and reinforced some of his theories on city crime and poverty, but no matter. They were no longer to be regarded.

Dad was remarkably composed that way. Everyone—doctors, friends, "experts"—agreed that one day he would have to deal with it. He'd break down and the full magnitude of what happened to him would envelop him and the emotions would pour out. No one could go through what he did and not send their brain into some sort of revolt against the experience. He was broken. One day, he'd realize it.

They didn't get it. They didn't know my dad. How could he break down? You have to be upset about something in order to have a breakdown.

Of course Dad got shot. *Of course* he nearly died. That's what happens. Who are the people who leave this world unscathed? Where do they live and how do we all get there? Sooner or later, life hits everybody in a big, sucky way. The surprising thing that had happened—the one, amazing, *unbelievable* event in all of this—was that Dad had lived through it. It would have made much more sense to him if he had died. Not that he wasn't grateful to be among the living, but from the moment the first bullet entered his stomach the most likely outcome saw him dead and rotting in a grave a few weeks later, not trying to figure out how best to resume his duties at the Shop in his new, broken condition.

He'd put enough money in a savings account that the temporary loss of income didn't interrupt our lives in a significant way, but nearly a month out from the shooting, we were fast approaching a time when it wasn't going to be enough. Nothing, least of all the mortgage, would be served by further delays in the return to normalcy.

Besides, Dad was a bit of a workaholic. That was an itch that needed scratching.

To others it may have seemed a suspicious peace, but for Dad this was the only way he knew to be. His zen-like disposition toward the entire event and its punishing consequences required no calculation. It wasn't that he was going to have to deal with it one day. It was that he had dealt with it so quickly and in his own way everyone had missed it.

* * *

For me, it was no different. With Dad's future recovery now fully manifested in the present, it was hard to think of any downside to the entire affair. We had all been shaken out of the malaise of familiar routine life and into something I found terribly, terribly wonderful. This was a time of experience and importance. Of feeling important. There would be something to take from all of this when it was over. Some grand lesson or greater understanding of life, the universe—all of it. People told us over and over again that everything happens for a reason, and I couldn't wait to find out what that reason was.

A couple years earlier, during the fourth grade, I spent a lot of time in the school library going through each and every biography of the presidents of the United States of America. Lincoln, Washington, Grant, Wilson, Adams. My favorite was Teddy Roosevelt. Nearly all of them suffered some great tragedy in their youth after which who they would later become began to come into focus. It was even a familiar trope in my comic books. Batman's parents were killed and Spider-Man's uncle met the same fate. The scriptures proved it too. Joseph was tossed into a pit and sold into slavery. Isaac was nearly sacrificed by his father, Abraham. Experiences, especially ones based in tragedy, changed a person into something more than he would have been otherwise.

I didn't really think I'd become president. And Dad had survived so Batman was a no go. Maybe a prophet. It was possible I might be righteous enough for that. I was sure there were plenty of other things I could be that were pretty important as well, but I had a hard time thinking of any. A captain of industry? No, I didn't really want that. Time would tell. No doubt, in the end, my life would be a great story. And this was chapter one.

8

SUPERDAD

Dad was born in 1949 in Taft, California, but grew up farther north in Folsom. Grandpa, a World War II vet, worked as a guard at the local state prison that housed the criminals whooping it up on a pretty fantastic Johnny Cash album. Grandma said Dad was an active and happy child, but lonely. His only sibling, Jim, was older by four years and they fought often. All of the other kids in the neighborhood were the same age as Jim, leaving Dad in constant search of something to do.

By age four, Billy Heasley, a twinkly-eyed little boy with a round, open face, was well known as a notorious troublemaker and record holder for most flower beds trampled in the county. He was the town's youngest repeat offender, earning him the well-deserved nickname Dennis the Menace. An unusual day for Grandma was when Billy *wasn't* brought home by either the dog or the police. The dog was a Nazi like that.

To rein him in and keep him at the house, Grandpa tethered Billy to one of the clothesline poles in the backyard with a small chain tied around his waist. A glass of water and food at his side kept him hearty while he played. His pet turtle, also fitted with a little chain tied to a stake in the ground, kept him company. A nearby willow tree provided them both with ample shade, if not enough cover from prying eyes. When a report was filed claiming Grandpa and Grandma were abusing Dad, the police showed up. After seeing the setup for themselves and who was tied to it, they agreed it was for the best.

When he entered school, Dad was immediately pegged as "retarded" and sent to a special class away from the other kids where administered alienation taught him everything he needed to know about those who presumed to know what was best for him. Dad's actual problem was school itself. He wasn't stupid. He was just an energetic kid who couldn't be bothered with the rote repetition of busy schoolwork. It was too easy. Once, in high school, a particularly frustrated teacher told him, in her estimation, just exactly how stupid he was. Dad got mad and figured he'd show her and he aced the next test. Naturally, she failed him for cheating. Lesson learned, he went back to not giving school much of his attention and time.

He was a trumpet player. To make extra cash as a teenager, he played with the bands at local bars. When he joined the Army during the Vietnam War, he auditioned for and won a spot as a member of the President's Fife and Drum Corps, playing "Hail to the Chief" and other selections from Nixon's personal soundtrack. Though he loved the music and it kept him from fighting overseas, it was a three-year stint under the thumb of the ultimate authority of the military and he hated it. Once, fearing a promotion in rank, he insulted the camp cook and threw a plate of food in his face. He never achieved a rank higher than private.

After happily exiting the Army with an honorable discharge at the conclusion of his enlistment, Dad did everything he could to find a way to earn wages without someone else making decisions for him. Jobs working as a teller at a bank and as a co-manager at the newly erected Blackbeard's Family Fun Center in Fresno only confirmed his need for self-reliance.

So, he started his own business selling and distributing fish bait wholesale to mini-marts and drug stores across California's Central Valley and throughout the Sierra Nevada Mountains. With time, the inventory at Bill's Bait and Tackle expanded to include candy, food, toiletries, soda, alcohol, and cigarettes. And, of course, guns.

* * *

Dad reported back to work on February 17, 1989, four weeks to the day from the shooting. Two weeks prior he had been in critical condition, and now there he was, smiling at the regular customers glad to see him back and conducting business as usual. The only differences now were twofold: his wheelchair and a new, albeit tiny, hole in the back wall.

In March, my brother Logan joined the local Little League, and Dad honored his prior commitment to coach his team. Even if it had to be on wheels, he was determined to fulfill his promise. The kids on Logan's team, a band of misfits Dad was saddled with after being late to the draft, listened to his every word and ran every sprint he ordered. He was a rolling miracle, a figure of fascination who commanded respect. It hardly even mattered whether he was any good at coaching or not (he was).

Dad didn't need to be mobile to bark at the kids and send them on laps around the bases, but some of his finer coaching tips were lost until he graduated from the chair and into a walker in early April. His wounds had mostly scarred over, though the muscle underneath was still in a state of repair. He drafted me into being an assistant coach of sorts, a part I played to my ignorant best. It was I who ran after the ball when the "A" for effort kids got up to bat, a task requiring no discernible skill and to which I was therefore well suited. Dad's only mistake was in misinterpreting my hustle for enthusiasm and using the assumed opportunity to teach me a thing or two about pitching.

It was after the other kids had gone home. He sent Logan over to home plate and took me out to the mound. He told me to face due east, worked me like a puppet to show how to bring my leg up for the windup, and how to not let it get away from me for the pitch. I humored him because throwing a baseball with accuracy wasn't entirely unpleasant and I wasn't half bad at it. Besides, I could tell it was important to him.

"Well, what do you think?" he asked after about an hour of entirely unnecessary overtime practice. "You've got an arm on you, son. How about that?"

"Yeah, not too bad," I said. "It's pretty cool."

"What do you think, you wanna throw a few more?"

"Nah."

"No?" Dad looked crestfallen.

"Nah. I mean, it's cool, but it's not changing my life or anything." Dad was killing me with that look. "I'm just—you know, I'm not really into sports."

"But I thought—you're a good pitcher, son. With a little more practice, who knows what you could do."

I looked at the ground. We didn't have these conversations very often. He gently encouraged me and my brothers to be excited by what excited him, but baseball was about as far from our shared love of science fiction as you could get. Unless it was lamenting the death of Lt. Yar at the hands of Armus, the black sludge monster, I just didn't care. He knew that. "All right, all right," he finally said like a defeated puppy told in no uncertain terms that fetch time was over. "Let's go on home."

Dad wasn't perfect. He could be a little bigoted sometimes and loved to tell jokes about dumb Pollocks. When he'd get the chance during the day at work, soap operas were his entertainment of choice. He could be impulsive and selfish, buying new cars without telling Mom and then coming home with a big stupid grin on his face like he'd won a trophy from some imagined contest with the dealer. He was too shy at parties and then, if you got him talking, he wouldn't shut up. I got into the habit of apologizing for him as I got older and everyone always told me the same thing: "No, it's all right! Your dad's an interesting guy."

By May, Dad was out of the walker and on his own two feet again. It made coaching easier but walking more of a chore, so he used a cane. This was when he looked his smallest. In the walker he got around with a slow, laborious shuffle, but that was a noble effort. A show of strength that could only be described as herculean. The rickety unsteadiness and sort of half lurch Dad did with the cane was more "old grandpa" than "thirty-nine-year-old brown belt."

No one else saw him this way. Dad's second pre-shooting commitment was to serve as a chaperone for my sixth grade camp up in Sonora, California. Gold rush country. (It was my one-week consolation prize to Logan's multi-month coaching sweepstakes win.) When he entered the camp, he did so as the conquering hero. My friends had been fascinated by the story for months. Now, there he was. Live, imposing, and in the flesh.

Comfort and independence being the issues that they were for Dad, the whole class made the trek up to Sonora in a school bus while we went up in the silver mini-van I'd put a bullet in years earlier. Dad refused to travel any way other than in style. With us was Matt Bybee, my hockey-less friend, and his father. Brother Bybee volunteered to be a chaperone as well, but, unfortunately for him, on the second day of camp he fell extremely ill and had to head back home to have kidney stones removed.

That made Dad the sole male adult in charge of all the boys in my entire class. No one was upset by this (except perhaps Matt), as Dad more than lived up to the hype. When a pillow fight broke out one night in the cabin that served as our dormitory, Dad was right in the middle of it. Matt and I hid in his private room to avoid getting hit.

Twelve-year-old boys swing pillows about as hard as they play kickball. Twelve-year-old boys with mortgages and a business to run hit even harder. We could hear Dad beating down boy after boy with mighty *thwacks* that were surely opening up skulls even as they inspired outbursts of laughter. Matt had this thing he'd do with his hands when he was excited where he would bring them up to his face and dance his fingers up and down his cheeks. He was excited now. "I heard Nathan shouting for us. They have no idea where we are!"

"So," I said, "now what do we do?"

"I dunno. Does your dad have any candy in here?"

"I think he does. Somewhere. Let me—"

Rattle, rattle.

Someone twisted the doorknob and tried to get in. We froze. They tried again.

Rattle, rattle.

"Brock? Open the door, son! Brock, are you in there?"

We opened the door to let Dad in, but only his foot entered. The rest of him stayed in the hallway while he spoke to us, one of his arms bent back with pillow in hand, ready to knock sideways any and all boys who dared walk by. "You guys comin' out?" he asked.

"No!" I said. "Are you kidding? It's crazy out there."

"All right then, your loss!"

Thwack! Down went another boy.

Dad tried a couple more times to get us out of the room and into the fray—he even offered a free hit on him if we'd join in—but we proudly and resolutely responded in the negative. Each time we made him go away disappointed, he smiled broadly before turning his full attention back to the fight and the next boy brave enough to incur his wrath.

On the nights when Dad didn't hand out concussions, he told ghost stories. The first night, a small group gathered at the side of my bed after most of the other boys had gone to sleep. By the second night, the whole population of the dormitory showed up. Dad had an entire repertoire of spooky stories and a gift for instilling a creeping, tension-filled dread into his narratives. Most ended in a "Gotcha!" moment, but others just kind of petered out with no real resolution, leaving the described horror hanging in the air and very much, possibly, out there. Right now. In the darkness. After a particularly gruesome telling of the story of the Zodiac Killer, one of the boys was later found in his bed curled up in the fetal position and sobbing. Dad held him until he calmed down enough to sleep.

Dad's favorite story to tell was "The Hairy Hand." It is about a farmer who is terrorized night after night by the slaughtering of his livestock. After the killing spree finally claims the town's sheriff, the farmer spends the last night in his locked room with a shotgun by his side. He falls asleep but is soon awoken by an odd feeling near his torso. Something underneath his bedsheets slowly crawls along his stomach. In a panic, he rips off the sheet only to see that—and this is when Dad's big GOTCHA moment would come in—it's his own hand! The possessed hand grabs a knife and makes short work of the farmer's throat, bringing him and the story to an end.

When it came time to choose a skit to perform for the other dorms on the final night of the week-long camp, it was an easy choice. We'd already spent the better part of the week trying to scare each other with our "possessed," mostly hairless hands by grabbing each other by the throat unexpectedly. No one questioned the appropriateness of the subject matter, least of all Dad. I was selected to be the farmer, and Matt played the Sheriff. Dad took up the charge of continuing his narrative duties with mock reluctance.

Our only real props at the small, outdoor amphitheater were a few blankets and a folding table to mimic the farmer's bed. Under the table sat my friend Nathan with a bottle of ketchup, ready for the right moment. As each night of the story passed, I got up and walked around to the "animals" (really just other boys playing dead) to discover the carnage and then head back to my "bed" for the night. Dad accidentally created his own catch phrase when, once they'd caught on, the audience raised their voices with his as he repeated the refrain "AND THERE WAS BLOOD EVERYWHERE!"

Finally, the big moment came. I returned to our makeshift bed for the final time and threw on the blanket. Nathan hurriedly poured a bowlful of ketchup into one of my hands underneath the covers, while my other hand grabbed the butter knife in my pocket. I slowly let it inch up my stomach and toward my throat. When the reveal came, I made a motion of slitting my throat with my "hairy hand" and brought the generous helping of ketchup up to my neck and head with the other. It smelled terrible, like someone threw up a week-old pizza on my face.

But it was worth it. The audience gasped appropriately at the sight of my bloody visage and then cheered after one last "AND THERE WAS BLOOD EVERYWHERE!"

It was strange seeing Dad work a crowd like that. He was good with the one-on-one, but his vulnerabilities usually came out in social settings. Put him in a room where the chief goal was to mingle, and he looked like a scared, caught rat. Put him up on stage . . . well, I had never seen him up in front of people like that before. But now, after a long week of hiking, sarsaparilla sodas, campfires, pillow fights, and ghost stories, he put on a masterful show. That was *my* dad up there.

* * *

After school let out at the beginning of the summer, Dad made some changes to the Shop. New security cameras went up, and a new front door was installed with a nifty feature that made it impossible for it to be kicked in like the night of the shooting. The plan was to not get robbed again. It didn't work out.

Dad never regained the physicality he had before the shooting, but now he had finally tossed the cane aside and stood firmly on his own two feet again. He wasn't going to be running long distances anytime soon, but he was more powerful than his pronounced limp otherwise suggested. It led some to think Dad was weaker than he actually was and to underestimate him. One doofus in particular.

It is sensible when selling a thing that can kill to render that thing inert. That's why the display gun with the yellow tag Dad mistakenly grabbed to fight back the night of the shooting didn't fire. It may very well be that in the history of arms dealing no weapon has ever been loaded until after purchase. You, as a customer, are welcome to handle it, pull the trigger, and check the chamber, but you are not allowed to stuff it in your pocket. You can't run out the door with it. And don't even think about getting in your car and driving off with it on the passenger seat. That's a big no-no. Doofus did it all anyway.

Dad, suddenly lighter on his feet than he had been in months, shouted out to one of his employees to call the cops and ran outside as fast as his scarred-over, pockmarked legs could carry him. Doofus was already racing out of sight down the road. Dad jumped into his own car and took off after him.

The Idiot Robber Doofus took a hard turn into a dirty country road to try to lose Dad in the wide, open spaces of farmhouses and abandoned barns and fields. It didn't work. Dad stayed on his tail and followed close behind, through the cloud of dust kicked up by the car ahead of him and down roads that only tractors dared to tread. It was in one of the fields that Doofus activated the next phase of his master plan: run like the dickens on foot.

Dad was right behind him. He abandoned his car, pulled out a very-much-not-yellow-tagged weapon from the waist band of his pants, and tore off after the guy with a speed that neither of them guessed the crippled store owner capable of. He caught up in a flash.

"Freeze!" Dad shouted. "Get down on the ground! Give me the gun and get down on the ground!"

Doofus obeyed and got down on the ground. Dad approached him, ordering him to stay face down. He retrieved his stolen firearm and placed his own gun directly behind the man's head to keep him there until the cops arrived. When Dad told the story to us later, there was one thing he made very clear: He absolutely would have shot that guy.

Dad was back. Not "back from the dead," but legitimately, in every way, *back*. He was the way he was before, mostly. The bullet wounds had sealed themselves up enough that they didn't need daily care. He could play and roughhouse with us again and, in no small part because of the notoriety, business at the Shop was better than ever. I had seen him orange and ugly, full of puss and wheelchair bound. And now, like something out of an action movie, he was running down a thief in a field.

In a field!

II

THE HERO

9

THE WRONG SIDE OF TOWN

I woke up to a helicopter's searchlight shining into my bedroom. I deferred to the sand in my eyes, buried my head in my pillow, and tried to block it out, but it was no use. I told myself a helicopter in the backyard was sleep-induced craziness and that the light was probably a passing car. The sound that woke me up in the first place? Probably a crowing cat or something.

Then I remembered cars don't drive through our backyard and Dad shot all the neighborhood cats with Logan's BB gun, scaring them away permanently.

Whup, whup, whup.

That sound . . . it was spinning blades.

I went to the window and pulled back the blinds. I winced as the full force of the searchlight poured in. The helicopter hung low in the sky, but our tiny patch of dying and tunneled out backyard grass was not a suitable landing pad.

The alarm clock read 1:00 AM. I still had plenty of time to get back into bed and have a decent go at sleep again, but I was curious now. I stumbled out of my room and headed down the hallway toward the living room to find out if Mom and Dad knew why we were being invaded.

The other half of the house was entirely lit up. I found Mom sitting on the couch, casting nervous glances toward the large living room window facing our street. She was alone.

"Mom," I said. "Why is there a helicopter in the backyard?"

"Brock!" I had startled her. "It's the police! They're out tonight. They're looking for someone." She was dressed in the ratty, old, sentient pink robe she always wore in the morning before getting dressed. One look at her dark, puffy eyes told me she'd hardly slept at all. And she wasn't happy about it.

"What happened?"

"We don't know yet. Your father heard gunshots and it woke him up. When we went outside to look, we heard the sirens going up and down our street and saw the lights and police everywhere. They're still at it."

Our house sat on a single strip of neighborhood three rows wide and one block long that once upon a time served as the model home tract for the much larger neighborhoods in the surrounding areas. This made Buckingham Way fairly isolated, with only a spacious, undeveloped field to the south and an AM/PM mini mart/gas station on the corner to the north to keep us company. The mini mart served as an allowance-guzzling temptation to every kid who lived on our street, but it was closer still to the busy intersection at Cedar and Ashlan, thus rendering it mostly forbidden while I was in the lower grades. Now that I was twelve years old, the AM/PM was an almost daily destination. A one-stop shop for Pop Rocks, Slush Puppies, five-cent peanut butter cups, and, as I was about to find out, illegal aliens.

"Wait, where's Dad now?"

"Oh, you know your father. He grabbed his gun and took off to see what's going on."

My neighborhood had been turned into a war zone, and Dad was out in it. This was awesome.

We didn't have to wait too long for him to come back. Out of breath and as excited as I'd ever seen him, the gun in his hand complemented Dad's pajamas splendidly. "I made it to the mini mart. Police everywhere. There are two bodies on the ground near the storefront—two federal agents! I spoke with one of the officers there, and he told me an undercover sting operation went sideways. Something to do with illegal immigration. When their contacts figured out the agents were cops, they shot them both. In the chest."

Mom's eyes went wide with fright. "Wh-where are the shooters now?" She was in the middle of her worst nightmare. Our lives were finally back to what passed for normal, and now this. Whatever else she had been feeling the night of the shooting nine months earlier, it wasn't surprise. The Shop was on that side of town. Our home was safely all the way over on the other. We lived near Blackbeard's, the Family Fun Center where Dad used to work as a manager. Family Fun, with video games, miniature golf, and waterslides. The only thing people were supposed to get hit in the chest with around here was brightly colored golf balls.

"The shooters got away and could be anywhere by now," Dad said. "That's why they're doing the search in our neighborhood. They've got them trapped within a one block radius of the store, but they don't know where they are within that radius. That's what the helicopters are for."

No way!

"Bill," Mom said, fully freaking out now. "I'm waking the kids. I'm taking the kids and we'll go to my parents'. We'll be safe there. Let's just leave."

Uh, no. No, I did not want to leave. This was not a time for Mom to be Mom. Couldn't she just not do that for one night? There were so many houses within a block of the mini mart. What were the odds the bad guys would come to see us? All of our lights were on and there was a military-grade (probably) helicopter circling overhead. We were in the safest place for miles!

"No, sweetheart," Dad said. "That's not how it works. They're not letting us or anyone else leave. The whole block is quarantined within the search area. We can't go outside of it and no one else can get in."

Yes! It was September 6, 1989. I was supposed to be entering the seventh grade at Tioga Middle School in about seven hours. Depending on how long the quarantine held, I could potentially skip my newest first day of instructional misery.

The great lie of the sixth grade was that we'd actually accomplished something. In reality, my graduation from Thomas Elementary was a pointless demarcation of educational progress that signified nothing more than moving two blocks north to a different school. The carrot was not given, it withdrew even further. There were ten more years of schooling still to go (at least). Almost double what I'd done so far. Seventh grade meant starting all over. At the bottom. Before kicking us to the curb, my sixth grade teacher made it quite clear to her students that we could look forward to an increased workload with multiple classes and teachers, and gigantic eighth graders who suffered no fools. In seventh grade, there would be no mercy. All those fourth graders we'd been picking on? We were going to empathize with them in a way that would make our underpants crinkle.

I had spent the entire summer in worried anticipation, culminating in a nausea that not even the A-Team circling outside could put at ease. I knew, with the kind of certainty that can only come from ignorance and fear, that seventh grade was going to be the absolute, most miserable experience of my life.

Unknowingly, those federal agents died for my right to not go to junior high. I could only hope their sacrifice would not be in vain.

"Stay away from the windows," Dad commanded us. Of course, he was at the window looking out at the street as he said this. He was in the zone. "I'm going back out."

"Bill, no!" Mom protested—more out of habit than hope.

"You'll be fine. Just—just keep the doors locked. There are police everywhere, Jill. I won't be long; I need to see if there's anything I can do to help."

"Bill. Bill, come on. What do you think you're going to do out there?"

"I'm an extra set of eyes. It's still early enough in the search that I might be able to catch 'em. I'll be all right. I've got my gun. It'll be all right."

"Bill, they don't know you! Let the police handle it and stay here inside with us. Just stay with us."

"I'll be fine. And so will you. Don't wake the little ones, stay inside, and I'll be back as soon as I can to check in on all of you. Brock, you listen to your mother."

"Bill . . . " Mom started in again.

"Okay," I said. I knew why Mom was so worried, but she didn't need to be. Dad knew what he was doing. He probably had more experience with gunfire than any of the officers out there. No way anyone would be getting the drop on him again. If he said he could help, then he could.

Dad left again and Mom and I turned on the radio for news updates. Soon, the noise woke up Logan, and he groggily made his way out of his bedroom to join us. The three of us huddled together, waiting for some sign of progress on the search. I felt restless. I tried to stick close to Mom, but I couldn't help wandering over to the window to see if I could spot anything . . . or anyone. The street would have been dark but for the flashlights darting in and out of the bushes and the dance of spotlights overhead tracing figure eights up and down our street. Everything was lit up and flickering at once, like an unstable crash of lightning that lingered too long. I wanted to be out there too. It all looked like so much fun. Then, I heard the bullhorn.

"SIR, GET BACK INSIDE OF YOUR HOUSE. RETURN TO YOUR HOME NOW OR YOU WILL BE ARRESTED. WE WILL ARREST YOU."

Dad's second trip outside was considerably shorter than his first. With his gun out and his lack of uniform, he'd been causing no small amount of confusion for the officers and agents who were on the scene. They insisted that he stop "interfering." Dad respectfully but reluctantly obeyed and came back inside.

As the early morning night dragged onward, the search continued with no word of progress, and no sign of resolution. Every passing hour brought us closer and closer to 7:30 AM, the latest we could possibly leave for school and still arrive on time. It was all going to end one way or another. It was the "another" that frightened Mom.

What would happen after the men were found was the real question. Suppose they should start shooting. Where would the bullets go? Our living room? McKay and Tyler's Room? Dad's legs as if magnetically attracted? (I was tired. This made sense to me at the time.)

None of us went back to bed, least of all Dad. He stayed on high alert. By 7:00 AM, there was still no word, and I started planning my truancy. There could be no blame and no guilt if the police themselves prevented me from attending school.

At 7:15 AM, Mom made us all go through the motions of getting ready for school. I knew it was pointless; fortune smiled upon me. The search had been going on for hours, and the odds of the entire event ending at precisely the time prescribed by the Fresno Unified School District were slim. It was pretty clear which direction this was going. The first day of seventh grade would be a bust.

At 7:30 AM, it was reported that both of the men who shot the agents had been caught, the last one having been found in the house directly behind us, the one with which we shared a fence. Nestled away for most of the night in our neighbor's garage, the slipperiest shooter was the only person who got any sleep that night.

My stomach dropped. I could have easily claimed sickness or fatigue. Either one would have been true, but neither would have been legitimate. Seventh grade was going to begin, and I, unfortunately, was going to be there for it. I would have to find my way through a new maze of outdoor hallways to my many, many classes. I would have to meet all those teachers. I had made an enemy of a friend over the summer, and I'd have to see him, too. I would have to endure another year. The fear—entirely unbecoming of a son whose father survived an armed robbery, ran down thieves in fields, and chased after killers in the dark—was very real.

10

A FRIEND IN NEED

Isaac was tall and brave enough to wear a mullet. I'd never thought much about the color, quality, and texture of clothing before, but it was obvious his made him the authority on everything cool. He introduced me to pastels. We met in the fourth grade when all of my closest friends were put in a different class with another teacher. He caught me sketching one day and admired my nascent talent for drawing the most realistic superhero muscles of anyone at school. He was new and looking for a friend. That was me.

No one knew more about superheroes and comics than Isaac, least of all me. I had only just barely discovered the magical worlds that could be hidden inside flimsy, brightly colored newsprint via a *Superman IV: The Quest for Peace* movie adaptation I found on the spinner rack in a mountainside mini mart high up in the Sierra Nevadas while on the bait delivery route with Dad. The (for some reason) always wet, all-brick store was frequented mostly by fishermen and people whose idea of a next-door neighbor was someone who would take no less than ten minutes to come over for a quick game of shoot-that-thing-that's-wandering-through-my-property-right-now. It was about as unlikely a place as I could ever hope to find such a book, and yet there it was.

Each page of the comic held about five or six little miracles of illustration Isaac told me were called panels. Moments were captured in micro, with each successive panel suggesting movement and flow and pace in a way that had me eager to turn each page and disappointed when I reached the last one. The connective tissue between the panels—the moments of action missing—was left to my imagination. I participated in the telling of the story, filling in the details on my own. If Clark Kent walked up to a phone booth in one panel and Superman flew away from it in the next, then a world of story could have happened in between. Or a simple changing of clothes. It was up to me.

One of the first things I did in the week following my discovery was to go to the Thrifty Drug Store near our house and see what other comic book adaptations were available. Sure enough, on a low shelf, there they were. The Transformers had their own comic book. So did G.I. Joe, Alf, and Chuck Norris and his Karate Kommandos. Even the Care Bears had one, and it wasn't too bad, really. With their mighty Care Bear stare they vanquished evil with the power of the emotional spectrum! It was easy to think of them as sensitive but short superheroes with a grooming issue. Isaac scoffed at such a notion. He was a purist.

"If you're going to read comic books, you have to read Marvel."

"I do," I said. "Look, it says 'Marvel' right there on the cover." Sure enough, Marvel had an imprint for books featuring licensed properties called Star Comics. My defense was weak and I knew it, but I offered it up anyway, tentatively. Isaac's eyes went tight.

"This is for little kids," he said, taking the comics away from me and examining them with all the stink his eye could muster. "Marvel makes these, but they're not the real Marvel. The real Marvel is the real superheroes. Spider-Man. The Fantastic Four. The Incredible Hulk. The Uncanny X-Men. Especially X-men."

"I've seen those."

"Good. Now start buying them."

Superheroes were powerful, faced complex personal and moral issues (marry the clone of the dead girlfriend or no?), and they never, ever fought evil with something as passive as staring. Except for Cyclops. He shot optic beams from his eyes. Optic beams, *not* emotions.

Isaac's bedroom was a refuge, providing sanctuary for a battalion of action figures that remained untouched by the brothers and sisters he never had. Stacks and stacks of bagged and boarded comic books filled up boxes that hadn't been accidentally kicked in by scrimmaging little brothers. I was a dog and his room was my four-color bacon; I salivated enviously every time I entered.

It was on the floor of Isaac's bedroom that we spent hour after hour lining up our respective comic collections to see how much square footage they could cover and to trade the ones we'd grown bored of. Some days we'd reenact the entire third act battle of Tim Burton's *Batman*, pitting the Caped Crusader and the Joker against each other with lots of plastic-on-plastic violence, thanks to Isaac's pristine, complete set of figures and vehicles.

With Isaac leading the way, I gladly went straight down into the geek rabbit hole.

* * *

I was eleven when Mom's brother, Uncle Scott, approached me in the summer of 1988 about the possibility of manning his shaved ice stand in a nearby parking lot for a few hours every Saturday afternoon. Just me, by myself. I wanted to do it, badly, but I knew Mom would be instantly against it. I could already see her "Not my baby!" face.

Money was on the table. I had to find a way to stop that face.

I knew that as soon as she heard about the job all Mom would think about was the burlap sack that would go over my head as the kickoff to my kidnapping. My solution: hire Isaac to help me out and use him as the better dressed kidnapping bait. To my astonishment, my ploy was effective and she agreed to let me work at Hawaiian Ice to make the people their fruity, cold confections so long as Isaac was with me.

This was how, at my first real job, I became both employee to my uncle and boss to my friend. Like no one should ever do.

The job description was simple enough. All we had to do was make the shaved ice, change the monies, and listen to R.E.M.'s *Green* over and over again. (It was the only cassette tape in Uncle Scott's boom box. I became more certain with each passing Saturday that this R.E.M. was a band of toothless vampires who could only subsist on a diet of bleeding ears.)

I handled the ice carving duties. The trick was getting the blade to hit the block at just the right angle so the flakes of ice were so fine they would group easily, but not so big they'd coalesce into hard chunks like they would on a snow cone. If the flakes could stay somewhat separated, then, once they hit the tongue, they'd just melt away. There was a real art to it and I was the master.

Isaac's job was to douse the manmade snow with the many flavored syrups. He didn't care so much about the money. As an only child, he was, essentially, the kid version of rich. With nowhere else for their middle class money to go, his parents gave him whatever he wanted. For Isaac, working at the stand was about hanging out, getting drunk on Tiger's Blood, and heading over to Thrifty's afterward for our weekly reading purchases.

Uncle Scott paid our wage of three dollars an hour directly to me. It was a small price to pay for time with his family and away from his sunny, sticky real estate at the strip mall. He probably knew but did not care that more often than not he was actually paying us to laugh ourselves silly, get into cherry and bubblegum flavored fights, and otherwise unknowingly frighten off the customers. I paid Isaac his cut out of mine, usually amounting to three or four dollars. It wasn't much, but it didn't have to be because Isaac came to work in a flying limousine with gold-plated wings. Sometimes we were paid more money than we'd made that day, but that didn't stop Uncle Scott from asking us back the following year.

We began our second tour of duty in June of 1989, about five months after Dad's shooting, during the long summer of dread. This time, I came to the job with a more mature sense of our responsibility and a thought toward what it must look like to passing motorists as they witnessed a reenactment of *Lord of the Flies* with streams of syrup.

Isaac was a handful that way, even a year later. He got worked up easily, letting his imagination and adolescent inner juices run away with him. He hopped around our small patch of asphalt like a madman, kickboxing the air and spouting off insane ideas in a multitude of funny voices. More than once he reeled me into great battles of cosmic importance (no dispute too great that it couldn't be solved by a well-thrust, imaginary light saber), and I did my best to bite the line. Did he honestly think yelping monkeys minding the store would promote sales? He didn't seem to care one way or another.

As the summer wore on, my impatience grew. Curbing Isaac's behavior became a regular part of my job responsibilities, and I was proving to be terribly irresponsible. I couldn't let Isaac get bored and stop working for me, but I also couldn't let Mowgli the jungle child stink up the stand with money repellent. I was part employer/part cruise director and I hated it.

The solution was Caleb.

Caleb was nearly the physical opposite—rotund where Isaac was lanky—affable, and shaggy-haired. He was given to sweating large beads in the summer that collected on the tips of his hair. He was into comic books, too, but not as much as me and Isaac. Was it by choice? I doubted it. He lived in an apartment, not a house, so I assumed Caleb's lack of printed superhero was for want of funds. That seemed so unfair.

With only four Saturdays left in the summer before school started, it made sense to ask Isaac to step aside in favor of Caleb. Isaac didn't need the money, and there was very little left to be made anyway. But, it would mean a lot to Caleb.

I called him and told him my idea. He just wanted to know one thing:

> **CALEB:** You're sure Isaac is okay with this?
> **ME:** Yeah. Uh huh. Why wouldn't he be?

It took me a couple more days to call Isaac. I had to make sure Caleb's parents were going to approve, and I didn't want to bother Isaac with something that wasn't final yet. It wouldn't be fair.

I knew Isaac would see immediately what a good idea this was. When he picked up the phone and said "hello," it was the first time I noticed he spoke with an annoyed edge in his voice. I wondered if it always had that quality. I decided it did, then explained the situation.

> **ISAAC:** So, that's it? I don't get to work at the stand anymore?
> **ME:** Yeah, you know, you've done it a lot already and Caleb actually needs this. I figure that's what's fair for everyone, right?
> **ISAAC:** How is this fair?

Okay, that was more than annoyance. That was anger. Definitely anger.

> **ISAAC:** Caleb hasn't done it once. I've been there since last summer!
> **ME:** I know! That's my point! You've had all this time and Caleb—Caleb hasn't. Look, uh, I didn't think this would be a big deal. Maybe we could do this—maybe if you guys trade off? There's only four Saturdays left. Maybe you take two and Caleb takes two? I'm sure he'd be okay with that change. He won't care.

ISAAC: You already talked to him about this?
ME: Well, yeah.
ISAAC: This is something the two of you talked about already. That you decided together.
ME: Yeah, sort of. I just wanted to make sure he wanted to do it in the first place. It's not a big deal. This doesn't have to be a big deal.
ISAAC: Yeah, it is. It's a pretty #$%#in' big deal.

Whoa, whoa, whoa. What was happening?

ME: Dude, don't do that. Don't talk like that. Come on. Don't–don't cuss, all right? I get that you're mad, but—
ISAAC: I'm not doing two weeks. Tell Caleb I'm not doing two weeks and he's not doing four.
ME: N-no. I can't do that! Isaac, c'mon, I already told him. The two weeks, that was something that I just—that's not—That's not fair to him. He didn't do anything wrong. I'm sorry, okay? I really didn't think you'd have a problem with it. I really did think you'd be okay. I'm just trying to help him, that's all.
ISAAC: #$%@ you.
ME: It's just four weeks. The summer's almost over!
ISAAC: #$%@ you. I was here first. #$%@ YOU.
ME: It's not even that much money. You don't need it like he does.
ISAAC: I don't $#@*in' care.

Isaac's voice got quieter, but not because he'd lowered it. The phone had moved away from his mouth. I heard a faint "Fine, do whatever" before an angry click.

I had been shaking since before Isaac picked up the phone. Four weeks later, on the first day of seventh grade and facing our first reunion since the phone call, I hadn't stopped.

11

THE FIGHT

An hour earlier we'd been held hostage in our home by the fear of killers lurking in the neighborhood. Now, it was first period, my first day of seventh grade at Tioga Middle School. This was so much worse.

"In this class you'll be learning the very, very basic math you need to move on to the eighth grade." My new math teacher (literally the only subject he taught—so weird) spoke with pure hatred. For his job, for his life, for us—I didn't know what. "I expect you to pay attention as closely as possible and do all of the homework. Only by paying attention will you learn anything. Some of you may be unfamiliar with this concept. That is why you are in this class."

I ceased caring about math when the betrayal of everything I held numerically dear known as fractions was introduced. *Doesn't mean I'm stupid*, I told myself. *I just don't like math.* I had always been one of the smart kids, and I still clung to that distinction. Mr. Everything Sucks and I Am Alone had other ideas.

"There is another class I teach sixth period where the students are much, much smarter than you all are. If you're lucky, you'll get to move to that class next year. Perhaps even next semester if a miracle occurs and your brains unexpectedly show up. For now, we suffer through this year together. Open your books."

I had never heard a teacher talk like that before. At first, it felt like a joke. Why would he spend half the class making us feel bad about ourselves? When variations on the "you're stupid" speech were repeated nearly every day that first week, I decided that teaching could be just a job, something that had to be done and was loathed. That had never occurred to me before. As I considered the rest of my new teachers in this context, I noticed that many of them conducted the business of instruction with the kind of impatience that could only come from wallowing too often in the familiar. There was a clear disdain for students that bled from every word.

The goal of learning at Tioga Middle School was entirely secondary to surviving the day, for all parties involved. There was hardly a morning I didn't ride my bike to school on an empty stomach because the nausea that hit me upon waking would not allow breakfast. The only thing I looked forward to that first week was lunchtime.

The sixth graders from the other elementary schools that funneled into Tioga brought with them rivalries and a rougher crowd than I was used to. The "FIGHT!" calls usually went out during our thirty-six-minute break for eating when we could freely roam, but the small campus wasn't exactly constructed with the audience needs of gladiatorial combat in mind. The trick was being fast enough to get to a fight before it broke up or ended, and yet still leaving it quickly enough to get to the next one in time. That is, of course, unless the cry of "GIRL FIGHT!" went out. Those fights were rare and far more punishing, so we raced to them no matter what else was happening. They were the only fights with the potential to continue even after they'd been broken up by school administrators. Them girls was crazy that way.

An unfamiliar darkness dwelled at Tioga. My friend Nathan and I rode our bikes together to school in the mornings, and his tires were slashed twice that first week and at least once every week after that. During my second week, as I put my books into my locker one afternoon, a boy I did not know approached with an offer to sell me drugs. He actually used the word "drugs," making it much easier to remember what I was supposed to say "no" to. I politely declined, and he politely went his way, which made him seem all the more evil to me. His cordial demeanor was a trick, I was sure of it.

Showers after PE were naked and communal, the greatest of all the evils perpetrated at the school. Not as hilarious as they thought? The boys who whipped our bare backs with the wet towels they'd twist into rat tails. I wanted to whip them back, but I would have felt bad for doing so and, had I ever actually done it, the rat-tail boys would have retaliated with far more ferocity, that much was certain.

At Tioga, I was always on my guard. Always waiting for the next insult, the next surprise, or the next attack. For that reason alone I should have seen Isaac coming at me from the angle he did. I knew it wasn't going to be easy seeing him again. I knew from his silence during the last few weeks of summer he was probably still mad at me. I knew words would have to be said. I just didn't think it was going to be those words.

"C'MON! You wanna FIGHT?!"

The first time Isaac tried to fight me it was the second day of school. For the next few weeks afterward he came at me, goading me again and again with no success. I absolutely would not fight my friend.

His final petition for violence happened during the fourth week of school and, as always, a crowd gathered. I was determined they once again go away disappointed. I didn't want to fight. I didn't know how to fight. I had always gotten by in elementary school because of my mouth, not my pugilist skills. If a bigger kid was ever upset at me, I'd pair up a "Yo Momma" joke with words with more than three syllables and leave him confused and everyone else laughing. Isaac knew my charms and was immune to them.

"You wanna fight?" he asked me for the last time.

"No," I said definitively.

"You a p##@? Fight me, you #@$%er."

"Look, just leave me alone, all right? Just leave me alone and I'll leave you alone."

"What are you gonna do if I don't?"

"N-nothing."

He got right up in my face, as per the rules of the pre-fight. We stood chest to chest, me looking away from Isaac's ever narrowing eyes and he boring a hole into the side of my head. The time and place of most fights were usually decided on beforehand by the participants involved, but I hadn't set anything up with Isaac. I never scheduled our little dances of aggression, nor could I imagine ever doing so. (I thought it was an asinine practice in the first place. If you want to cause someone harm, why would you warn them ahead of time? If I wanted to fight someone, I'd drop them coming out of a bathroom or sucker punch them while they had half a school pizza stuffed in their face.)

The summer was over. Hawaiian Ice had packed up. How did fighting me fix anything? And who were the skater punks he was suddenly hanging out with? Why couldn't I just have my friend back?

"I'm just gonna go," I said, pleading with him to stop. "Okay, Isaac? I've been telling you—I don't want to fight you."

"Yeah?" Isaac puffed out his chest all the more. "Well, I'm gonna beat the #@$+ out of you, you $#@%er."

"Whatever."

"$#@% you." And with that he pushed me, hard, in the chest.

"I'm not fighting you," I said. "I'm not fighting at all. I'm sorry, all right? I'm sorry I ever brought Caleb on. If I could go back, I wouldn't do it. I didn't know you would—"

"I don't $#@%in' care about that! You're such a scared little $#@+."

Yes. "No, I'm not." Yes, I was.

"C'mon!" He pushed me again, harder than he ever had before. I took a stumble backwards.

"No!" I shouted. "Forget you!" And, as I had learned to do, I turned around and walked away. I knew if I didn't give Isaac what he wanted—if I didn't push back—then he couldn't get as mad as he needed to be to really come after me. This usually led to the playground fight connoisseurs coming up to me afterward and advising that I "shouldn't be such a p##@ and let that guy push (me) around like that." Courting embarrassment wasn't high on my list, but giving those guys a thrill was even lower. My back to him, Isaac was left with no other recourse than to cuss up an even bigger storm and hurl obscenities at me. I wanted so badly to just turn around and let him have it (verbally, of course), but I didn't.

WHAM!

My knees went bloody as they made contact with the pavement. My head followed, my face landing with a hard splat, mouth open to swallow grains of dirt left behind by dirty sneakers. At first, there was no pain, only the thought of how ridiculous I looked being shoved to the ground feet over butt. There's no real shame in being the one attacked from behind, but I was sure that anyone else would have folded less comically. I already looked weak for not fighting back. *Now,* I thought, *I just look stupid.*

The laughing confirmed it.

I got up, enraged. Isaac hit me from behind so hard I was sure I had whiplash. At home, Logan and I took turns running away from each other during fights, depending on who was the most mad. The most mad was usually the one who was in the most pain. The most mad wouldn't care about how much he was hurting the other, only that he was. I wanted to kill Isaac.

In a rage, I ran up to him. I wanted to punch him in the face. I wanted to punch him in the face so hard his jaw would crack and break and he'd cry like the baby he was. Instead, I maintained and declared once again, "I'm not going to fight you!"

Isaac put both hands on my chest and pushed me again, as hard as he could, throwing me back again. "BUT I WANNA FIGHT YOU!" I caught myself before hitting the ground.

Everyone around us—the fight connoisseurs, my friends, Isaac's skater friends, the girl I liked in English class—howled and chanted: "FIGHT! FIGHT! FIGHT!" It was finally on, they were sure of it.

I narrowed the gap between me and Isaac again, getting back in his face. I stood there, not sure what would happen next. I only knew that backing down was impossible, but also that I would not throw a punch. Whatever the cost, I would not hit Isaac back.

Before anything else could happen, a whistle rang out. Everyone dispersed quickly. Isaac pushed me one more time, effectively pointing out to the vice principal who the problem was. A large woman at once entirely focused on what we were doing and completely disinterested in whatever the problem actually was, she sized us up and made her decision instantly.

"Both of you, come with me."

Back in her office, we were invited to explain our conflict. I went first. Isaac eyed me like I was the single most contemptible thing he'd ever seen in his life. His version of events made me sound as though I was the worst kind of liar, playing games behind his back and cheating him out of what was rightfully his. I didn't recognize myself. And I didn't recognize Isaac.

The vice principal leaned forward. "What we have here is a disagreement between two peoples." Really? Obviously she had attained her high position on the strength of her keen observational skills. "What we don't have is respect. Respect for each other. Respect of this school. Do you two know what respect is?"

No, of course I don't. I'm an idiot. "Yes," I replied.

"Until you two can respect each other and your classmates, I want you to stay as far away from each other as possible. I don't want to catch either one of you near the other or it will be detention for you both."

Did she even listen to my side? "Tell him that!" I said. "I didn't do anything! I want to leave him alone—he won't let me!"

Isaac sold my point: "%&#@ you."

"That's ENOUGH!" the vice principal roared.

It was my final betrayal. I didn't even pretend I had instigated anything. I tried to put everything on Isaac, and he hated me all the more for it. The vice principal scolded Isaac one more time before dismissing us. Once we were clear of the office, he gave me one final shove.

"You heard her. Stay the $%#& away from me."

Until that moment, I never actually believed Isaac wouldn't be my friend again. My experience had always been that, whatever the problem, friends would forgive and forget the next day. I figured eventually it would be the same for me and Isaac. Now, I knew I was wrong.

Isaac was now my archenemy. But, I didn't accidentally make my Lex Luthor go bald. He had a mullet and I'd "cheated" him out of twelve bucks. Now and forevermore he would hate me. My intent didn't matter, only what he wanted and the fact that I wouldn't give in to him and let him have it. And, just like Superman could always count on Luthor to bust out of prison and threaten the city once again, I knew it wasn't over with Isaac.

As I went off to sixth period, I got more in tune with what I had put my body through. My heart was racing, my knees and back hurt like crazy, and I was on the verge of tears. I hadn't been in the principal's office since the third grade, and even then it was as a witness to a fight I had nothing to do with. Now I was one of *those* kids and there was no going back from that. Soon, the vice principal would spread the tale of the fight and the drama surrounding it to my teachers and the other administrators in the school. I was now "trouble." I hated that. I wanted to be thought well of. I didn't want to be "trouble" or in it.

Dad wasn't about to let that happen. Later that day, he sat me down and we talked, just the two of us.

"Your mom went down and talked to the vice principal earlier this week," he said.

What. "She did? Why?"

"I wanted to know what she had to say about that kid trying to sell you the drugs. I was working, so your mother went instead. You shouldn't have to deal with something like that, not at your age. Neither one of us was very happy about it."

That didn't sound like Mom at all. I had a hard time imagining her facing down anyone, much less a woman twice her size in a power suit. "What did Mom say?"

"Just that. That you had been offered drugs and it was unacceptable.

We wanted to know how big of a problem this really is and what they're doing about it."

"What did the vice principal say?"

"She said—get this—she said 'Drugs? There are no drugs at our school.'" For his imitation of the vice principal, Dad went into the slightly higher-pitched, lilting voice he reserved for the imitative mocking of authority. He sounded like a very fey British diplomat.

"That's not true!" I said. "I'm not the only one who's been offered drugs. Everybody knows who the stoners and the dealers are. She really said that?"

"She did. Look, son, your mom and I have been thinking . . . you're coming home with more and more of these stories and now this thing with Isaac. We don't like it. We don't like it for you. You are dealing with things at school that you shouldn't have to. We have an idea that I want you to seriously consider."

There was something I did not know. The day after the shooting of the federal agents at the mini mart on the corner, Mom and Dad signed papers on a new house in nearby Clovis. Fresno averaged about one hundred murders a year, Clovis about one. Though the cities were so close together that out-of-towners could scarcely tell when they were going from one to the other, the difference in general safety and—more important to my parents—the quality of the schools could not have been greater. Soon, there would be no need for me to put up with Tioga or the Fresno Unified School District. Or my math teacher. Or the vice principal. Or Isaac.

"But," Dad continued. "The house won't be ready until the next school year. So, here's what we're thinking . . . "

Public schooling was over. I would now be homeschooled. I would end my time at Tioga after a little more than a month in classes and start over by myself at home. I'd have some catching up to do since nothing I'd done at Tioga would count toward the homeschooling curriculum, but without the distraction of kids who belonged in cages and the continuing threat of getting knocked to the ground, I'd catch up soon enough.

All I heard was "no school." I was in.

12

HOLLYWOOD

During the first couple months of homeschooling, I nearly lost the calluses on my Nintendo thumbs. None of the work I'd done at Tioga Middle School counted, so there was no time to waste on princess-rescuing frivolity if I was ever going to make up for the lost six weeks. But, no matter how hard I worked, I just couldn't seem to get ahead.

My parents had contracted a homeschooling service for my books and curriculum. There was an educational professional out there, somewhere, to whom I submitted all my work, but it was entirely up to me to figure out how to use the materials and lessons provided. I was quickly overwhelmed by the new curriculum and the responsibility of teaching it to myself. The thick textbooks seemed written in another language, and the density of content sent my mind into revolt. If I hadn't liked math much before, I now found it impossible. Science, normally a subject I enjoyed, betrayed me and turned into some made up abuse of the alphabet called "chemistry." I wasn't a huge fan of the assigned books in English class at Tioga, but at least I understood what happened in the stories and why. The novels I read for homeschool played chicken with my intelligence, throwing unfamiliar words at me every other sentence and forcing me to dive into a dictionary to figure out just what in the world Hester Prynne was doing with that minister.

For two months I struggled, my efforts yielding nothing more than frustration and confusion. It was only when I finally got to the point of giving up all together that it was discovered I had been given all the wrong materials. All of my books, from science to English to history to math, were not only from the wrong grade level, but they were all from grades far above my own.

Mom and Dad fired the homeschooling service and my education moved to plan C—which was really just the same as plan B but with a different company. By then, the holidays were fast approaching. Plan C couldn't even begin until after the new year.

In January of 1990, I started the school year all over again. My time at Tioga still counted for nothing, and my eight weeks of accidental high school was equally invalid. I now had one semester—five months—to get an entire school year's worth of work done.

I played even more Nintendo instead.

At first, Mom and Dad didn't even notice. I went through the motions each morning of at least trying to do some schoolwork, but my patience for the much-too-large mountain of worksheets and tests that never seemed to diminish always ran out. And quickly.

After lunch was game time. *Metroid. The Legend of Zelda. Blaster Master. Battletoads. Goonies 2. Defender of the Crown* (Dad's personal favorite—he played as much as we did). *Rygar. Super Mario Bros. 3.* My real textbook was *Nintendo Power* magazine. I studied hard to know what the latest and greatest games were and how to conquer them. Through sheer dedication and strength of will, I completed every grass, desert, water, and lava level thrown at me. What others called "wasting time," I called work ethic.

This was my pattern, week after week. A little bit of schoolwork to satisfy my mother, a whole lot of game time to defeat our would-be digital overlords. Sure, I did my assignments—some of them, anyway—but I also took advantage of any justification to leave my textbooks behind.

Justifications like a Hollywood crew rolling into town, determined to make a spectacle of Dad's harrowing tale of survival.

* * *

Rescue 911 was a network television program that featured true stories of people in trouble who had been saved by the miracle wrought by Alexander Graham Bell and a magical three-digit number. The show struck a dramatic yet celebratory tone, hailing the work of police and rescue services across the United States. Three reenactments of traumatic and inspiring events were staged a week, buffeted by on-camera interviews with those involved. It was a lot like *America's Most Wanted*, except you didn't pee yourself afterward for fear of home invasion and death by multiple stabbings.

Most rescues ended happily. The show's sensibility was generous toward both its subjects and its viewers, refusing to dole out guilty, vicarious pleasures by exploiting the victims and their families for cheap emotional drama. It was a reality show before the term was coined and rendered connotatively crass. We watched together as a family, though sometimes it was all too real and Mom felt compelled to leave the room.

To host this weekly exhibition of everyday peril and frantic phone dialing, the producers enlisted the aid of the most talented and powerful duo in all of Hollywood. Together, they had smoked up the small screen for years in such classics as *The Twilight Zone*, *Star Trek*, and *T.J. Hooker*. They'd even put out an album or two. Only William Shatner and His Glorious Hairpiece had the skills to guide viewers in and out of the commercial breaks. The Shat. Captain Friggin' Kirk. It was as though the *Rescue 911* producers were gunning for the coveted Bill Heasley demographic.

The show found the subjects of its segments by calling local police stations across the country. Since *911* focused so much on casting local law enforcement and paramedics in a positive light, the Fresno Police Department was quite eager to have this nice, friendly faction of Hollywood swing on by. Even nearly a year later, after hundreds of murders and robberies had made their way through the news pages, the Fresno PD knew exactly which story to pitch to the producers.

For Dad, this pretty much constituted what he imagined to be the greatest thing ever. His longtime devotion to all things Shat and Kirk finally found its nirvana in the now single degree of separation between them. His first question for the producers wasn't "How much will we be paid?" or "Will the shoot be catered?" It was, "Do I get to meet William Shatner?"

The answer was, "No, but you do get an autographed picture."

Good enough.

Dad's second question was if he could play himself on camera. The producers were adamantly against it. The last thing they needed was a guy who hadn't properly dealt with his trauma freaking out on set. Dad's eerie calm, instead of being reassuring, concerned them all the more. There were many things to worry about during the one-week shoot: filming in multiple locations, interviews with over a dozen of the people involved, and complicated special effects and stunt work. Nowhere on the schedule was there room for recording proof of Dad's need for therapy.

Dad found their worries to be, quite frankly, stupid. He was tired of other people telling him how he should and should not feel. He begged and pleaded and reassured the production company, the on-site producer, the director—he would have taken his case to the guy holding the boom mic if he thought it would have done any good. Eventually, through measured persistence, reservations were set aside.

Though it's a scant three hours away from Los Angeles, Fresno is mostly useful to Hollywood as shorthand for Podunkville, USA, in lazily written late-night talk show jokes. With its flat streets and squat, unadorned buildings, there's just not much about Fresno that's immediately cinematic. A production crew in town was a big deal. Someone had actually dared to turn a camera on our "little" town of nearly half a million people. They completely took over not only the Shop, but also our house, our lives, and what we talked about at the grocery store. For the entire length of the one-week shoot, we were either on the front page of *The Fresno Bee* or the top story on the local TV news. At church, a friend took to humming the mostly tuneless *Rescue 911* theme song, following me around like a puppy, and asking questions about movie stars I had no connection with.

The men and women in the production crew were something of a disappointment. We had expected egotistical, acerbic Hollywood types chomping on cigars and asking Dad if he would mind having a pet monkey to provide comical reaction shots as he's shot to pieces. Instead, they were perfectly respectful, lovely people. They took seriously the responsibility to not cheapen the gravity of Dad's situation while still maintaining some sort of broadcast standard. They wanted us to have nothing but a positive experience and catered to our every need and desire (by which I mean we ate a lot of Kentucky Fried Chicken).

Our every day and night was commandeered by the filming. My regular, half-hearted homeschooling routine was upset so badly there was no need for even the pretense of doing my schoolwork. Hollywood, evil influencer of children, successfully destroyed any lingering ambition I may have had to finish my giant work packet of death. A real-life motion picture show was in town. Now *that* was something to study.

My father, to his everlasting credit, had instilled in me a deep love and appreciation of all things cinema. He didn't pore over movie magazines like *Starlog* or scour the Scholastic book orders for anything movie or (better yet) *Star Wars* related like I had obsessed myself into doing, but he was known to "work late" now and again. Then, the next day, he'd tell us all about the movie with the confusing title we all had to see together. "Trust me, Brock," he said one day in early August of 1985. "You'll love *Back to the Future*."

Even then, I didn't completely understand what we were in for. I knew that the making of a segment on *Rescue 911* would hardly be representative of the experience of what it must be like to shoot a big studio film, but all of the essential ingredients—cameras, lighting, a director, a producer, the sound guy, makeup artists, even a stunt man—were there.

I found out rather quickly that a television shoot is mostly about the waiting. The real work wasn't in what anyone did while cameras were rolling—that was actually the smallest part of it. Our drab, overly brown living room was transformed into a pleasing, dynamic space through what seemed like endless hours of prep work by the lighting guy and the sound guy and everyone else who pulled on that drapery or closed that window. It took *forever.* If you blinked, you missed the actual seconds when the camera rolled. But, no worries. Wait some more and soon the scene or the interview or the insert of a car driving down a dark road would be filmed again. And again. And again. Each minute piece of action had to be repeated multiple times to accommodate different camera angles and the mysterious, punishing demands of the totalitarian director who ordered "Again, one more time," over and over again.

As bored as I sometimes was by the process, Dad was very much the opposite. Take after take, his smile and stamina never waned. When the time finally came to perform THE moment, the director gave Dad one last chance to back out. If ever he was going to have any psychological or emotional difficulty with the recreation, this was the scene during which that would happen. He would be required to again watch as two men, with guns, kicked in his door and fired their weapons at him. Tiny charges tucked away inside of the glass display cases were ready to blow apart in concert with the blanks fired from the guns. Other charges on Dad's person would mimic the bullets that hit him. The impact would be nothing like what he felt on the actual night, but there would be strong, abrupt sensations in the same places and he would need to react and fall to the ground with precision. And without having a freak-out. That it wasn't real might not matter in the moment.

The stunt man, on call and ready, grabbed a donut and sat down. If anybody was gonna go down in a red haze of colored corn syrup, it was gonna be my dad. He'd bled for this once already and this was his reward. Everyone else could worry about him if that was what they needed to do, but no one would be taking his acting debut away from him. In the spring of 1990, fifteen months after he was shot, my father giddily reenacted his real-life action hero experience.

Logan and I were forced to go hang out in the trailer across the street from the Shop, far away from the psyche-damaging pretend violence. Because of the multiple set-ups and the fact that their screen time was brief, the two actors playing the shooters were already in there, waiting. So, for most of the night, right up until it was time for them to go into the Shop and play their parts, it was just the four of us.

"Hey, hey," the one closest to the door said as we opened it. "Who's this now?" They both sat at a little table in what looked very much like my grandparents' motor home. "Who we got?"

"I'm Brock, and this is my brother, Logan."

"Well, all right," the other one said. "Pleased to meet you both. I'm Carl, this is Will. You fellas enjoying the shoot?"

"Yeah!" Logan said.

I wasn't so sure. "It's okay,"

"Pretty boring, right?" Carl said. "I feel ya, I feel ya. You know who's having all the fun is your dad."

"Yeah," I said. "I wanna see but they won't let me."

"Just as well," Will said. "They're gonna run through it thirty times before they're ready for us. Be glad you're in here with the pretty faces."

"'Pretty?'" Carl asked. "That why we're wearin' masks in this scene?"

"Nah, man. We wearin' masks because we're *too* pretty. They don't want us outshinin' their dad, the star. Look at this mug, huh?" Will jutted out his chin and stroked it so we could get a good look. Logan and I just grinned. "Why else anybody wanna hide that? Obviously, I should be the guy behind the counter, not the guy with the machine gun. Don't tell nobody this, but I'm really more of a gentle soul."

"Fool, look at you," Carl said. "You hear this guy? Man, their dad is straight up white. You think you're so good you can play white?"

"Maybe. I got style, man. I'm versatile."

"You ain't *that* versatile."

"Whatever. Why you gonna bring me down like that?"

"Why you—why you don't look in *mirrors?*"

They both laughed uproariously at this, and we laughed with them. It was entirely possible I was looking at the two coolest people I'd ever met.

"Hey, you dudes want some Twinkies?" they asked.

How was this a question? "Sure!" I shouted. They invited me and Logan to take the seats beside them.

"We got a lot of 'em. Have as many as you want!"

I couldn't help but think about how unusual it was to be alone with two adult black men. I'd never had any real interaction with black adults before. At school, my friends had many different skin colors and were from countries whose names I couldn't pronounce, but I'd never met any of their parents. These men didn't seem all that different from anyone else I knew, except for the fact that, perhaps owing to their occupation, they were quite a bit funnier. And, they had Twinkies. Lots and lots of Twinkies. Being sequestered in the trailer? Not so bad.

Our family was going to be a piece of entertainment, and I happily broke unnaturally colored bread with the villains. What had been tragedy was now fun. What had been scary was now pretty much amazing. The wait in the hospital, the many visits to the ICU, the day after day of cleaning out Dad's bullet wounds—none of that seemed to matter as we laughed and ate ourselves into early diabetes with the two men who would try to "kill" my father later that night.

13

TALKING TO A DEAD MAN

Under the cover of night, the Shat emerges from the space between a collection of police cars and an ambulance, dressed in a tight suit just a little too small for him.

> **WILLIAM SHATNER:** Bill Heasley owned a small bait and tackle shop on the outskirts of Fresno, California. Six days a week he ran the register and waited on customers himself. Until the night of January 17, 1989.

At the pronouncement of the date, the Shat dropped his voice an octave to a sort of half-whisper. Never had the enumerated orbit of the earth sounded so grave. It's doubtful Dad heard anything beyond the first two words of the opening line. The Shat said his name. Whatever came next was gravy.

Everyone who was remotely involved in Dad's rescue gathered together in the fall of 1990 at a Chinese restaurant in Fresno to see what they looked like with an extra ten pounds and drink in celebration to a few more. Ours was the second segment of the second episode of *Rescue 911*'s second season. Dad sat right in the middle of the crowd, nearest to the glow of the screen. Once the Shat faded from view, the place went quiet.

The re-creation begins with a prelude to action, showing Dad packing up the guns for the night. Outside the Shop, two men in sneakers and masks jump out of their truck to the strains of a ghostly electric guitar, their submachine guns already drawn. A quick edit later and the gunmen kick in the door. Then, another quick cut back to my startled father, his head snapping up to see them. A close-up on the barrels of the raised guns. Shots fired. Dad's body tumbles backward, shaking with the impact of each bullet.

I knew it wasn't real. But still . . . Dad knew how to react believably to bullets hitting and sinking into his body. This must have been what it was like.

The quick edits continue. Display cases exploding. Glass flying everywhere. Dad dropping to the ground as soon as the barrage of bullets pause long enough to let gravity take him there. The shooters rushing desperately to collect as many weapons as possible into the large sack they brought with them. Dad, already breathing heavily as he mistakenly grabs the display gun in his attempt to fire back. Another spray of bullets when he fails—back and forth and back and forth. Finally, the shooters back out of the Shop, firing just a few shots more for good measure.

It was startlingly violent, but it wasn't particularly moving. I'd seen the raw footage on playback months earlier after a good amount of begging and betting that the fatigue of the late-night shoot would make everyone forget why they'd sent Logan and me away in the first place. The action seemed plain and unremarkable then. I remembered the (hilarious!) actor firing the last shots and shouting, "Bang! Bang! Bang!" as he did so. It was hard to take any of it seriously.

What I didn't expect as I sat and watched the finished version of the scene with everyone in the Chinese restaurant all those months later was what happened next: a piece of real cinema artistry tucked away inside of the pop-reality infotainment that rocked me sideways.

The shooters leave, the door swinging closed behind them with a furious *SLAM!* Its lonely echo trails off. The quick edits stop. The camera—now at an omniscient, unflinching overhead angle like a security camera that was never (but should have been) there—slowly pans to survey the destruction to the Shop. Dad is unseen, but his heavy breathing rises up once again to overtake the soundtrack—this time completely. The pan finishes to reveal my defeated father on the ground, his body ravaged by bullets and propped up against the display cases. He doesn't move with the exception of the rising and falling of his chest with every desperate clutch of a breath.

The camera lingers. The thought for anyone watching is the same: he is alone and he is going to die.

Cut to the outside of the Shop; an eighteen-wheeler passes by with a roar on the otherwise empty stretch of highway, frustratingly unaware of the drama that's just taken place inside. After it's out of sight, all that's left is the silent street and the dimly lit Shop. All is still and nothing more happens.

And it's achingly clear: nothing more is going to happen.

Emotion blindsided me. A sick, pit-of-my-stomach feeling I had never felt before in connection to the shooting of my father took over. My heart pounded, pushing furiously against the inside of my chest as the onscreen image finally, fully enlightened an event I thought I knew so well. It was one thing to hear Dad's matter-of-fact retelling of his story. That was life lived made into trivia and conversation. This other thing, though, this dose of devastating reality through the remove of a television show made for a paradoxical perspective I wasn't prepared for. It cut me somewhere deep, in a place within I didn't know existed. It *hurt.*

I looked over at my in-the-flesh father watching the show with rapt attention. He was just a few feet away. Healthy. Had we truly come so close to losing him?

Getting shot and left for dead on that floor meant Dad felt hopelessness. It meant Dad felt real *pain*. Not the kind of pain you recover from, but the kind of unrelenting pain you die from. It meant that life as he and I and everyone else knew it was ending and he faced that possibility alone. That the most unlikely hope—recovery—had turned into outcome didn't take away from the experience of those moments of unknowing. What was felt was felt, and what was hurt bore scars. I had been so sure in my knowledge Dad would be okay that I had never taken the time to honestly consider what he had to pass through to get there.

The despair he must have felt. How tempting had it been for him to give up? It would have been so much easier and less punishing to bleed out and let himself slip from this life. Did that cross his mind at all? It would have crossed mine. He proclaimed in the 911 call audio he was going to die. I had dismissed it as pessimism. What if it was a cry for relief?

I fixed my gaze upon the television and tried my best to not think about it. I felt my eyes welling up. I nearly cried, but I held it back for two reasons: 1) I had yet to cry about the shooting at all, and I wasn't about to start then, and 2) The lady paramedic who called my mom that night was there and she was really pretty.

The show cut to the beginning of the 911 call, completely ignoring the "incidental" incident of the 411 call. (If there is a battle for "_11" supremacy to be fought, this would have been the perfect time to stage it. I wanted the incompetency that nearly cost my father his life brought to light and the employee at Information Services publicly flogged with spiked phone cords. Mom felt much the same way. The producers explained that the show only had so much time, and details like that didn't serve their purpose of highlighting rescue services, even if it was an interesting aspect of the story on its own. They didn't need the additional color. I understood the reasoning; I just didn't like it.)

I'd heard 911 Operator Diane Vargas's voice so many times on the audio recording and she always seemed so calm. Her on-camera interview for the segment told a different story.

> **DIANE VARGAS:** I wasn't sure how bad he'd been hit. I tried to get from him—through questioning, through tone of voice, through voice inflection—how bad he is, medically. Mr. Heasley was not going to make it. I was talking to a dead man.

The segment moved quickly to show the changeover from Ms. Vargas to EMS Dispatcher Dan Lynch, the man who took the call over from her that night. I finally had a face and a mustache to put with the bull-headed demeanor and orders to stick things up butts.

> **DAN LYNCH:** You could hear the pain; you could hear the fright in his voice of what just occurred to this man. . . . And, as the call gradually progressed, you could hear his breathing grow more rapid and deeper, which is a sign of shock. This guy was on his way out.

Cut to the ambulance carrying EMT Steve Braun and paramedic Lori Stevens finally arriving at the Shop and not getting out of their vehicle. For a good portion of the time that Dad struggled inside, they just sat in the ambulance right outside and waited. Helpfully, the Shat explained:

> **WILLIAM SHATNER:** The paramedics were the first to arrive, but they are not allowed to visit violent crime scenes without police protection.

Even more helpful was Lori Stevens' next comment:

> **LORI STEVENS:** We put ourselves on the scene, but the scene was not secure because there was no law enforcement there. I can't do Bill any good if I'm shot. I can't do him any good if I'm dead. We just pulled back across the street. If we had to get out of there quickly, we could.

A battle of narrative supremacy ensued. With raw charisma and three seasons of *Star Trek* backing him, the Shat got in the last word on this matter:

> **WILLIAM SHATNER:** They could only wait, helplessly, until police arrived.

To illustrate the frustration the paramedics felt, an insert shot showing Steve the EMT banging the steering wheel of the ambulance repeatedly with his fist as it sat parked in the darkness flashed on the screen. At this, the entire restaurant roared with laughter.

According to the show, this scolding of the steering wheel happened at roughly the same time Dad told Dan the Dispatcher to relay a message to his family. Dan communicated the feelings the conversation inspired well, his mustache quivering with his lip as he reenacted the call.

> **DAN LYNCH:** "Tell my wife that I love her and tell the kids to be good." That was pretty emotional for me at the moment. It was like, "I'm the last voice between their father and their family?"

We obtained a copy of the audio from Dad's 911 call about a month after the shooting. The desperate, halting grabs for breath and the grit and anguish in his voice was unlike anything I'd ever heard come out of him. Multiple listens and sharings with curious friends and relatives had made my family sort of numb to it. Or rather, to most of it. No matter how many times I heard it, Dad's plea that we know that he loved us and to be good always filled me with both gratitude and great anxiety.

It's the timing of it. It's toward the end of the call when his life is a slippery thing and he's feeling it—he doesn't need to be told. "Be good."

These were not my father's last words, but they may as well have been. Better than any will or testament, his words and wishes then, in the moment of death if not the fact of it, were recorded.

"Be *good*."

When he was later robbed of the chance to repeat his dying words at the moment of his actual death, it didn't matter. It had already been said.

And it was a heck of a lot of pressure.

14

EDITED FOR TELEVISION

Before the show went to commercial, Steve the EMT pounded away one more time at that infernal steering wheel. This sent everyone in the restaurant right back into giggle fits, making our room possibly the only one in America viewing *Rescue 911* as a comedy. Much ribbing of live-and-in-person Steve the EMT ensued.

Everyone who had been featured so far were almost universally harsh in their assessments of their own appearance and performance, and their colleagues and friends took great pleasure in validating them. Compliments were reserved for Dad. It was agreed he did the best job of anyone and that he was a natural stunt performer. I wondered what they'd all think of me. I knew the producers had used some of my interview. I prayed I'd said something halfway intelligent.

When the show came back from commercial, everyone quieted down quickly. The Shat graced the screen once again, recapping everything for those whose memories didn't go back further than two minutes. The "actual call" resumed just in time for Dad to speak his final words to Dan the Dispatcher.

"Call my wife. Tell her to get the El—"

We had asked Dad what he intended to say before getting cut off, but his memory of the call was fuzzy at best. The pain he remembered quite well, thank you very much. But half-uttered sentences? No. He guessed he meant to say "Elders," meaning the Elders of the Church, and that he was anticipating needing a blessing once he arrived at the hospital in the event he lived long enough to receive it.

Rescue 911 didn't care about any of that. Before the viewers at home even have a chance to process the implications of the phone going dead, sirens wail again and a police car pulls up to the Shop. Inside is Sergeant Jeff Johnson of the Fresno PD. He was the first to see Dad in the flesh that night.

> **SGT. JOHNSON:** It looked like there'd been a war inside that one small area, about twenty square feet. It didn't take but a few seconds for me to check the store and make sure nobody was there lurkin' in the shadow which would endanger Bill or me. And then my attention's drawn to Bill.

The paramedics rush in after Sergeant Johnson gives the all clear. They cut off Dad's pants and shirt, both of them wet with red. (This was the first time the stunt double had to step in. Fake bullets? Fine. Real scissors? No way.) Now, finally, with the clothes off and the skin revealed, the physical results of the violent shooting are shown in all their family-appropriate glory and intensity.

On the stunt man's back we clearly saw a tiny circle of red syrup measuring a few inches in diameter. Reality was far worse. Dad described the blood as "gushing." As he lay there that night, waiting for the police to arrive and crushing those recycled soda cans, he stole a look down at his legs and surveyed the damage. From the new, sticky spots on his bullet-ridden legs he saw blood squirting into the air—actually shooting upwards and spilling onto the ground, creating a massive red pool all around his body. There was no way to depict that reality and maintain a broadcast standard. I couldn't help but be disappointed.

> **SGT. JOHNSON:** That's when the shock really hit, when I saw his condition. My first thought was, um, y'know, "Call the homicide team." Even though he was still breathing and everything else, that was one of the first things I did after the paramedics had came into the room.

The paramedics rush Dad out of the Shop and into the ambulance. On the way to the hospital, laid out on a stretcher and dying, Dad picks back up on his earlier theme from the 911 call. Through his breathing mask he makes his case. The person by his side to hear it is Lori the Paramedic.

> **LORI STEVENS:** He just knew he was gonna die. He knew he wasn't gonna make it, and Bill was grabbing at the things that mattered most to him. He kept saying, "Tell my wife I love her. Tell my wife I love her. Please, you've gotta tell my wife I love her. I know I'm not gonna make—tell her, please tell her." And I said, "Okay, Bill. I promise. What's the number?" So he gave me the number and I repeated the number. He says, "Yes." I said, "Bill, I'll tell her. I promise." He says, "Okay," and I think a bit of calmness came over him.

All of this while we were eating dinner. We typically did our dancing after dinner, and dancing is what we were doing when the call to Mom came in. Rationally, I knew there was no way for us to know until someone elected to tell us about what was happening, and yet how wrong was it that we ate fish sticks while Dad bled to death in the back of an ambulance and declared his love for us?

There's a weakness to the presence of a person whose body is mortally wounded, a feeling of "away-ness" that's unsettling when the person is right next to you. Seeing Dad on TV, again on the stretcher as they wheeled him through the hospital's hallways, I was brought back immediately to that week just after the shooting when his life hung in the balance. Again, the re-creation felt more intimate than the reality. Again, I was brought nearly to tears.

All the facts of the night had long been known to me, but now, pulled together and distilled into a continuity focused solely on the peril of the whole event, even those of us who knew the outcome—aka everyone in the Chinese restaurant that night—could not help but wonder if the man disappearing behind the double swing doors to surgery would live. This was the power of narrative. We weren't just seeing a reduction of our experiences into a compromised, abridged version of that terrible night. We were witnessing an unveiling. The story had not been imposed, it was discovered.

Dad's surgeon pops up on screen to describe his immediate medical issues: shock, massive blood loss, bullets possibly whizzed into major organs and arteries, and so on. We get it: he's bad off. But, at least now he's in the safe hands of the doctors, freeing up Lori the Paramedic to make her call.

> **LORI STEVENS:** That phone call was awful. I was so scared. I had no idea what I was going to say; I had no idea what *to* say.

Finally, Mom. With her dark, almost black hair and pale skin serving as backdrop for the vibrant makeup on her face, she looks quite pretty. Her big blue eyes shine out brighter than usual as she bluntly explains her frame of mind that night.

> **MOM:** The phone rang and all I wanted—all I could think was, "Let's hurry this up because I want to be back with my kids."

In a nice bit of intercutting between their two interviews, Mom and Lori the Paramedic reenact their conversation almost as if they are actually talking to each other. Mom speaks nervously, but then she always did.

> **MOM:** I've relived many, many times in my mind what it may have been like for him. To me, when he said in the [911 call] that he loved me, means more to me than anything he's ever given to me.

Mom's eyes visibly water as her words warble out. The camera lingers, leaving us to ponder what she's just said during a half second of silence that seems longer. A church organ swells. The face of the sad, pretty wife (widow?) is replaced by a congregation singing a somber hymn. The implication is clear: Bill is dead and this is his funeral.

It's a bit of a mean trick.

> **WILLIAM SHATNER:** Doctors worked on Bill for three hours to try to save his life.

A familiar face emerges from within the congregation. It's Dad, singing right along with everyone else.

> **WILLIAM SHATNER:** With five bullets still inside him, Bill has survived.

However unfair this turn in the storytelling, it effectively mimics in brief the long held breath Dad's family and friends had to endure both that night and in the weeks that followed. There is a real, earned sense of relief in seeing Dad hale and hearty, standing in the midst of those who cared for him most as though nothing happened. His survival is impossible to believe, but it's real all the same.

During their talks, the producers learned how important Dad's religion was to him and how involved everyone at church was with what went on that night and in the following months. Representing that by filming inside of sacred halls for the first time in *Rescue 911*'s short history was an effective way to pay tribute to that aspect of our lives. The overtly religious material remained purely visual, however, presented by the show without commentary.

Still, one thing is clear: Dad is a faithful man, surrounded by faithful people.

> **DAD:** I'm not a person that's been afraid to die. Uh, what concerned me more than anything was, of course, that I would not be with my wife and kids. And that's really the only thing that I was thinking about at the end, that I just—that I would miss them if I did die.

Dad never expressed himself with too much animus. There was a lack of the need to persuade in his tone and in the way he carried himself that belied the impact of his immediate physical presence. Silent unless spoken to, seemingly wider than he was tall, he looked more than a little intimidating even when supposedly at rest. It was only when he spoke—as he did toward the end of the *911* segment for final, definitive confirmation that he was still alive—that he seemed remotely approachable. He spoke plainly, without overstatement or hyperbole, his passions rising up to express genuine delight and little else.

So, it was easy to mistake a statement like "I'm not a person who's been afraid to die" as the humble, modest explanation of a man who kept cool even in the face of the greatest danger. The American viewing public could be forgiven for not recognizing they'd just heard my father's philosophy on life.

15

HOW IT ENDS

Up until his time in the Army, Dad had given religion very little thought. He was baptized into The Church of Jesus Christ of Latter-Day Saints at eight years old, but because the local congregation met some forty miles away from where they lived, my grandparents took him to the much closer nondenominational churches. Dad forgot entirely he was baptized and remained ignorant until his enlistment. It was his dog tags that made it plain: *Religion: Mormon.*

After the Army, he entered college at Fresno State and started working part-time at a bank. Dad's life was his own again, and he spent it in the way that most pleased him—smoking, drinking, and going to bars. His roommate, a pothead, was the closest thing he had to a friend during what was mostly a lonely, aimless time. Their mutual irritation meant the arrangement didn't last long. Lost and not making much of a go at life in the early 1970s, Dad moved back in with his parents, beating the Millennials at their own game by about four decades. It was time to take a hard look at his life.

The smokes and the booze were killing him and turning his body into something he didn't recognize. So, he quit. Cold turkey. He threw out all of his liquor and chucked the cigarettes and never looked back. I once asked him how he did that and he told me he "just got tired of feeling miserable all the time. It didn't make any sense to keep doing the things that made me feel that way. It was easy."

Dad thought back to his dog tags. They had that inscription on them, *Mormon.* He grabbed a phone book, found the nearest church building, and popped in one Sunday to check out the local congregation. As he approached the church building and entered the foyer, a darkness crept over him. People entered and exited and moved through the hallways and passed right by, but no one spoke to him. He felt uncomfortable. So, he turned around and left.

The next weekend, he went back. He didn't feel like he'd really given the Church a fair shake, but if that awful feeling came back, that would be the end of it.

Sure enough, the darkness returned as soon as he entered through the doors. This time, however, the bishop of the local congregation spotted him and pulled him into his office for a chat before Dad had the chance to leave. The darkness immediately lifted, never to return. Dad's curiosity was piqued. He dedicated himself to learning everything he could about this church he was supposedly a part of.

Dad's investigations into the Church went a long way toward satisfying the part of him that sought answers to the big questions: Who am I? Why am I here? Where am I going next? He was a student of history, a big fan of fantasy and science fiction. The gospel of Jesus Christ was another complicated mythology—and future history—to sink his teeth into. One he came to believe had the added benefit of being true.

I was barely into first grade when Dad and I started having long theological discussions together. They almost always happened whenever I accompanied him on his bait and tackle delivery route. The long drive from the base of the San Joaquin Valley up through the foothills and into the Sierra Nevada Mountains gave us a chance to talk uninterrupted for hours at a time. The sky never got bigger than when we drove along the cliffs of Highway 168, its view more expansive than anything I'd ever seen from the flatlands of the valley. Vertical fields of pine trees and rock faces dotted with power stations and marked by side roads stretched off into the distance, nearly all the way back to Fresno. The higher we ascended, the fresher and colder the air got. The mountains were cool and clean. Fresno was warm and dirty. Against that backdrop and with time on his side, Dad didn't think there was anything my six-year-old brain couldn't handle.

We talked about the American origin of the Book of Mormon, the stranger discourses of Brigham Young, and the life before this one, when every single person who was ever born on earth joined together to follow Christ to come to this world with a veil of forgetfulness and a charge to find their way back home. (Even Hitler!) Our earliest conversations centered on the book of Revelation and the Second Coming of Christ. Dad told me stories of death and destruction and blood running in the streets and a persecution of the members of God's Church on a level that hadn't been seen since the time of Christ. I believed his every word and took it upon myself to warn my friends.

"You'll try to kill me," I told my friend Chris over a backyard lunch of mayonnaise sandwiches and juice. He was a few months younger than me and lived just across the street.

"No, I won't," he oh so naively insisted.

"Yes, you will! Just wait."

Chris thought about it. "When?"

"I dunno. Later. When we're, like, twenty or something."

"Why?"

"Because I'm Mormon! It's gonna happen, you'll see."

I upset Chris to the point he forgot all about his juice box. "Well, I just won't kill you then," he decided. "I'll tell everybody not to and I won't do it. They can't make me."

"You won't be able to help it. It's okay, though. I already forgive you."

It was a hard thing to explain to outsiders, but death could be a light subject in my father's house. It wasn't this macabre thing to him because he didn't fear it; he looked forward to death and the knowledge it would bring. The most he'd say of the physical part of dying, as most do, was that he hoped it would be as quick and as painless as possible. What was exciting was the aftermath. The glorious passing from one mostly difficult life to the next, a relief from the trials and tribulations of the world and a passport to a new, more mysterious existence and new experiences.

Dad's assertion to my mother, even before they were married, was that he was going to die young. For him, it was simply a fact that hadn't occurred yet. And, like anything that can confidently be described as "fact," Dad's disposition toward it was very matter of. As much a given as his past as a soldier in the Army or as a trumpet player or as a troublemaker, so too was his curtailed future. His certainty came from his unquestioning belief in the source of his severe intel, God himself.

Shortly after getting reacquainted with the Church and joining it consciously, Dad's curiosity about God's planned purpose for him became his primary concern. To satisfy this curiosity, he received a special type of blessing called a patriarchal blessing. Any member of the Church may obtain one, but all who do so are advised to receive it only when they feel they are ready. One of the most sacred callings in the Church is that of the patriarch, whose sole purpose is to give patriarchal blessings.

The blessing is that which God wants the individual to know about the possibilities of his or her own life should they choose to stay on the path of righteousness. It's not fortune telling so much as potential telling. The patriarch is, then, a conduit for the blessing, which is believed to be given by the power of the Holy Spirit. All patriarchal blessings are recorded and transcribed, with copies sent out both to Church Headquarters to be put on file, and also to the recipient and subject of the blessing for their own study and reflection.

Immediately upon receiving his patriarchal blessing, Dad was mostly—almost completely—dissatisfied with it. He felt it was generic in the extreme. It was full of the kinds of platitudes and advisements one would hear in even the most basic of blessings. A blessing of comfort or for better health might have read much the same way. He knew that living a life righteously had its rewards. But . . . what rewards? What, specifically, potentially, did life have in store for him? It seemed that God did not want him to know much at all.

Not willing to accept the blessing as it was, Dad went back to the patriarch and quizzed him to try to get some idea of what might have gone wrong. When the man had no further answers for him beyond what he had already given, Dad turned to other local Church leaders, reviewing with each of them the contents of his one-page blessing (a massive disappointment in and of itself—Dad had heard of blessings three or four times as long). He was counseled again and again that the blessing was not the final word on anything and that he might find its meaning expanding with time. Many of the leaders he spoke to admitted that it did seem like a very generic blessing as far as these things usually go, but that it must be right and must be all he needs. Dad studied the blessing all the more, praying for greater insight.

There was a particular line in Dad's blessing that kept jumping out at him: "Your children will remember you." It puzzled him, gnawed at him, and niggled about in his mind until its meaning became something more than what was contained within the scope of the words alone. At the time he received the blessing, he had no children, nor had he even met my mother. The easy inference from this one line was that his single status was most likely a temporary state, but he was convinced there was more to it than just that.

Your children will remember you.

Why would his children need to remember him? Where was he going that they would have opportunity enough to reflect so significantly upon him that it would justify a specific mention in his patriarchal blessing years prior? If his children were going to remember him, did that not also mean that the converse might be true if he did not live his best life—that they might forget him?

Dad became convinced that this one short sentence was not of the same general character of the rest of his blessing, but rather a significant signpost that pointed the way toward his mortal end. He came to believe with certainty that the choice of wording was specific, that the "children" were indeed children—not adult sons or daughters. He could think of only one reason to be away long enough from his young children that there might be some danger they would forget him, thus causing God to comfort him with the knowledge that this would not be the case: he would have to be dead.

The knowledge of his early demise sunk in deep and turned into certainty. It defined Dad, allowing him to live a life of peaceful anticipation. Death, when it came for him, was something he would welcome. It was part of the plan. He told my mother this when they started dating. He let her know she was involving herself with a man whose time on this earth would be short. His assertion was so strong she believed him and, especially once they were married, it was something she worried about constantly.

But I didn't. How could I? Our long talks produced one sure effect upon me: it never occurred to me to fear death. Dad made it seem wonderful and fun and not this scary, unknown thing. The possibility I might not live a good, righteous life kept me up at night, but not death. Never death. Death—the fact of it, the physicality of it—was, if anything, funny.

Dad still returned home from work quite late even after the shooting. Mom, having no way to contact him if he wasn't answering the phone at the Shop, would pace. We knew his absence at dinner probably meant Dad was dealing with a customer or caught up in conversation with a guy at the gas pump who thought all he'd asked for was directions. Meanwhile, Mom wiped away gallons of snot and did her best to keep her four boys from uprooting the house by its foundation. She would invariably ask out loud at the most exasperating point in the evening, "*Where* is your father?"

To which my reply was always the same: "He's probably dead."

I thought this was hilarious. She, not so much. "What if he really is?" she'd say. "How do you think you would feel?"

"Fine," was my every time response. "He's either gonna come home or he's not. He'll either be dead or not. Nothing I say or do is going to make any difference."

Such frankness didn't sit well with Mom, but she knew it would only encourage me if she kept the argument going. On the few occasions she would keep after me, I'd take it much further, describing how Dad could possibly be lying lifeless and mangled on the side of the road. As I got older, I took it even further than that.

"Maybe he got shot. Again."

The dark humor made Mom visibly uncomfortable, which made it all the more hilarious to me. They were just words, funny only because they were so inappropriate, sure, but still funny and, coming from me, powerless. Hadn't Mom heard this stuff from Dad for years anyway? If she could just learn to laugh about it, it wouldn't be such a big deal.

* * *

After Dad is rushed into surgery, *Rescue 911* cuts back to Mom. This time, with him sitting beside her.

> **MOM:** Bill's my life. Bill's my world; I love Bill very much. He's made my life very happy. Scares me to think that I . . . might not have married him. That I came close to not marrying him.

It's an odd moment toward the end of the *911* segment. Dad is quiet, listening to Mom and passively accepting everything she's saying. Mom's eyes dart to the side briefly, as though even she wonders what in the world she just said and why in the world she felt the need to say it. Then, her gaze lines back up with the camera as she waits for some sort of instruction on what to do next. It's a pause that lasts the broadcast equivalent of an eternity. Even casual viewers have to wonder, "What's going on?"

Then, Dad seizes the moment. He comically shrugs his shoulders and raises his eyebrows as if to say, "I have no idea what she's talking about." Mom stares forward, oblivious, and he rounds off his behind-her-back performance by silently chuckling. It's a welcome bit of levity that doesn't play into the narrative of the story being told at all, but it was easy to see why the producers chose to include it. Everyone at the Chinese restaurant roared their approval.

The sad truth behind the silent chuckling was that Dad proposed to Mom no less than three times and she turned him down flat all three times. She was young, attractive, and nineteen years old. Dad was twenty-four. He had been through the Army, gotten rid of his vices, joined the Church, gone to college, and couldn't stop talking about dying. A catch to be sure, but Mom wasn't ready like he was to settle down and take the next step in life; she had yet to even venture near the stairs. After his third proposal rejection, Dad looked at the situation honestly and asked himself just how much of his short life he wanted to waste on this girl. He dumped her and they both moved on.

For the next year, Mom and Dad led mostly separate lives, crossing paths about as much as you'd expect for two people who'd met at a church dance. Mom lived at home with her parents and worked at the nearby JC Penney department store. One night, she spied Dad with another woman as they passed through. She recognized the blonde as one of the tellers at the bank where Dad worked, and something stirred terribly inside her. The next day, she called him out of the blue and proposed. He accepted immediately.

They married in December 1974. In January 1977, I showed up to ruin their lives as they knew them. To my father's delight, I was soon followed by my three brothers. There was a time when Mom thought a pity stare was just how strangers greeted each other.

Interviews with spouses and family members, along with dramatic footage of the surviving victim walking along their neighborhood sidewalk or enjoying a family BBQ, were typically *Rescue 911*'s last stop on the way out to commercial before the next segment. All of us, even my youngest brothers, had been asked to sit down for interviews. McKay and Tyler were too young to care or respond with coherency. Logan, just two years my junior, could have done an interview if he'd wished, but he claimed to have more important business to take care of than his broadcast debut. Something to do with bicycles and homemade ramps.

The coveted last interview spot was all mine. Unfortunately, when my freckled, janky-toothed visage graced the screen, what had once been excitement at the prospect of being on national television soon turned into everlasting embarrassment.

My greatest concern had been my appearance. I took great pains to pick out my best shirt and used product for the first time in my life to slick my hair back for the interview, but it didn't matter much under the hot lamps they set up around me. My hair dried out and lost its shape, and under the glare of the supernova lights it was impossible for me to look anything other than pasty white. Well, past*ier*, anyway.

I shouldn't have been so worried. Once I *heard* the chosen clip, my appearance was the least of my concerns.

> **ME:** I think what kept him alive was his will to live and . . . his will to . . . see us grow up and stuff. And . . . cuz he really cared a lot about us. I really love my dad. A whole lot. I'm really glad he's around.

Did the producers hate me? I had been asked so many questions and *that* was the answer they chose to go with? Between the lights and the camera and the pressure of knowing that anything I might say would be preserved forever, I had been terribly rattled. Maybe this was the *best* of what I'd said. What a horrifying thought. Steve the EMT and the steering wheel? An Olivier-level performance by comparison.

I could only imagine the production meeting where the need to have the most inane, stuttering talking head possible to finish out the segment was established.

> ***PRODUCER A:*** *Hey, you know what we need for the end?*
> ***PRODUCER B:*** *What's that, Stan?*
> ***PRODUCER C:*** *Yeah, Stan, tell us. Whaddaya got?*
> ***PRODUCER A:*** *Okay, picture this, boys . . . we get the funny-lookin' kid, whatsisname . . . [snaps fingers] Bart . . . no . . . Brooke?*
> ***PRODUCER C:*** *Brock.*
> ***PRODUCER A:*** *Yeah, that's it. Brock. We stick his interview up there at the end, a choice bit, y'know? Something where he uses the phrase 'and stuff.'*
> ***PRODUCER B:*** *We got a lot of that.*
> ***PRODUCER A:*** *Perfect. Okay, but the thing is—stay with me boys, this is where it gets good—the thing is we set him*

> *up first by showing that clip where they're playing football with the dad and the pass to Brooke—*
> ***PRODUCER C:*** *Brock.*
> ***PRODUCER A:*** *—right, whatever—the pass gets intercepted by his younger, littler brother! Whaddaya think?*
> ***PRODUCER B:*** *Say . . . that's pretty good, Stan!*
> ***PRODUCER C:*** *Genius!*

For the record, the director told me to let Logan catch the ball.

Besides the obviously intended humiliation, the brief flash of Dad playing football at Woodward Park and getting tackled by his boys effectively illustrates just how high-functioning his post-shooting body really was. In those first few years afterward, unless you happened to catch him in his short shorts going for a swim, it was hard to tell anything bad had actually happened to him.

My thunder was further stolen by the Shat when, at the very end of the segment, he once again asserted his dominance by refusing to let me have the last word. As my narration over the (rigged!) football game concluded, Captain Friggin' Kirk came back on screen to wrap it all up for us.

> **WILLIAM SHATNER:** The suspects in the shooting incident were arrested within a week and were subsequently convicted and sent to prison.

Cut to commercial. Everyone in the Chinese restaurant cheered and slapped backs. And partied until real late. I was left with two emotions to close out the night: a sobering pride in my dad, and utter humiliation. I scolded myself; I hated being like this. Why did I care so much what people thought of me?

III

THE ENEMY

16

THE NERD HERD

Our new home in Clovis sat on the eastern edge of town, nestled in a maze of mostly yet-to-be-built houses directly across from Clovis High School. Past the development and in the nearby countryside was nothing but open fields, a cemetery, stores selling cattle feed, and a water park. The four bedroom house was a plus-one bedroom step up and the suburban castle Dad had always dreamed of. Three-car garage, spacious kitchen, cavernous living room with a vaulted ceiling, and plenty of room for a pool. The backyard was the biggest of any in the entire housing development—Dad made sure of that.

A new home meant a new school. Actual school. Only the uncurious new school district and my ever-so-slightly above average intelligence prevented my wasted year of homeschooling from halting my calendar-mandated academic progression. My teachers at Clark Intermediate didn't need to know I missed out on most of the seventh grade, and they never had reason to suspect it might be the case. In fact, they were so easily fooled that junior high seemed to me be little more than an educational rest stop.

Dad's *Rescue 911* segment aired during my second month at Clark. The timing, I thought, was perfect. I was the new kid at school, and I knew the notoriety I would get from being on national television would be a great shortcut to social acceptance. Unfortunately, the second month of eighth grade is two months too late.

The only sure gap in my learning from my year off from public school was in the social arena. I was their same age and gender, but most of the boys at Clark had made some sort of giant maturity leap from hanging upside down on the jungle bars to leaning against the gym wall and making lewd comments about the bodies of the passing girls that developed oh so courteously faster than ours. I had some serious catching up to do. Catching up I wasn't entirely sure *how* to do, but that I prioritized above all things. Even my friends.

It didn't take long for me to find my tribe at Clark. A comic book slipped out of a backpack and read between classes was the only clue I needed. The boys had all been friends since grade school, but that didn't matter. They accepted me immediately. Together, to my astonishment and regret, we were known as the Nerd Herd.

We discovered this hard fact while, of all things, walking down a school hallway and minding our own business. I was out in front and had momentarily forgotten that if another student came my way, it was my responsibility and my responsibility alone to establish a three-foot radius of safety and space.

"Get out of my way, Nerd Herd!" the girl with the big, dangly earrings and a confidence I instantly admired said as she pushed past me.

I recoiled in horror. "Was that very, very round girl talking to me?"

I looked over at my friend Jack for confirmation. "I think so," he replied. Jack was shorter than me, which made me uncomfortable. I liked being of average height and felt no need to stand out one way or another. Jack sometimes made me feel freakishly tall.

"What did we do to her?"

Our friend Chester ran up from behind and demonstrated exactly what he saw. "I think you brushed her when she walked by, like this." He bumped me hard enough so I nearly fell over. Chester never did anything subtly. Paul and Michael, right behind him, snickered.

Jack took a leap at me and thrust his hands forward. "Next time, just push her back, Cyke." I cringed. Jack liked calling me Cyke, after the field leader of the X-Men, Cyclops. I knew it wasn't very cool, but I did like the nickname—both because the steady, righteous Cyclops had always been my favorite X-Man and because, in a way, it was like I was being called their leader. As the new guy, it was flattering. Admittedly, my credentials were pretty solid—I came up with the best origin stories for the characters in the comic books we never got around to drawing.

"If you were Wolverine," Chester said, "you could have just popped your claws—SNIKT!—and been all like SHWOOM, SHWOOM!"

Chester was the tallest. He imitated the five-foot-three-inch Wolverine by crouching down low and miming vigorous slashing motions. His heavy backpack, barely tethered to his arms by their loose straps, flung about wildly as he hopped around and made war with the air. I looked around to see who might be watching. Only everyone.

"Wolverine sucks," I said, dampening Chester's spirits. (Because he did. What kind of hero uses knives? Chester just liked him because he was shady and drank lots of beer. Wolverine was tough, sure, but it's much harder to be tough and do the right thing. Cyclops did it in style. Who did Jean Grey go home with at the end of the day? Oh, that's right, *Cyclops.*)

The guys were my oasis and my lifeline after the big move across town. We were all passionate about something, be it movies or anime, but mostly comics. Our sleepovers at Chester's house were long, glorious matchup sessions where we fought imaginary battles between the Hulk and Superman and anyone else we could think to pair up. I enjoyed such matchups and imaginings—they were *fun*—but the thing my new friends couldn't understand was that such discussions and their attendant physical manifestations were not appropriate on campus.

It was like Isaac at Hawaiian Ice all over again. Our spot was a patch of grass by the flagpole, in the center of the school and in full view of the entire student body during lunchtime. I could never let loose like they did. Chester, God love him, didn't care that he looked like an overgrown six-year-old way outside the sandbox. Jack giggled *a lot*—and that was when he was at his coolest. Paul and Michael lived in a world where it wasn't the disapproving eyes of our peers watching us disdainfully from behind the nearby trees, but warlocks and evil mutants.

I wasn't blind when I met them. I knew when they first befriended me Jack and his friends weren't the most popular guys in school. *No problem,* I thought. *Just gotta work my way up.* But that's not how social strata work in junior high. You start at the bottom, you stay there. There's no ladder. There's only the hand of the god of popularity, whose judgments are swift, inscrutable, and final. I didn't know why Jack, Chester, Paul, and Michael were the only guys who asked me to hang out with them, but they were. They were good guys. The best.

"Nerd Herd." That's what she'd called us. I was a nerd. Worse, I was in the Nerd Herd. *Nerd Herd.* It rhymed so it had to be true. When I was on campus, I wanted only to retreat as far into my oversized shirts as possible, until the collar covered my newly-ripe-with-acne nose and I could walk among my classmates unknown, if not unnoticed.

No, I was sure they noticed me. They *all* noticed me. Because I was in the Nerd Herd.

The airing of the *911* segment did nothing for me. (Which, given my performance at the end of it, *of course* it didn't.) Even when Dad came down to my new school as a guest speaker to talk about his experiences, that did next to nothing. All I got out of that spotlight was a morsel of forced interaction with the popular kids. They asked me the same questions everyone else did after hearing Dad's story.

> *Did they ever catch the guys who did it?*
> Sure, yeah. It took a while, but they got 'em. They both went to prison.
> *Good!*
> Yeah, then one of them got out on good behavior.
> *Really?*
> Yeah. And then he killed a cop.
> *Oh.*

Such conversations went nowhere. *I* went nowhere. The label had been applied and the stone and the marker already set.

Here Lies
Brock William Henry Heasley
Son.
Brother.
Nerd Herder

Nothing I could do at Clark Intermediate would stop my well-known nerdity from rendering my existence inconsequential to the hundreds of classmates who would have had no idea who I was but for my injured father and the silly, graceless company I kept.

That had to change. *I* had to change.

When the eighth grade and my time at Clark drew to a much needed close, I knew I had to make the hard choice. Though we were all moving on to Clovis High together, I was done being an awkward outcast, and I was done with the Nerd Herd.

17

BREACHING BRUTE PROTOCOL

Fact: *In 1991, it was social suicide to be directly associated with nerds, either in truth or in the minds of others.*

The foundational precept of the system of popularity all high schoolers must adhere to dictates nerds are on the bottom of the social food chain. Somebody had to be the bottom and they were elected long ago, probably at a time when noogies were doled out with wooden clubs and successfully making fire was tantamount to pushing Coke bottle glasses up your nose and snorting out the quadratic formula. The nerd is rambunctious and "weird," studious and particular about things no one else cares about, and above all, he (rarely, if ever, she) is awkward in conversation. Alone, these qualities do little harm to one's social standing, but together they make one unpopular and undesirable. Being a nerd is not conducive to landing a girlfriend or walking by jocks safely without the threat of violence. This was the system. It wasn't up to me. My friends at Clark Intermediate were outcasts because they weren't calm or crass or cruel or conformist enough. I could not—*would not*—be an outcast with them.

Whenever I saw Jack or the rest of the Nerd Herd on the Clovis High campus, I headed in the other direction. Or, if spotted, I walked away politely and explained I had other, more pressing matters to attend to. Which I did. I needed to find someone else to hang out with. I spent the first week of high school eating lunch by myself and trying to remember if I'd even had a plan beyond "leave the Nerd Herd." Luckily, my desk mate in biology came to my rescue when he turned to me and asked the one question I'd hoped no one would: "Hey, who do you hang out with at lunch?"

Tom Mariner was blond, good-looking, athletic, and into cars. Only a fat gut and a sex change could have made him any more my opposite. And even then he probably still wouldn't have had the body image issues I did.

I averted Tom's eyes for fear of discovery. Was there a true answer to the question that didn't leave me looking like a complete loser?

Well, I used to hang out with these guys who were very good friends but not even remotely cool, so I ditched them to eat sandwiches by myself near the library. Because everyone knows the last place you'll find nerds is at the library.

No, I couldn't tell him the truth, but I couldn't just lie to Tom, either. Best to leave out the details.

"No one," I finally responded.

"Didn't you used to hang out with those nerds?"

Dang it. "What nerds?"

"You know . . . c'mon, you know."

"Uh, yeah. But not anymore."

"Heheh. Good. You can't hang out with nerds like that."

"Oh, I know. That's why—that's why I don't."

"Cool."

I'd passed some kind of test with Tom in that moment, I knew that much. But I couldn't figure out what the test was for or why he had me take it. Maybe I was a lot better-looking than I thought I was if he had also come to the conclusion I didn't deserve to be saddled with the Nerd Herd as friends. Maybe the god of popularity had accepted my sacrifice and now smiled upon me.

The feeling I deserved death by massive, karmic humiliation slowly took over the more Tom spoke.

"You should hang out with me," he said. "You and I could hang out at lunch."

"Really?" I was both bewildered and flattered. "Where do you hang out?"

"Oh, anywhere, y'know?"

"Yeah. For sure." No, I did not know. What did that even mean? I decided it didn't matter. Whatever Tom was proposing, I was for it. All in.

I didn't want to be Dad. Time and again he told me all about growing up alone and unwanted and without friends all the way through high school. He didn't think people found him interesting. He didn't imagine they wanted to be around him. This left a deep impression on me. If someone like my dad could end up alone, what hope did I have? But, here was Tom to rescue me. Maybe Dad's fate didn't have to be mine. Maybe Dad was just one Tom Mariner away from popularity and friends.

If he had been, he certainly would have had one up on me.

* * *

Tom and I usually began our lunch period by taking the lazy way around from the cafeteria to the snack bar in our pack of two, making fun of all the people we wanted to be like along the way. Inevitably, with nowhere else to go, we'd end up settling in behind the home economics building near the dumpsters because nobody of consequence went near the dumpsters and thus our chances of discovery as rootless campus vagabonds was nil. Our goal: to not be seen in any one place until our position in the popular hierarchy was secure. People who don't see you being a loser have to assume you're much cooler than you actually are because of the lack of evidence that suggests otherwise.

Part of our regular route was through the science building. One day, while walking through the first floor hallway, we happened upon two letterman-jacketed seniors. They sat on the floor at the midpoint of the hall, backs leaning against the opposing walls, ogre-sized feet stretched out toward the middle. One of them had high, spiky hair and the other a forehead so prominent he might as well have painted it green and started smashing things.

Tom and I had just as much right to walk the hallways as anyone else. The brutes had chosen to sit there, like that. There was no way to walk around them. We easily stepped over their feet without touching either of them, with nary a lag in our stride. Apparently, to do so was a serious breach of brute protocol.

"Stupid chicken-legged freshmen," a voice behind us said. "Did we give you permission to walk by?"

Did we need it? No. No, we did not. I turned around and explained that very simple fact to the two brutes as politely as I could and with as few words as possible so they would understand. "It's not your hallway. We'll walk where we want to walk."

Before I turned back around to resume my march out of the building with Tom, I glimpsed the spiky-haired brute rising up from his golden throne on the floor. "WHAT did you say to me? WHAT DID YOU SAY?!"

"You really gonna make me repeat it?" I called back.

"Shut up, Brock," Tom whispered desperately as we picked up some speed. "Just shut UP!"

"Come back and say it to my FACE, freshman!" Spiky Hair shouted.

Without turning back around again, I, the suicidal teenager with no idea what was wrong with me, shouted as loud as I could into the hallway, "YOU HEARD ME THE FIRST TIME!" And then, just a little quieter (though not nearly enough), "Morons!"

That did it. We had already made it to the exit of the building, but, just as the door was closing behind us, I looked back to see the two brutes getting fully up off the floor, one of them yelling, "Let's get 'em!"

"TOM! GO!"

Outside the building, Tom and I had two options: either we could run into the loving arms of a group of adoring cheerleaders who would recognize our loner status for the very 'James Dean' appeal it held, or we could be stupid freshmen and run back into the science building via the outer stairwell to the second floor. Since multiple women vying for our attention had been such a problem in the past, we bounded up those stairs as fast as our chicken legs could carry us.

At the top of the stairs I looked back down. What I saw sent me into a panic. "He's right behind us!" I screamed. Funny. Only Spiky Hair was after us.

Tom wasted no time throwing open the double doors leading us back inside the building. We ran as fast as we possibly could down the upstairs hallway, leaping over the bewildered science nerds sitting on the floor waiting patiently for their next class. My heart raced ahead of me. We needed to reach the other side of the building and the indoor stairwell or we were dead. And after that? Down the stairs back to the first floor of the building and out the front doors to salvation!

I looked back. I wanted to see just how fast this brute could run. Pretty fast, as it turned out. It was possible he had earned that jacket.

"Don't look back!" Tom shouted.

"RRRAAARRRRRR!" Spiky Hair screamed (or would have in the cartoon version of this scene).

Fast as we could, we rounded the corner and leapt down into the indoor stairwell. We had made it to the first tier of stairs and nearly to the second when, suddenly, there was brute number two, Hulk Smash, coming up the stairs right toward us. We stopped, turned, and tried to go back up the way we came. We couldn't. Spiky Hair was descending. He caught up to us and went straight for Tom, grabbing him with gigantic, adult-like paws and pinning his arms behind his back. Tom wasn't going anywhere. We were both trapped.

Hulk Smash came right up on me in the stairwell and got up right into my face, putting us eye-to-sternum.

How would Dad play this? I wondered. He may have had his insecurities, but he was no coward. Not like me. But, he also had a gun and forearms with the circumference of a large watermelon. Unfortunately, the school frowned upon packing heat, and I was still firmly against throwing a punch and, to be honest, exercise.

There was only one play: not backing down. I knew the brutes, whatever my crime, wouldn't respect me if I folded. We'd just be inviting more abuse if I did; I'd seen enough after-school specials to know that much. Besides, I had backed down with Isaac repeatedly, and that hadn't worked out so well for me.

Out of the corner of my eye I saw Tom being forced into further submission as Spiky Hair put the squeeze on. My panicked friend threw me a look that seemed to be asking, "What are you *doing?*" I honestly didn't know. Yet.

Hulk Smash snarled at me, licked his teeth, and, speaking to his insecurities, said, "You better watch your smart little freshman mouth. Apologize to us."

"Tell me what I said and I'll apologize to you," I challenged back.

"You know what you said."

"So, tell me." He couldn't. A brute's short-term memory is short indeed.

"Do you want us to kick your pasty freshman butt? You got a smart little freshman mouth on you, and I think you need your butt kicked."

Tom's eyes plead with me to *just apologize!* The part of me that was usually in charge screamed something similar. "Tell me what I said and then kick my butt. Here we are. I can't stop you." Certainly not at that range . . . or ever. "Unless you're afraid?"

That was it. He was afraid. The look came over Hulk Smash's face at once—he was afraid to beat us up. The brutes had expected to intimidate us and make us cower and beg for our lives, and instead we called them on their bluff. If we weren't going to apologize, what were they supposed to do? Let us go? Not without looking foolish. Not with their self-respect intact. Our butts, they *needed* to be kicked.

So, Hulk Smash did what any red-blooded American does when there's a job that needs doing and he doesn't want to do it—he called in the Mexicans. Up at the top of the stairs looking down on us was our audience—two Hispanic sophomores in full gangsta regalia who had been watching the entire stairwell confrontation. Where they came from, I didn't know, but as Hulk Smash cast his eyes about in search of his dignity, he finally found it in them.

"Hey, we'll get those two Mexicans to beat you up!" he shouted, pointing upward. "Hey, you two, come beat up this . . ." *chicken legged freshman*. Right. It was sounding less like an insult and more like the guy was admiring my gams.

To my surprise, the 'Mexicans' obeyed orders, let loose, toothy, enthusiastic grins, and went into tough guy mode, cracking their knuckles on their march down the stairs toward us. "Yeah, yeah we'll take care of him for you. Sure, sure. Yeah, let's kick his butt! Let's do it!"

I wondered if they might have knives.

"Don't forget about this one," Spiky Hair reminded them as he held up Tom just a little bit higher.

"Yeah, yeah—him too. We'll beat 'em both up for you, man!"

Once they got closer, I recognized them. I knew these 'Mexicans'! They were not only in the same PE class as me, but their lockers were also directly across from mine in the same row. No one else in our row had aerosol deodorant, so, for about two minutes every day, I was a very popular guy. I generously allowed anyone near me, these 'Mexicans'—Diego and Miguel—included, to have use of the only deodorant in existence that can be safely shared between strangers without fear of contamination. These guys depended on me every day to get them through sixth and seventh periods without smelling like sweaty turds.

This was my superhero moment. I didn't have the muscles of Superman and I looked a lot more like Clark Kent, so the only way out was the Batman way—with smarts.

Spiky Hair and Hulk Smash let Tom and me go, handing us over to Diego and Miguel. While the brutes stood by with stupid, evil looks on their faces, my PE brothers-in-underarms took hold of Tom and me by our shirts and shoved us against each other and into the brick wall bordering the stairwell.

"Hey, you think you can talk like that to them?" Diego said to me. "Is that what you think? You think you can just say what you want, man?"

"You wanna say it to us?" Miguel got right into Tom's ear. "Say what you said to them. Say it to us!" A trembling Tom received the verbal assault while trying to stay as still as possible. "You flinching?" He failed. "Look at this white boy flinch!"

They still didn't recognize me. Even though we were close enough I could smell the cheese sandwiches on their breaths. They didn't know me at all. Still, it was the only play I had: "Hey man, if you beat us up, I'll cut off your supply of deodorant."

The two volunteer thugs stopped immediately and took a good long look at me. Slowly, recognition dawned on their faces. The brutes looked completely confused (as opposed to their default state, only mostly confused). They quickly let us go.

"Oh . . . yeah! Yeah, this guy's okay!" Diego said, now practically hugging me. "Look, look there's no problem here. This guy's okay. Everything's fine here. No trouble. You don't need to do that. Take the deodorant away? Really? Why you want us to smell bad for the honeys? Why you wanna do that, man?"

"I don't, man," I said. "We good now?"

"Yeah, man. We good. It's okay. They're okay, right?"

"Super fresh, man!" Miguel confirmed. "We gotta stay clean. For the ladies." Then he turned to the brutes and mimed putting on a fresh coat under his pits. "You know what I'm sayin'?"

Puzzled and now a little scared that they'd just picked on a friend of the 'Mexicans,' the brutes looked at each other and nodded their heads in agreement. The fierce 'Mexicans' patted us on our backs and sped us on our way. Without looking back, Tom and I took off for the door we had been trying to exit from in the first place. We burst into the outside sunshine, got as far away from the science building as possible, and recounted the story to each other with joyous, fearful delight.

The brutes never bothered us again, even going so far as to apologize the next day for what happened. I tried not to read too much into that.

My bid to move up the social ladder was a total failure, as I knew it would be, resulting in little more than a shuffle to the side on the bottom rung. Possibly, I was no longer even on the ladder. The lonely days Tom and I shared walking the campus, pushing back on bullies (just the one day, really), and out at the dumpsters never brought us the popularity and attention I sought. Tom had no more confidence than I did and was maybe twice as scared. He needed me just as much if not more than I needed him.

His good looks ended up really disappointing me.

18

GOOD INTENTIONS

You cannot be a member of The Church of Jesus Christ of Latter-day Saints without people having feelings about it. Whether it's admiration or disdain or fear that you're somehow sitting in self-righteous judgment of the other person even though you're just, y'know, sitting there, being a member of the Church is, for a lot of people, some exotic thing. There are many upstanding Latter-day Saints in the FBI, but also we think green Jell-O salad is an actual food that should be eaten by humans, usually at funerals. What I'm saying is, either we're trustworthy, hard-working people worthy of hiring, or we should be fled from lest whatever disease is the source of the horns on our heads (they're just tiny nubs) is contagious. There's not a lot of in between.

In high school, I was told quite often I was going to hell.

"I'm sorry, Brock, but you're going to hell."

"Excuse me?"

"You're going to hell."

"Okay."

My friend Saffron meant well. Why she chose that day in our history class to give it to me straight, I didn't know, but I did know she was only telling me about my dark fate out of concern and care.

"I'm only saying this because I care about you."

"I feel that. I feel cared for."

"I'm serious! I'm your friend, and as your friend, I want you to know the truth. You're going to hell."

As an overture to helping a person come to Jesus, 'you're going to hell' pretty much sucks. Though I knew it had been used for centuries in spiritual warfare (with, presumably, some degree of success given its longevity as a tactic), it was hard for me to imagine anyone—much less me who was most assuredly *not* going to hell—changing their ways with that hook. It's instantly offensive. As far as I was concerned, no one should ever be told they're damned for eternity by anyone less than all-powerful.

Even so, it was actually quite difficult to be upset with Saffron. She was pretty, had the most amazing eyes, and liked to touch people on the arm when she talked. She ranked as one of my very best "classroom-only" friends, always making it a point to at least say hi each and every day. Perhaps it was a calculated effort. Attention given in exchange for a listening ear.

"And why do you think I'm going to hell?" I asked her.

"Because you don't believe in Jesus!"

"Really? Whoa. I gotta stop reading the Bible then. It's not working. Like, at all."

"Stop it! You know what I mean!"

"Really don't."

"You believe in *a* Jesus, but not *the* Jesus. Not the right one."

"I wasn't aware there was more than one."

"Hello! The Antichrist?"

By my junior year at Clovis High I had pretty much given up on any hope of popularity or close friends. I did have friends at church, and we hung out at church-sponsored activities and sometimes on the weekends, but not at school. I now preferred to make the trek across the street and go home for lunch rather than wander the campus aimlessly. Instead of being by myself with Tom, I could just be by myself at home. We were basically friendly still, but, as seemed likely from the start, we had drifted apart. It started when he got a girlfriend at the end of sophomore year and he debated whether or not to give in to her pressure to sleep with him. It ended around the time I called her a whore. Okay, maybe that *was* a little harsh, but what would *he* call her?

Girlfriend. Right.

As far as school went, I decided to satisfy myself on a diet of friendships and restrict myself only to those relationships that existed within the confines of the classroom setting. I called this new paradigm of peer association "Frequent Scheduled Acquaintanceship" and, because I had labeled it with multi-syllable words, it felt like a legit approach to the remainder of my public school life. Not jockeying for acceptance anymore meant not having to face rejection. In a classroom, we were all thrown together. No need for invites. No one ever had to ask, "What is *he* doing here?"

This legally mandated, limited contact put me at a comfortable distance from everyone. Even girls, unfortunately. I dated here and there, but the girlfriend, like every other kind of close relationship, remained an unattainable goal. The distance was highly effective. I could go for days, even weeks, on end without feeling lonely or envious or resentful of those in the tight-knit groups and cliques whose memberships were always denied me. The negative emotions of jealousy and resentment, when they did arise, I transmuted into a layer of social armor suitable for saying and being who I needed to be in order to not clue people in to my actual, solitary social state. Which is to say: I knowingly used humor as a defense mechanism.

I, as the perpetual outsider with nothing left to lose, could get away with saying just about anything—be it blunt, outrageous, hurtful, or truthful—to inspire my fellow students to laughter. And I *reveled* in it. It was the one, true reward for my unwanted and chosen isolation, and it gave me an unapologetic, often rude, but always hysterical (to me, if no one else) connection with those around me. It was friendship (*ahem*, "Frequent Scheduled Acquaintanceship") as bloodsport. True, I got slapped on more than one occasion, but that just gave my punchlines an additional hilarious stinger.

"It's true," I told Saffron. "The Antichrist and I—we're best buds. We're gonna go goat killin' and sacrificin' later. You wanna join us? We need a virgin."

Gasp! "You did not just say that."

"You're right, I didn't. Uh oh. Now I'm a liar. Dang, I'm all kinds of evil today."

"Stop that!"

There were other benefits to being able to say whatever I wanted. I could afford to be bold in less crass, more spiritual ways as well. Not needing a social filter meant I had a much easier time sharing what I believed with others, whether they liked it or not. I had been taught in Sunday School from a very young age that "every member is a missionary," and I took the charge seriously, turning my social disadvantage to an advantage by loudly proclaiming even my passion for my religion with reckless abandon. I loved to talk about it, and the more disturbed the hearer by my boldness the better. Saffron and I had that in common. She could never pass up an opportunity to talk about her religion, either. Even to an outcast like me.

"We believe in the same Jesus," I told her. "How could you think we don't?"

"Because you believe in the Book of Mormon Jesus," she said definitively, as if she knew anything about it.

"Same Jesus."

"No, it's not. It's not the one from the Bible."

"We read the Bible, too. Same guy. Long hair? Beard?" I stroked my chin to exaggerate the beard's length. Saffron punched me in the shoulder and laughed.

"It's not the same Jesus!"

"Your guy has short hair? Trippy."

"You know what I mean!"

* * *

I used to hit small children.

Before my fifth birthday, it was well known throughout the church building where my family attended that if I didn't get my way there would be violence. Possibly blood. All kids shorter than me were to be beat on, and all toys were meant to be mine. I was selfish, combative, and given to fits of rage if my juice box was not produced by my poor teachers quickly enough. Because I was her first child, my mother hoped it was a passing phase and I was more normal than the looks she got from strangers otherwise indicated. There were plenty of signs she was dead wrong about that.

One Sunday, when I was three years old, Mom went to drop me off at the church nursery, like always, but was refused. She was told I was no longer in the same class I had been going to for the past year. I had been assigned to another room altogether.

"W-where?" Mom asked the nursery leader. My surly little self lingered at her side, my very presence a source of worry to all the carpet scrapers I shared a class with and who now looked with fearful anticipation as I once again darkened the nursery doorway.

"Just down the hall," the nursery leader said, pointing. "On the other side of the courtyard."

Only once we left were uneasy stares relaxed and toys once more brought into the light.

We walked—Mom thinking I must be pretty special, and me stomping the life out of any ants that dared cross my path through the outdoor courtyard.

At the end of the hallway we opened the door to a small classroom. Mom was shocked by what she saw. Sitting in the middle of the room was a pleasant-looking woman, her gritted teeth shining through a forced smile. Opposite her was another chair, empty.

"Is . . . " Mom began. "Is this the class Brock's supposed to be in?"

"Yes," the woman in the chair replied. "This is it."

"But, where are the other kids?"

"Oh, ah . . . you see there aren't any other kids in this class. Just Brock. This is a new class just for him."

"You mean you were called to be his teacher? Just his teacher . . . just for him?"

"That's right."

"But why?"

"The nursery leaders talked it over and just felt that Brock . . . this is a class where he can get the attention he needs. We're . . . we're really going to have a lot of fun in here."

Mom took a step back and let it sink in. "Is this because of the beatings?"

"Yes."

The mother of one of my young victims had moved her child out of the nursery and into the regular Primary classes with the older kids just to get him away from me. I could not be reasoned with, taught, or told what to do by anyone. Mom had learned, through trial and error, to be patient and give me my space. The teachers at church had reached the same conclusion and used the tools at their disposal to provide me with that space.

I cannot say why things changed for me, exactly, but I do know when. I was five years old, a year out of the nursery. An idea took root in my mind that altered my perception of myself and how I should behave: I was special, maybe even a big deal (probably a big deal). I knew, somehow, that God had a plan for my life and to make that plan work I needed to be different. I needed to be better.

So, I was.

I became afraid of Joseph Smith.

Or rather, I should say, I was afraid what happened to Joseph Smith would happen to me. He was special, too. God and Jesus Christ appeared in a grove of trees right before his very eyes when he was very young.

Later, they sent an angel to make nightly follow-up visits to his bedroom for further instruction. Because he was special. Because he was chosen. If I was special, then Joseph Smith and I were alike.

From that time forward and for the next couple of years, there was nothing more frightening I could imagine than an angel showing up suddenly, unannounced. If it had happened to Joseph, it could happen to me. I was terrified.

I took steps to ensure my safety. Joseph's first celestial visitation, from the Father and His Son, occurred because, after attending many different churches and being confused by the disagreements among them, he prayed to know which of all of them was the true church. Lesson there: don't ask questions or the glowy people in the white robes will come talk to you. That was easily avoided; I was pretty confident Joseph's answer that none of them at the time were true was on the mark anyway. He'd done all the work for me there.

The angel was a different story, though. According to Joseph, that guy showed up at the strangest of times—usually at night and despite the fact that his brothers were sleeping nearby. Logan sleeping in the bed across from me would mean nothing to an invading angel. He would just put some kind of spell or something on my brother to keep him asleep. (Not that he needed a spell at all—if Logan could sleep through his own snoring, he could sleep through anything.)

With no prior record of it, at age five I suddenly became very afraid of the dark. If angels liked to show up only when it was dark, then I had to sleep in the light. I insisted that either my bedroom door be cracked at all times, or that I have a nightlight. Preferably both.

I was too ashamed to tell my parents the real reason for my out-of-the-blue need for constant illumination, but they indulged me anyway. Fear of angelic visitation, if there could be such a thing, seemed like such a prideful phobia. As if I should be so special. But, that was the truth, wasn't it? I knew that I was. Special.

The older I got, the more challenging it was to live up to it. Life got complicated, and the right thing to do wasn't always so clear. Tests—whether to conform and use foul language or look at a magazine that inspired wonderful lusts or watch a movie I knew was inappropriate—were continually before me. I didn't pass all of them, but I always tried. If everybody else was doing it, that was usually a pretty good sign I needed to stay far, far away.

As a sixteen-year-old junior in high school, my feelings of having a grander purpose still lingered, but they were dim and had grown into a responsibility whose weight I did not feel I could bear. Joseph Smith, once a little older, was chastised by God for those times when his youth got the better of him and he entertained himself with trivialities and misbehaviors. The pressure to not similarly misbehave was always on. I knew that righteousness and absolute fidelity to God's commandments were a must.

I despised being a teenager. All of its attendant violent emotional shifts and wildness of heart only served as distractions from my real purpose, whatever that was. In this, I felt very alone. On the few occasions when I chose to share my feelings with friends and revealed my burden, they looked at me with bewilderment. The truth was, I wanted to be an adult. I wanted to set aside the laziness and hazy understanding of the world that came part and parcel with youth in favor of a life figured out and purpose defined. Thirty-five—that was my dream age. I would have given anything to skip ahead to it, a time when the questions marks of my life would be long demolished, when sense would be made out of Dad getting shot and its higher purpose, when I could know that digressions like my fight with Isaac were not held against me, when I would know, with surety, that all I had been taught in church and by my parents was all true.

Deep down, that was what really scared me. For all of my conviction and strong feelings about my God-intended purpose, I didn't really *know* anything about Him. Joseph Smith had his first vision at fourteen years old. In 1993, I was two years past that, and I didn't even know for sure if the Church he'd built up was God's one, true Church as he had claimed and I had been taught, or if it was just something concocted in the overactive imagination of a boy who didn't want to go to his Sunday meetings. I didn't *dis*believe his story. But, that wasn't good enough. Not when I had been promised more than that. I had been taught that a person could pray to know whether or not God was real and if Jesus Christ was our Savior. I could know for certain—for myself—if the Book of Mormon was true and if Joseph Smith was a prophet and if The Church of Jesus Christ of Latter-Day Saints was the only true church upon the earth. The answer to such a prayer would be an understanding that would go beyond faith to be much more. It would be knowledge.

According to my Sunday School teachers, God could give me truth directly by touching my mind and heart with His Spirit. This knowledge would make itself known in any number of ways, but most likely by a "burning in the bosom," according to the scriptures. That sounded uncomfortable to me, but I still wanted it. Desperately. I could imagine no greater gift. I wanted to *know* what was real and what was not. And I knew I just didn't yet.

But, I did believe.

* * *

"I believe in Jesus Christ," I told Saffron. "I believe He was and is literally the Son of God. Do you believe that?"

"Of course," she said.

"And do you believe He died on the cross for our sins and was resurrected three days later?"

Saffron thought about it a second. "Yes."

"Then we believe the same thing."

"No!"

"The same Jesus."

"No, it's not. It's different."

Really. "How?"

"I don't know. I just know that it is."

"And that makes me not a Christian?"

"Yes, because if you don't believe that Jesus Christ is your personal savior—"

"—which I actually do."

"—which you don't because the one you believe in is totally, totally different from the real one—then you're going to hell."

"Because your pastor says so."

"How did you know that?"

Because that's what it always came down to. Saffron wasn't the first person to have the "going to hell" talk with me. She, like so many others, only knew what some book with "CULTS" in big, block letters on the front said about us. A book that could probably be found on her pastor's shelf.

That was the most basic claim—that we were a cult. Other books said we believed we could become gods for the purpose of having eternal sex to make spirit babies, or that we performed blood sacrifices and secret rites in our temples. All of these crazy things were based on either outright lies, or the twisting and misrepresentation of some basic tenet that we did believe. The amount of disinformation out there was staggering. I'd heard all of it.

"Okay, look," I said as gently as possible. "Here's what I do believe. Like I said, I believe Jesus Christ to be the Son of God, the Savior of the world."

"No, you—"

"Let me finish. I believe that Joseph Smith was a prophet of God, just like Moses or any of the others. I believe we have a prophet on the earth today as well. That's not that radical of an idea. I believe the Book of Mormon to be true—the word of God just like the Bible is. These are the things I believe." I hated using the word "believe," but that's what was honest. "I know you don't believe the same way I do, but you have to at least trust me on what *I* believe."

"No, I don't have to," Saffron fired back. Her look was one of pity. "Because you don't know what you believe."

There it was. At Clovis High, and, for the most part, in the greater Fresno area, there was a strong contingent of the faith community who were a bit dogmatic about not only what they believed, but also what everyone else did as well. Mormons, in particular, were a target.

Sermons were often dedicated to discussing our beliefs at length and how to thwart our missionary tactics. Movies such as the infamous *The Godmakers*, a film made by a group of people who had left the Church, were widely seen in churches and through seminars. Once, a group of men from a neighboring church entered one of our buildings to hand out anti-Mormon literature in the foyer during one of our larger meetings. Special classes were even held during the week to confront "the Mormon problem." When Saffron told me I didn't even know what I believe, I knew exactly what her goal was.

"Next Wednesday, there's a class being held at my church," she said. "We're going to learn about the Mormon faith, and I think you'll find it interesting. You should totally come!"

"Really?" I said. "You want me there?"

"Of course! Anyone can come. Everyone's invited."

"I don't think it would be a good idea."

"Why not?"

"Because. Because . . . I, I don't know that I can be polite."

"That's fine! Come and listen to what we have to say, and you can say what you want to say, too."

"No, I . . . "

"Come on."

"It's lies, Saffron."

"Come see."

"All right. You know what? I will."

Yes, I would go to that class. I wanted to go to that class. Desperately, the more I thought about it. The teacher—whoever he or she was—was spreading nothing but falsehoods, and this was a chance to set them straight. All they did in that class was speak from ignorance. Somebody had to stand up to that. Why not me? Gone were the days in the 1800s when Mormons were tarred and feathered and killed for their beliefs. There was no real danger.

What could they throw at me that I hadn't already heard? I was well-read. I knew my Book of Mormon backwards and forwards, and I knew the Bible almost as well. I knew every accusation and every twisted truth. I would absolutely go to that class. It was the right thing to do.

"You are absolutely NOT going to that class."

My parents disagreed.

"Why not?" I said. "Someone has to." It was later that same day. I only told Mom and Dad about my plan as a matter of course. I couldn't imagine on what grounds they might object.

"No, son," Dad said. "There's no point. You're not going. Why do—why would you even want to?"

"Because they're teaching things that aren't true, and I have to deal with this garbage every day at school. I'm tired of it. I want to do something about it."

"That's not what we do," Mom countered.

"No, but it's what we *should* do!" I was yelling now. I got there awful fast. "We just let them say whatever they want about us and we take it and we don't do anything to fight back, and all that does is create more questions and problems."

Mom and Dad looked at each other sideways, doing that telepathic communication thing parents do that was so irritating. They thought I was crazy, but they were being irrational. If you don't fight back against the thing that's beating on you, all you do is get beat some more.

"Tell me what your plan is." Dad sat in his easy chair in the living room. I hated that chair. The way he reclined in it and held his hands behind his head always made him look so smug. "What are you going to do when the teacher or someone else in the class says something that you know to be incorrect?"

"I'm going to raise my hand and tell them they're wrong. I'm going to tell the truth."

"And what if they say something you don't expect?"

"That won't happen."

"How do you know that?"

"Because I've heard it all."

"Son." Dad sighed. "They will chew you up and spit you out."

"You don't know that," I said. "What's wrong with telling the truth?"

"Nothing. But you need to tell it where it will be heard."

Where had he heard that one, a fortune cookie? "I've already told Saffron I'm coming. I'm not going to break my word."

"You tell her your parents discussed it and decided you can't go."

"Dad, I'm not going to tell her that! Like some little kid!? Why don't you just come with me when I tell her? Bring a tissue. I might need my nose wiped."

"Brock!" Mom was appalled. Good.

"Son, tell her whatever you like then," Dad said. "Fact is, you're not going. Don't mention us if it makes you embarrassed or uncomfortable. Don't tell her any of that. Just tell her you can't go and need to be somewhere else at that time."

"That's not better!" I said.

"It's going to have to be, because it's the truth. Your mother and I have already decided."

I stopped listening. They tried to tell me something about following the Church's example by not challenging the lies and thus encouraging contention, but I was so angry I didn't even care.

19

SITTING ON A CHAIR WITH WHEELS

Dad's recovery after the shooting was quick and miraculous to all who saw it, but it never really ended. Even more than five years later, in 1994, the scarred depressions left behind by the bullet wounds still dotted his stomach and legs. No amount of time or body hair would ever erase or cover them properly, and they served as the only obvious marker of the increasing number of physical complications he suffered through afterward. Dad's old self had died, even if Dad refused to.

Financially, the time immediately following the shooting was a boom period, enabling Dad and a friend to partner up and start a second business in nearby Reedley. That store, Reedley Rod & Gun, sold firearms, fishing equipment, and military supplies. Even with his employees sharing much of the load, the increase in responsibility took a pronounced toll on Dad's body. With each passing year, the after effects of the shooting grinded on his hips more and more and fatigued him even on a typical day. The resultant limited mobility and weight gain atrophied what had once been habitual and near constant physical movement and activity. Every little thing required so much heavy breathing and stopping for a rest and going so, so, slowly. Even something as simple as walking.

Five years on and the tackle Dad took at the end of the *911* video was now a lie. Couldn't he run just a bit faster through the parking lot when we were late for a movie? Just a little? No, he had to hobble. He wasn't an old man, but he moved like one and, sometimes, he acted like one. His list of pains and the small, everyday tasks he needed help with was ever-growing.

And I was so, so sick of it.

It had been *years*. If I didn't know better (and who's to say I didn't?), I would have said he was milking it. He had been so active before, so go for broke at both work and play. Now? Now watching television challenged him. How hard was it to get up and find the remote himself? The phone? Before the shooting, I'd have never described Dad as one to sit and veg out. Now, he had a favorite chair. Superdad had retired. His kryptonite was football games and *X-Files* reruns.

"The shooting was a long time ago," I told Mom one day after school before Dad came home from work. A fresh batch of terrible, tiny, cooked-to-burnt-perfection Pillsbury cinnamon rolls sat on the kitchen counter. I gladly partook. "It's not like he was shot recently. He could suck it up, y'know, once."

"You act like it's a choice," Mom said. "Your father still deals with pain every day, Brock."

"Does he? No, look, I'm sure—" I popped another roll. "I'm sure he's still dealing with fallout from the shooting. But, maybe it's not as bad as he says. Maybe if he tried not thinking about it so much it wouldn't be as big of a deal. Power of the mind and all that. Instead, he talks about it all the time. What good does that do? There's always something wrong with him. Something new all the time."

"That's not how he is."

"Maybe you just haven't noticed it yet."

Mom dismissed me and my silly ideas with a scrunch of her nose. "It doesn't kill you to get him a glass of water once in a while."

"You said 'every day' wrong. It's pronounced 'every day.'"

"Oh, whatever." She pulled the cinnamon rolls away. I was on my fourth. "Things *are* harder for him now, Brock, but you act like he's making it all up! Why would he do that? You know it isn't like him to complain."

"I don't know that at all."

She looked at me funny. "Yes, you do."

Mom couldn't see it, but Dad was a complainer. A grunter now, too. He had grown weak. Not that there was anything wrong with serving my father—he deserved that much as the patriarch of the home, I got that—but did he need as much help as he claimed? Of course not.

It didn't help that Dad was now my boss. Earlier in the year, he started *another* side hustle as the manager of the Fresno Trap and Skeet Club, a local gun club catering mostly to wealthy old farmers and the gun enthusiasts who liked to tell their drinking buddies how much money the guy they hung out with that day made.

I was the gofer. I did everything from carting palettes of clay discs to the launch houses along the range, to raking the acres of leaves that littered the grounds, to selling ammo at the front counter in the clubhouse. When the shooters yelled "Pull!" I pressed the button to launch the targets into the sky. And when I took a split second too long to do it, they yelled at me. There was no official job description; I just did whatever needed to be done.

What needed to be done was whatever Dad told me to do.

He made the job miserable. For one year, every Saturday, I entered my loud (PULL! BANG! PULL! BANG! PULL! BANG!), dirty, sweaty hell. The days were long and physically demanding. I often worked four but sometimes six(!) hours at a time, right in a row.

No matter how hard I worked it was never enough for Dad. He pushed and pushed me to utilize every second of the day. Even when there was nothing to do he'd make something up to keep me busy: restack the boxes of targets, sweep the dining area, spray the windows clean. Again. I knew he did that just to make me mad.

Meanwhile, he often spent most of his precious time at the club chatting up the shooters and running inventory. Easy stuff. Nothing backbreaking for him. He used a golf cart to get around the grounds in lieu of walking.

By the midpoint of Dad's one-year tenure as manager of the Trap and Skeet Club, it was clear it wasn't going to be a moneymaking enterprise for him. Unfortunately, that was the task he had been entrusted with by the club's board of directors in the first place. Dad wanted badly to get out of the hazardous-to-his-health gun retail business. Instead, the club became only the latest in Dad's long line of failed replacement ventures.

My one outlet, the one way I had to get away from Dad and, to a lesser extent, Mom, was to simply leave. At the beginning of my senior year of high school I finally got my driver's license. This proved to be a huge boon for my few, mostly churchgoing friends and the numerous fast food restaurants dotting the city of Clovis. This was freedom of a kind I'd never had before, and it came at just the right time.

My parents were mostly supportive. I assumed this was because I was as unpleasant to be around as they were.

* * *

SLAM!

"Brock?" It was Mom. Up later than usual. "Is that you? Can you come in here a minute?"

Oh, come on. "I'm tired. Is it important?"

"We're all tired, son." Dad was up, too. And home. Great.

I rounded the corner of the foyer and entered the living room with a stink on my face so strong I was sure they could smell it. I really was tired. That wasn't something I'd made up just to get out of talking to them. Mom sat on the couch in her bathrobe, her hair wet and curly from a late-night shower, a cup of tea next to her on the end table. Dad's glasses were off and his feet up on the recliner. No news there.

"What?" I said.

"Sit down," Dad said. I didn't. "Your mother and I want to talk to you."

"About what?"

"You're late, Brock," Mom said. "We agreed you'd be home by ten o'clock every night and it's almost eleven. That is not—"

"I didn't agree to that. You guys decided that."

Mom rolled her eyes and shifted nervously. "Well, whatever. You're supposed to be home at ten and you weren't. We didn't know if you were in an accident or in trouble or what."

"You should have just gone to bed."

"I can't sleep when I don't know where you are," Mom said. "You know that."

"That's not my problem. That's your anxiety problem."

"Sit down, son." Dad noticed my shoes were off and that I'd been slowly backing away and edging toward the hallway. I had absolutely no interest in having this discussion with them. I just wanted to go into my room, close the door, and reread a comic book before drifting off to sleep. I sat down anyway. Dutifully.

"You're late," Dad continued. "This has been the pattern lately. You have a curfew for a reason; I've got work in the morning and your mother needs her rest. But here we are, staying up late and waiting for you again."

"No one is asking you to do that!"

"You don't have to ask, Brock," Mom said. "This is just what parents *do*."

"Well, don't. In my case, just don't. When you do that it's like you don't trust me. Why? What have I ever done to make you think you couldn't?"

"How about tonight?" Dad fired back.

"It's not you we don't trust," Mom said. "It's everyone else out there. You never know what other people are going to do. Especially at night. I know you wouldn't do anything stupid or get yourself killed on purpose."

"That's not the issue here." Dad spoke with a hint of irritation. "The point is, son, that you're not coming home when you're supposed to. We have told you repeatedly that your curfew is ten. Period. No discussion and no negotiation. That is what we have decided and whether you agree with it or not doesn't matter."

Silence. Dad had made a declaration and it was incumbent upon all of us to let it sink in. It was an unfair thing to do. I had countered, successfully, every single one of their points and what was Dad's recourse? Invoking parental authority to define the discussion on his terms. It was a pathetic attempt to reestablish control of the conversation, but all it really did was show further how weak his argument really was. If the only way he could regain control was to say, essentially, "Because I say so," then nothing he had to say—or would say—meant anything. "Because I say so" isn't a reason. It's frustration given veto power.

Dad himself broke the silence, making me laugh in the process.

"When was the last time you gave your mother a hug?"

"Haha!" I couldn't help it. The look on his face told me I should have. "Are you serious?"

He was. "Yes. Your mother tells me that you don't hug her anymore."

"So? She doesn't need a hug from me. That's what she has you for."

Usually the picture of calm even when I was at my most contentious, Dad tensed up. His forearms, the one part of his body that was all muscle and no fat, vibrated pure, silent fury. He grimaced, looking away from me as if he needed to remove himself from the situation for a second in order to maintain his composure. I knew that look well, and I knew to fear it. But not this time.

"Brock," Mom said hurriedly. "Why are you talking to us like this? It's like you're a different person these days."

"Well, yeah, Mom. I'm seventeen. I'm a different person every day. You can pretend all you want, but I'm not five anymore. Catch up." My secret delight at the level of anger going up in the room knew no upper limit. There was a natural high that came with sparring with my parents, and, if they were going to make me do it, then I was happy to resign myself to relishing the experience.

"We expect more than this from you." Mom looked genuinely hurt. Like I had taken something precious away from her. This wasn't about her, and I resented the guilt trip.

"I expect more than this from me, too," I challenged her back. "So, we're both disappointed."

I was on fire. There was nothing they could throw at me I hadn't already considered. The quickest way to deflate someone's point against you in an argument? Tell them they're right but that it doesn't even matter—that you don't even care. Mom and Dad were trying to appeal to my sense of self and responsibility, two things I felt the weight of more acutely than they could possibly know. I didn't need them to remind me I was supposed to be more than what I was.

"I'm not here a lot because of work, I know," Dad said. Was he getting his composure back already? I had to give him credit for his newfound ability to stay on point. "But, when I am here, I've seen it. I've seen you come home from school or from being out with your friends and then you go straight to your room without so much as a 'hello' or letting us know you're here."

"Brock," Mom said. "I don't need you to hug me. If that's not something you feel comfortable doing right now then . . . well, then, I understand. I just want you to acknowledge me sometimes. To acknowledge all of us. You disappear into your room every day to draw and read your comics, and we don't see you for hours until you leave again at night. Is it too much to ask that when you come in you say hi before going off and doing . . . whatever it is that you do?"

Oh, come on.

"This is ridiculous," I said. "Are we arguing over whether or not I say hi? Then let's fix that. Let's fix that right now. Hi, Mom. Hi, Dad. How are you both doing? How was your day today?"

"That's not helping things, son." *No, mockery usually doesn't, Dad. That's why it's such a great tool for driving you nuts.* "You know what we mean."

"Really? You think I do?" My voice grew louder. "Because no—no, I DON'T know. I don't even know the POINT of all this."

"Son, you need to stop th—"

"Because, right now, I'm tired and I'm confused as to what the problem is. Wait—I remember—I came home a little late tonight. Also on the list: I don't hug or say hi enough. Wow, I am so sorry. Oh, shame on me. Next time I choose to disobey you, I'll be sure and dial back the transgressions a little. Maybe it would be better if I did some hard drugs or drank some beers. Would that be better? Would that give you something real to be upset at me for? I know, I should just have copious amounts of unprotected sex. How about that? Because I could do that instead. If you prefer. Promiscuity sounds like a ton more fun than the sheer delight I must surely get from not hugging Mom. I could—"

"SON, SHUT THE HELL UP!"

I shut up. Dad's voice echoed through the living room despite the thick curtains over the windows lining every wall. Mom was stunned. I was way beyond stunned, I was afraid. I had no idea what had just happened. What had I said to inspire that reaction from Dad? I couldn't even remember. I was just having fun, right? Dad rarely cursed or yelled. He had just yelled at me. I was so instantly ashamed and I barely knew why. I had gone way, way too far. I wanted to throw up.

"SIT DOWN AND SHUT YOUR LITTLE MOUTH. This new attitude of yours is UNACCEPTABLE. This isn't some GAME for us. You need to—"

I ran from the living room before Dad even got a chance to finish. With tears in my eyes, I retreated to the safety of my bedroom and shut the door behind me as fast as I could. The last time I had reacted like that was six years earlier when Logan was doing his very best to annoy me as much as possible (one of his daily goals) and he finally broke me. I screamed at him within full audible range of my mother the most abominable four-letter curse I knew, followed by the word "YOU!" I shocked myself so badly I instantly began crying and ran to my room where I sobbed in my bed for the better part of a half hour. I never received a punishment for it. There was no need.

It did not seem as though I would be so lucky this time.

I hadn't been sitting on my bed and staring blankly at the wall for very long before Dad came knocking. Hadn't enough been said? I'd screwed up and said some horrible things and I obviously knew that. Why couldn't he just leave it alone?

"Son, let me in please."

No. "No, please. I'm sorry, okay?"

"No, son, I'm sorry. I shouldn't have yelled at you like that."

"Okay, thanks."

"But, you said some pretty awful things. Your mother is very upset."

"That's her natural state."

It was muffled, but I could still hear Dad exhale deeply from behind the door. "No, it's not."

I let him in. What was I supposed to do? It was his house.

He hobbled over and let out a little grunt, sitting down next to me on my bed. It buckled and creaked from his weight. For a little while we just sat there, silently. If he expected me to talk first, he could forget it. I felt terrible about what I'd said, sure, but that didn't mean I wasn't still mad at them both. My curfew was super early.

"Brock," Dad finally began. "I want to talk about what's going on with you."

"What do you mean?"

"I'm worried about you."

"Okay, I'm worried about me too."

"Don't start that, son. I'm trying to talk to you."

"Okay."

"So?"

"So what?"

"Brock, you can either talk to me or we can be here all night."

"Well, I'm already in bed."

Dad got up and grabbed my desk chair, my parking spot for the evenings when I wasn't out with friends. When I turned fourteen, Mom and Dad gifted me a drafting table for my birthday so I would have someplace comfortable to draw. The desk came with a chair with wheels for feet. Dad rolled it over.

"Sit," he ordered.

"Fine." I got up and moved with as much harrumph as possible.

Dad took my place back on the bed. "I'm worried about you," he repeated. "I feel like there's something going on with you, son, but for the life of me I don't know what."

"Everything's fine."

"So, the coming home late and the being rude to your mother—all of that is fine?"

"No, I guess not."

"Okay then, what is it? What's wrong?"

"I don't know how to explain it. I don't even know if I should."

"All I want to do is help. Whatever it is that's going on, I can—it's okay. Whatever it is, you can tell me. I want to help."

I wouldn't look at him. I was far more interested in a spot on my bedroom floor. *Now* he wanted to talk. Well, I didn't want to. I knew my dad. I knew there was no way he was going to understand me or what I had to say. I started talking anyway.

"I'm frustrated."

Dad just looked at me. He refused to read the world of unvoiced meaning in the two words I'd thrown at him. "Frustrated about what?"

"About everything."

"Such as?"

"Everything."

"Okay. What does that mean?"

"I don't know," I said, lying. "I'm just—it's like you said—I'm just angry all the time. The littlest things get to me."

"Things like what? What do you mean?"

"Like, if things don't go exactly the way I want them to—like if I'm doing bad in a class or my friends are being stupid, it's like I just want to give up and run away. I want to scream. And I get so mad at myself for that. Like, that's not okay. I should be able to control myself better than that."

"I don't know about that," Dad said. "Everybody feels that way sometimes."

"Sure, everybody. But not me."

"Why not you?"

"I don't know." I looked up at Dad. There was kindness in his eyes. I hated lying and I hated myself all the more when I did it. I looked down again. "Well, I-I shouldn't say I don't know. I think I kind of know, but it sounds stupid. I think it sounds stupid."

"Doesn't matter."

I looked at Dad again and I reminded myself. The chances of him understanding were just about nil. But I said it anyway.

"Have you ever read *Dune?*"

"I've seen the movie," Dad said. "Agent Cooper is in that."

"Right. And Sting."

"And Captain Picard."

"Yeah, so in the book Paul Muad'Dib talks a lot about his future and what he's destined to do (he's the one that was played by Agent Cooper). Eventually, he'll become the emperor of the universe and wage jihad throughout the cosmos or something (that's mostly epilogue), but at the beginning of the book he doesn't know any of that. He can just feel it, like it's this thing inside of him. He calls it his 'terrible purpose.'"

"Okay . . . " Dad was hesitant. He had to be wondering where I was going with this. Having never said it out loud before, I was too.

"Sometimes—well, for a long time I've been feeling something kind of like that. Maybe my purpose isn't exactly terrible, but I feel like I'm supposed to do something . . . great? I don't know. That's my point—I don't know. I can just feel it. All the time. What's hard about that is—whether it's true or not or vain or not—what's hard is this pressure I feel to live up to it."

"Okay," Dad said again. "What do you mean 'live up to it'?"

"Like, however good everyone else is, I have to be that much better. That's my responsibility."

"That's a lot to carry. Let's say you're right, son, and you might be for all I know. It wouldn't surprise either your mother or I if God has a great plan in mind for you. So, let's say you're right. What's the problem? If it were me, I'd be really glad to know a thing like that. The only plans God has for me that I'm aware of is to die. And everybody does that."

Pity party from Dad. Shocker. I moved the chair around with my feet a little even though I knew I wasn't going anywhere.

"No," I said. "No, you don't want it. It's a burden. Like, you know I hated working at the club. Part of that was just because I felt like I was wasting my time there. If I'm supposed to be doing something important with my life, then anything less than that is just a distraction."

"You're saying working at the club wasn't important work? It was work, son. All work is important."

"Dad, come on. I was your glorified errand boy."

"Everybody starts somewhere. You think I like everything I do every day? I don't, but I do it to provide for your mother and you boys. That makes my work important."

Real pearl there, Dad. Not what we were talking about. "I don't have a fam—this isn't what I'm trying to talk about. I know what you do is basically important. The point isn't that I hated working at the club, it's that working at the club isn't what—let me start over."

I got angry all over again. Why was I even trying to explain this to him when he clearly couldn't understand?

"Here's the thing," I said. "This is the thing. Now. Currently. I'm not really sure there is anything I'm supposed to do anymore. Yes, I've felt this 'terrible purpose,' but is it real? Is it not? I don't know. It's fading. I still feel its pull, but I really don't know if I'm not just making it all up because I like to feel special. (I mean, who doesn't, right?) And if it's not real, and I still feel it so acutely, then what's wrong with me? I feel like I've lost my certainty. I don't know how to be like that. I don't know how to not be sure. I don't feel like I know anything anymore."

"Anything?" Dad looked surprised.

"Pretty much . . . yeah." Too far, too far! I didn't want to go there. And yet . . . "Okay, you know how last month I went to the temple with the youth?"

Making the pilgrimage to the LDS temple in Oakland was a twice-a-year affair for the youth in our ward. The temple is as sacred and rare a place on earth as you're likely to find—so going there was a big deal. Even taking away the fact that we always stopped at one of the two McDonalds in Los Banos on the way up to Oakland, sometimes during Shamrock shake season, it was a big deal without that.

"Yes," Dad said. "That was, what? Two Saturdays ago?"

"Three," I said. "So afterward, on the bus, everyone was talking about how strongly they felt the Spirit in the temple. About how even in the waiting room the Spirit was strong. But the thing is that I—*I* didn't feel *anything.* I felt nothing—literally nothing. I wanted to. I prayed for it. But I didn't feel anything."

"Okay."

"'Okay?' Dad, this is a major problem. This is how I've been feeling lately. Not just about the temple. I feel like I've lost touch with . . . things. Everything I hang onto to make sense of the world and God and the universe seems so far away right now and nothing is clear. I feel abandoned. I don't know the things I should know."

Dad paused. He seemed to be searching for the right thing to say next, but it was obvious that he didn't have it. I let him off the hook.

"Like, for example, I don't know if the Book of Mormon is true."

"That can't be right," Dad said, a little relieved. "I've heard you share your testimony in church. You know the Book of Mormon is true. I've heard you say it."

"No, I've said that I *believe* the Book of Mormon is true, but I don't *know* it is. I'm very careful about that. Most people say 'I know,' but I don't on purpose. Because I *don't* know. Not like they say they do."

"But isn't it—" Dad looked confused. "Either way you slice it, aren't we talking about faith here? So you say you believe and they say they know. I think you're putting a lot of emphasis on one word."

I was dumbfounded. I recoiled, pushing myself back in the chair with wheels. Did he really not get this? This was crucial. This was everything. "Dad, I'm not the one putting the emphasis on the word *know*! That's the way it is in the scriptures!"

I leapt out of the chair and grabbed my set of scriptures off the nightstand. These verses were so well-known I couldn't believe Dad wasn't connecting with what I was talking about. I turned to Moroni 10, the last chapter of the last book in the Book of Mormon. I read verses 4–5 out loud to Dad:

> And when you shall receive these things, I would exhort you that you would ask God, the Eternal Father, in the name of Christ, if these things are not true; and if you shall ask with a sincere heart, with real intent, having faith in Christ, he will manifest the truth of it unto you, by the power of the Holy Ghost.
>
> And by the power of the Holy Ghost ye may know the truth of all things.

"*Know*," I said emphatically. "It says you'll *know* the truth. That's what I want. According to this, that's what I have a right to ask for. I've asked and I've pleaded with God to let me know. I've been studying and doing everything I can and I just feel like I'm getting more and more confused as time wears on and I'm getting nothing. If you put a gun to my head—right now if you had a gun to my head and you asked me if I believed in the Book of Mormon, I wouldn't say yes. I don't know what I would say, but I wouldn't say yes. Meanwhile, everyone around me feels the Spirit in a freaking waiting room. All I want to know is what's true. The more I don't get that, the more I feel like the ground is shifting beneath me and nothing I've known or thought I knew makes any kind of sense. I'm so unsteady it's ridiculous."

There. Get it now?

"Okay," Dad said. "What do you think you need to do next?"

"I don't know!" Had he been listening at all? "You tell me. How do you know the Book of Mormon is true and the Church and all of it? Like, how did you find out?"

"Well," Dad said as he leaned back on my creaking bed. "You know the story. I knew I was Mormon and I wanted to find out what that meant. I studied as much as I could and my testimony just kind of grew from there over time."

"No, I know that. What I mean is . . . when did you *know*? Like, really know. When did the Spirit tell you?"

"The Spirit never told me," Dad said. As though this was not the biggest flaw in the foundation of his faith ever. "It just made sense. I've never felt a burning in the bosom or any of that."

"Then how do you know?"

"I just do." Dad's matter-of-factness was starting to irritate me. "Like I said, it makes sense to me."

"But how can that be good enough? What if you find something that makes more sense?"

"That won't happen."

How could he know that? His faith was based entirely on his own understanding of things. And he was . . . happy with that? Begrudgingly content? It was like Dad had settled, spiritually speaking. He'd found what fascinated him most and held the most promise and decided to stick with that until the end. That's not faith, that's loyalty.

All of our endless conversations about deep points of doctrine and the mysteries of life after death suddenly came into focus. Was the gospel just the greatest of all possible mythologies to him? Were commandments the prime directive he followed with the hope that they would take him to the stars? Did he enjoy his investigations into the peculiarities and the speculations so much that they actually constituted his faith entire?

"Son," Dad continued. "I prayed for years—years—and I never got the kind of answer you're talking about. After a while . . . I just figured God decided I didn't need one."

This was unbelievable.

"You shouldn't have given up!" I shouted. "Who are you to say how long your wait for an answer is? Maybe if you'd kept on trying then you would have gotten an answer!"

"No, I don't think so. He just doesn't speak to me the same way He speaks to you."

Ha. If he only knew. "I wouldn't say that. He's been pretty quiet lately."

"Okay," Dad said, fixing on another tactic. "So, why can't you wait? Why this hurry to have an answer now? You can just keep praying."

"Because . . . " Was I really going to say it out loud? "I don't—to be honest, I'm not sure if there even is a God anymore."

I felt my gut do back flips. I scolded myself for saying it out loud. *You just made it real, dummy.*

Dad couldn't look at me. My statement was shocking, but it wasn't shock that registered on his face. He looked sad. Disappointed. I wanted that look to stop. I wanted to stop talking entirely, but now I couldn't. I had some stuff to get out.

"This—this is my confusion. Is there a God? Isn't there? If there is, why isn't He talking to me? I really don't know. And if I don't know that, then nothing in my life makes any kind of sense. Where does the pressure to be so good come from? Is that just me driving myself crazy? That's what it feels like. Did Logan tell you about our fight the other day?"

"Your mother mentioned it to me."

"He wouldn't give me the keys to the car, and I wanted to kill him. I pushed him against the wall, grabbed at his pockets, and screamed and screamed at him. Over keys. Know what I did afterward? I came here into my room and sat on the bed and I was just shaking. I felt awful. Sweating and shaking and I couldn't stop."

Dad just looked at me like he would at a stranger. I kept going.

"I felt so bad, like I was really losing it. Sometimes I think about that—about what it would be like to just give in and go crazy. Logan called me a lunatic. Maybe I am. What if I am? I feel pulled toward that. Like, that's a real, almost tangible temptation for me. A part of me wants to deny everything I've ever been taught or thought I knew and just let my mind go into whatever dark corners it wants. I think that would feel really good. And then I'd be free of all responsibility and I wouldn't have to deal with any of this."

I shook hard with fear. I'd never dared say any of this stuff out loud, and some of it was a surprise even to me. Much more so to Dad. Which is why he said what he said next:

"Brock, maybe you need to see a therapist."

What? "So, you think I'm crazy."

"No, I'm not saying that. That's not for me to decide. I'm just saying that maybe—maybe there's someone who could help you better than I could. Maybe a psychologist."

And just like that, Dad broke my heart. It was okay for me to think I was crazy. But Dad? Dad was supposed to tell me I wasn't. That these thoughts I was having were okay, even normal. That's what I'd been hoping for. The fact that Dad didn't think they were devastated me. It told me he didn't know me well enough to know I would work this stuff out eventually. He didn't have that kind of faith in me.

I was angry and he was wrong. Dad's physical weakness may have been a new thing for him, but now I knew Dad had been spiritually weak for a long, long time.

For Dad, what was true and what wasn't was a matter of cold fact. I had suspected, but now I knew without a doubt that he couldn't possibly understand my drive to make God fulfill His promises to reveal truth to me personally. I had shared the most hidden part of myself, hoping for an understanding from him that not only wasn't coming, but that I had already known could never be. My entire life and all my anxieties were wrapped up in something Dad didn't even think was important.

What did I expect?

20

THE FLOOD

It was a rare Saturday night when the church wasn't being used for a social or a wedding party, so we had to take advantage of it when we could. Robby's father, the bishop, entrusted him with the key to the building for some reason, so he went to open it up. The rest of us—Pete, Aaron, my brother Logan, Travis, and myself went to the store to purchase snacks—chips, candy, ranch dip, candy, sodas, pretzels, mini donuts, and candy. I could have done without the pretzels and with lots more candy, but everyone else insisted that candy, candy, and more candy was enough candy.

The church was a lonely building on the northern tip of the southern half of Clovis. It was so obviously too small for its purpose that the Church discontinued the model right after construction was completed. Across the street lay a field, and behind it were the cookie cutter homes more typical of the landscape of the area. Our own, slightly less-affluent homes were about a mile away.

We set up camp in the main hall, a carpeted basketball court used as a classroom on Sundays and for not-so-squeaky basketball games on Wednesday. We opened all the doors to the hall for ventilation and grabbed the soft chairs from the women's meeting room to sit on. Always our DJ, I hooked up my portable stereo from home to the building's PA system and inserted the mix I'd created especially for that night. Within minutes, the music of Led Zeppelin, the Grateful Dead, Tom Petty, and Nirvana could be heard throughout the entire building, and only by us.

Driving that train/
High on Cocaine/
Casey Jones is ready/
Watch your speed

We hoped. I reminded myself that God, should He be out there and looking in on us, knew that I did not personally pen the lyrics to the Grateful Dead's "Casey Jones." I was simply the latest victim of its catchy and addictive melody.

While I made the church's halls slightly less hallowed, everyone else set up the food on one of the long rectangular tables in the middle of the room. All together, it was quite the spread. Within striking distance, next to the abundance of sugar and saturated fat our teenaged selves would soon consume with ease, was the round table at which we'd be parked for the next several hours. And at that table? The game.

It was always the same game for there could be no other. Over the years we had honed our play and carefully worded rules had been established to ease the tensions brought on by our unanimous, absolute will to win at any costs.

No mergers.

One-time only rent exemptions.

No deal-making except during your turn.

No speaking during a deal unless you are addressed by the deal maker.

The lessons we learned to inspire these codes of in-game conduct had been hard ones, but they had been worth it. Arguments and storming out of the room in a rage no longer plagued us. There was only the game.

We began as Zeppelin's "Black Dog" rose to levels the church's meager, in-wall speakers could barely handle. Chips crunched and soda cans popped. The first properties sold established the early front runners. Taxes were paid by the unlucky, and beauty contests won by the fortunate and not-so-fair alike. Any spilled candy or fallen chip crumbs were picked up quickly. There could be no trace of our visit once we left or the privilege of being there on our own might be revoked.

By the end of hour one, all properties had been sold.

During hour two we began our hardcore deal-making. Things got heated, but the rules kept our aggression in check.

And then, it happened.

Without warning, all ten doors to the main hall closed simultaneously of their own volition. We stopped the game just as suddenly, and all eyes darted about the large, cavernous room as we searched for some sort of clue as to the reason for this unexpected defiance of the law of physics. We stared blankly at one another, half-frightened and half-curious.

Silence.

And then . . .

WEETWEETWEETWEETWEETWEETWEETWEETWEET!

The fire alarm. It was ear-piercing. We looked each other over. No one seemed particularly guilty. We sniffed the air. Nothing burning. We plugged our ears. Still too loud.

I turned off the music.

Had we done something unwittingly? We were confident no one else was in the building, a fact which sadly meant no adult was present to tell us what to do. Then again, we had Pete.

Pete was the guy you wanted with you when things went wrong. The son of Clovis's chief of police, his ability to pull useful knowledge out of a hat to solve any problem or predicament was rivaled only by my ability to pull a useless bit of trivia out of thin air for those occasions when my natural body language just wasn't getting my unique personality across. He was a good foot taller than the rest of us and had the greater mass to match. If you weren't afraid of him, you were probably his friend (and even then . . .). Outwardly, every little thing about him hinted at his natural talents. Like telling us what in the world was going on.

Pete was able to surmise pretty quickly why the doors had closed. The locks that held them in place automatically demagnetized anytime the fire alarm was set off. Apparently, the spooky time delay between the demagnetization and the actual alarm sounding was an extra feature the designers threw in for kicks and giggles.

While we all stood helpless in the middle of the room, Pete opened his hat and pulled out the fact that the master control panel for the entire church building was next to the bishop's office. This, in theory, would give him direct access to the fire alarm itself and he'd be able to shut it off.

I suggested we fan out and try to find the source of the fire in the meantime. Everyone agreed and took off in a mad dash. If the building burned down, we all knew who they would blame.

Throughout the building, barely audible below the screeching of the alarm, were the sounds of dozens of doors opening and closing. Bravely, I trekked to the women's restroom and stepped inside to assess the situation. So that's what it looked like.

WEETWEETWEETWEETWEETWEETWEETWEETWEET!

It didn't take long for us all to find the absolutely nothing that was going on. No fire, no sparks, no danger of any kind that we could see. Things made less and less sense as the alarm continued to drone on and on. We grouped back up with Pete at the bishop's office to see if he was having any luck.

No dice.

"Stupid thing isn't letting me in," he said. "You need a key. The fire department should be here soon. I called them already just in case."

"Well, that's good," I said. "Why do you think it went off?"

"I dunno, dude. You sure you guys checked all the rooms?"

"Yep."

"Even the girls' restroom?"

Three of us replied, "Yep."

The thing we did not know and that the firemen were more than happy to explain to us once they arrived was that the alarm didn't go off because of fire—it was because of water.

Holed up in the main hall with no windows or view to the outside, we had completely missed the seriously biblical weather going on outside the church. Nothing in the skies before we entered had even suggested this as a possibility for the evening. We had been so busy listening to Tom Petty doing a free fall we had no idea about the torrent of rain coming down so hard and so heavy it triggered the fire alarm. Which was something that could happen. Who knew?

Having now cheated death and properly secured the women's restroom, the firemen left us and the church fell quiet once again. We returned to our game. I cranked the music back up. Chip and candy consumption resumed.

I don't know how anyone heard it. It must have been in between songs. We couldn't figure out what it was at first, but it sounded like someone shouting and POUNDING on the front doors to the church. I imagined a sopping wet, desperate, strung-out heroin addict wearing weather-eaten boots and looking inside with hunger in his eyes and his tongue on his lips. No doubt he was drawn like a moth to the flame of the lights we'd forgotten to turn off, the promise of warmth and shelter shining like bright rays of hope from the sacred edifice. Was he absent-mindedly fingering the blade in his pocket? Or was it already drawn and behind his back?

We all ran out to the foyer. There, at the door, stood Dad soaking wet and screaming at the top of his lungs. We opened the door quickly.

"WHAT ARE YOU GUYS STILL DOING HERE?!" Dad shouted, forgetting he was now inside. "The whole town's flooded. You need to get out NOW."

"Are you serious?" I said. Heavy rain was one thing, but a flood? Clovis doesn't flood. I'd never seen Fresno or Clovis flood in all my life. And, it wouldn't have been above Dad to drive all the way out to the church to act hysterical as part of a joke.

"Yes," he confirmed. "Leave your stuff and let's get out of here. We'll come back for it later. Your mother is worried sick about you guys. Come on! Let's go, let's go!"

"But we—just give us a second and we'll get our—"

"Son, there's no time. If you wait here much longer you're all going to be stuck here till morning. Pete, I don't have enough room in the van for all of you. Can you take Robby and Travis?"

"Sure, yeah," Pete said.

"All right, I'll take Aaron—he lives near us—and Logan and Brock, obviously. Follow me closely and stay on the same path I do until we get to the high school. I know the way through this, and if you don't go where I go you're gonna end up like the other fools trying to drive through it."

I grew up during drought years. I had no idea what real rain was like, but the five seconds it took us to get from the doors of the church to the inside of the vans was a swift education. We were all instantly soaked head to toe, just like Dad.

Some say there's nothing to see and never anything going on in the Fresno/Clovis area. They're mostly right. Even the weather and natural disasters usually just move on by. Both cities get only mild tremors from the largest of earthquakes, and the snowfall a mere forty-five minutes away in the Sierra Nevada Mountains just can't quite reach the valley floor. But that night? That night Clovis went below sea level.

The city was not set up for this amount of falling water. It rose up over curbs and climbed its way onto front yards. The top halves of stalled cars littered the streets, their drivers forced to sit on the hoods and wait for either help or drainage.

I loved it. I'd never seen my hometown look anything like this. There was something kind of beautiful about the way the streetlights shimmered across the waters of the city's new, crisscrossing rivers. Like a white trash version of Venice.

Dad had a working knowledge of the new topography from having already driven through it once on his way to get us. He navigated his way back through it all slowly, making sure we stuck to only the most shallow parts of the streets. The van was far too low to the ground to pull out of deep waters, especially with all the weight it carried. Dad made left turns where he should have turned right because a straight shot home was only going to get us into trouble. Only the correct detours would allow us safe passage.

I tried to imagine the father of one of my friends doing what Dad did that night. I couldn't. My guess was that a big part of why Dad came to get us was because Mom couldn't stand the thought of us potentially spending the entire night at the church with only gummy bears and dinner mints to sustain us. But, I also knew this was Dad in his element. It was a crisis, and he could do something about it. These were the times in which he thrived. And smiled broadly.

"Dude," Aaron said to me after our third wrong turn. "Your dad is pretty cool."

Oh. Yeah.

21

THE LAST TIME

Dad placed his hands on my head, and the men gathered in a tight circle around the chair I sat in. They stacked their right hands over his, one on top of the other, each of them courteously supporting the weight of those above their own to not overburden my bowed head. I could feel the meat of Dad's palms dig in nonetheless.

Up against Dad's, my own hands looked relatively frail and elegant, easily swallowed up in a handshake with men or very husky boys. They wouldn't have looked out of place on a woman and made for perfect partners with my tiny, slender wrists. I wondered if my hands might fill out at some point or if I'd always see bone where Dad had so much muscle and flesh. I was eighteen years old. *By now if ever*, I thought. But still, as a man, I hoped for a brighter, more masculine future.

Focus.

The room was deadly quiet. Feet and butts on metal chairs shuffled in the silence while the cylinder of men did their best to get into a comfortable position. There was no telling how long they would need to stand around me. That was up to Dad. They bowed their heads and closed their eyes and waited. Finally, my father began.

"Brock William Henry Heasley, in the name of Jesus Christ and by the power of the Holy Melchizedek Priesthood which we hold, we place our hands upon your head and confer unto you the Melchizedek Priesthood and ordain you to the office of Elder with all the rights, powers and authority thereof."

I was five months out of high school and two months away from going out on a volunteer mission for the Church, just as I was supposed to. Whatever other questions I had about life or God or any of it, this much was a given: I would go on a mission. I was about to turn nineteen and that was the age of eligibility. It was time and I had spent my entire life preparing for it.

My call was to serve in Arizona to teach Spanish speakers the gospel of Jesus Christ in their own language and dedicate my life entirely to the Lord for the space of two years. It was an assignment I received only days earlier. It was an assignment I desperately did not want. I had no hesitation in giving up my family, my friends, dating, school, my new job at the movie theater and (for that matter) movies, television and comic books. But English? I did not want to give up English.

I didn't want to admit it, but my call to serve—handed down from the prophet and President of the Church himself—seemed more than a little uninspired. My call gave me doubt I didn't need. Spanish? I got Cs in Spanish. Barely.

I hadn't moved on much at all from the night Dad questioned my sanity. I remained in a state of default belief, but that perfunctory hope still refused to bear fruit. My willingness to serve a mission was a child's commitment, founded on a child-like faith based more in trust than understanding. I felt some guilt about that. Could I go door-to-door preaching something I only *wanted* to be true? It seemed I would have to. What else could I do? Go to college?

Unlike Dad, I'd never stopped asking what was true. I knew that was the coward's way out. If I accepted the stories of the scriptures even in part, then I had to accept that God sometimes tests His people's patience. He—I was certain—now tested me. I clung to that idea, though my behavior did not always indicate I was anywhere near passing the test. My prayers were more token than diligent. Just long enough to feel like I was doing my part and just often enough to annoy God with all my constant pleading.

I made my bed with belief. Belief, I told myself—not knowing—was enough. But I was wrong about that.

I concentrated, closed my eyes even tighter, and pushed all other thoughts out of my head. Dad continued the blessing with his own words.

"We bless you with a desire to read from the scriptures regularly. As you do so, you will find the counsel within the words of God and

His prophets that will have the most meaning to you. We bless you with strength and a willingness to serve . . . "

I wanted to remember this moment, what it felt like to sit there and receive the power and priesthood of God. The power to act in God's name was, I knew, no light thing. I would now be able to serve in the Church in a leadership capacity, if so called. I would be able to give blessings of healing and comfort. I would be able to enter the temple fully, and experience all of its attendant blessings. I would serve God and the people of Arizona as an *adult*—as a man.

Would there be a moment when I felt the power enter my body? What could a thing like that possibly feel like? I didn't know, and the longer the blessing went on, the more it seemed I would never know. It was just another blessing, not at all unlike the countless other blessings I'd received from Dad on the first day of school or when I was sick.

"We bless you with faith and understanding. We bless you that you will have His Spirit with you as you fulfill your priesthood callings and attend to your duties; that you will have joy in His service and be mindful of what you—"

Dad stopped talking. He stopped cold.

And hard. I felt tremors in his fingertips as they dug more deeply into my scalp. The duration of the pause grew to an exceptional length, beyond awkward silence and into "Did he fall asleep?" territory. My head grew hot. I listened intently and only to Dad's breathing, waiting for the next piece of advice or insight. It wasn't coming. *Why this pause?*

Finally, he continued—but now, his voice was different. Shakier and lower.

"Brock . . . you are about to encounter many challenges. Hard times are ahead of you both in your mission . . . and in your life. There will be great trials, but your Father in Heaven has every confidence that, as you trust in Him, you will overcome them. In the name of Jesus Christ, amen."

The men surrounding me echoed my father's "amen."

I felt the life drain from me. My entire body seemed to consist of only one organ: my stomach. Which felt awful. I had no power to give over to my limbs, no ability to speak. My eyes opened, but I saw nothing. My mind raced ahead of me, overwhelmed with thoughts and empty at the same time. Not a thing or person in the room was of consequence.

What did Dad's final words mean? "Hard times?" Like what? Why would he say that?

Somehow, I managed to get up from my chair and stumble through a half-hearted round of shaking hands with the men who participated in the blessing. Dad was last and we embraced.

I turned around and walked back to my seat next to my family, who were there as witnesses and as support. The "room" we were in was really just a section of the main hall of the church partitioned off by a vinyl curtain. Directly above our heads was a basketball hoop folded up into the ceiling (as it always was when not in use—no one was fooled, our meeting was in a gym).

Mom beamed. My brothers looked like they couldn't have cared less. Now that it was over they would return to their respective classrooms. Except it wasn't over.

"And now," the bishop said, "I'd like to ask Brother Heasley to come up and share his testimony with us."

I got up without thinking. "No," he said. "The other Brother Heasley." What other Brother Heasley? Why was the bishop so confused? He pulled me by the arm toward a space my father did not need to occupy. I felt a little embarrassed and wondered why the room was so big and everyone so far away. They all sat at the ends of long, long tunnels.

Dad's testimony was short and sweet, as it usually was whenever he was called upon to share it. There was little that made him as nervous and uncomfortable as having to stand in front of people and deliver any kind of impromptu speech.

When Dad was done, the bishop turned to me and indicated it was *now* my turn. I moved back to the center of the room while Dad took his seat next to Mom.

I lifted my eyes and did my best to focus them, but it was difficult. "I feel weird," I managed to say. "There's, ah—there's no other way to describe it. I suppose that explains my behavior just a minute ago."

I got a few pity laughs, but they could just as easily have been snickers. My intent was to then bear my testimony—to share with everyone all that I believed and how excited I was to go on a mission (leaving out the hatred of Spanish part).

Instead, I could not speak. Because I can't talk while I'm crying.

The tears so completely overwhelmed my face they blocked my speech and plugged my nose. I was overcome by . . . emotion? Is that what it was?

At first, I did not know. I bit my lip to keep from blubbering and scolded myself for the wretched display that was my face. Meanwhile, everyone waited, staring at me. If I'd been able to speak without sputtering, I probably would have ditched the testimony and just started apologizing.

My mind was clear. I had no explanation for the unnerving, involuntary, and vulgar convulsions of my body. *This is being done to me,* I thought. *I am not choosing this.* If it's possible to have an out-of-body experience while remaining in one's body, then that's what was happening. I felt . . . something. And it was intense. But, I could neither define it nor halt it. This went on for a full minute and a half. I was a victim, publicly tortured by whatever force had taken hold of me.

I started to put together what was really happening. Strange, unfamiliar thoughts barged their way into my mind, an intelligence I neither possessed nor was capable of generating.

I realized I was not the victim of what was happening. I was the beneficiary. It was as though all the emotion had cleaned me out, breaking apart all other feelings and thoughts so these new ones had a place to go. This new, vast space filled almost to overflowing with knowledge—more pure and refined and exact than any I had ever known. It rushed in so powerfully and with such clarity that neither natural occurrence nor imagination could possibly explain what was happening.

Here, now, was the answer I had longed for.

Any concerns I had about where I was or who was in the room with me fell away as I received my gift. I knew God was real and that Jesus Christ was the Savior of the world—my Savior—and that His gospel and the Church were true. It was all true. It could not have been simpler or more plainly stated in my mind. No proofs were presented. No facts clicked into place leading me to one, inevitable conclusion. I just *knew.* Better than I had ever known anything and, I suspected, better than anyone could ever know anything at all.

I gave into my tears and I welcomed them. I didn't care what my face looked like anymore as I sobbed a pure, joyful gratitude. This was my moment, and if it had to happen with so many surrounding me, then that was their dumb luck. To know what is true—really, *actually* true—what gift could be greater? It was one I had quite nearly given up hope of receiving. Why me? Why now? I had no idea.

That's when I got mad.

Really, genuinely *angry.* It rose up inside of me as I thought about all the people—all of my brothers and sisters out there—who didn't have what I had in that moment. How was that right or just? I had gone so many years without an answer, but I at least knew where to look. How many people didn't even know that much? How many didn't know the right questions to ask? It did not seem right to me that anyone should be denied the truth I now possessed, for any reason. The reality of an adversary was so clear. There was a force in opposition to truth that would do anything to stop people from obtaining it. A devil.

A desire for physical, punishing violence rippled through me. In that moment, my skin was just a container for my spirit and my rage. I felt like I could take on Satan himself and turn him into a bloody, pitiable mess. It wasn't right that people didn't have what I had in that moment. I knew. I knew the most basic function of the universe and my place in it. My heart ached for those left wanting, and my emotions turned from gratitude and anger to a deep sorrow. It didn't have to be this way. *It shouldn't be this way.*

I became conscious of the room again. Several minutes had now passed without even one word escaping my lips. I tried saying something just to see if I could.

"I . . . I am . . . "

The tears started back up and I clammed up again. I both wanted to experience and live inside of this moment forever, and see it end immediately. I averted all gazes, but from the sounds of the creaking chairs those in the room with me were feeling more than awkward on my behalf. No doubt they wondered when I might finally sit down. So did I.

I let another minute pass before attempting to speak again.

My sincerest desire was to somehow communicate to everyone in the room just exactly what I felt, to give them a piece of it, but I knew that was impossible. Instead, I said very simply and with a power behind my voice I didn't know I had: "I . . . know that Jesus Christ is my Savior and that He lives. I know the Church is true and that we have a Father in Heaven who loves us and knows us. This I say in the name of Jesus Christ, amen."

* * *

Dad chose to drive me the one thousand miles to the Missionary Training Center in Provo, Utah, himself. It was cheaper than a plane, and if there was one place where Dad and I didn't have any problems getting along with each other, it was on the road. We wanted to take our time and see the sights, so we stretched it out. Three days, just the two of us.

We piled my two suitcases into the silver Volvo station wagon. The large black trench coat I would wear during the Utah winter for the next nine weeks (and never again) hung on a hanger at one of the back windows. We said our goodbyes from the street in front of our house. Mom cried. I hugged her tightly and told her I loved her. I told my brothers the same. Two years was a long, long time.

I couldn't wait for it to start.

We took the southern route, and in Las Vegas we stopped for lobster and sleep. Dad talked all through the Mojave Desert about how on the Strip you could find the cheapest, most delicious lobster you'd ever tasted. The best part? It was all you can eat.

He wasn't wrong—it was very good—but why did it have to be Vegas? Was it necessary that our waitress serve us eyefuls of cleavage along with our food? Judging by the other servers in the restaurant and their equally low-cut tops, the answer was yes. Bad enough were the showgirl-enhanced billboards greeting us on our way into town. Did the local dining also have to be so immodest? Surely, at those prices, the restaurant could move the lobster without the sex marketing.

Las Vegas seemed a sad, depressed town to me. Everything in the city was in the service of pleasure and the trapping of attention and time. I felt like an alien visitor to a foreign land whose customs I couldn't understand. *So this is what being a missionary feels like*, I thought.

My first and only previous journey to Utah was just a few months earlier during a road trip with my friend Nathan. My favorite part of that trip was when we finally got out of the long, boring nothing that was the Nevada desert and first entered the mountains of Utah just past St. George. Fall was on the horizon, and there was a sharp bite to the cold rushing by outside, but it wasn't so bad we couldn't roll down our windows. Since my friend's car stereo status remained at "stolen," our only playback option was the boombox we put at my feet on the passenger side. We sang along at the top of our lungs to Barry McGuire's "Eve of Destruction," and it was glorious. Now that I was with Dad and back in those same mountains—surely the most beautiful I'd ever seen—I was intent on recreating that experience and feeling.

Mr. McGuire would have gone over well with Dad. His firm belief was that no good music had been produced past 1970 and that people hundreds of years in the future would still be singing along to "Red Rubber Ball" while the correct pronunciation of Nirvana fell by the wayside. I knew that belief put Dad squarely in the same camp as those who could not understand how a cardigan sweater could be worn ironically, but I was confident it was ignorance and not taste that held him back. There was a lot of good stuff out there. He just never took the time to hear it.

"Dad, I've got a tape," I told him. "Mind if I play it?"

"Think you should?"

"Why not?"

"President Tanner just set you apart as a missionary two days ago, son. You think listening to heavy metal is the best thing for you right now?" Every kind of music Dad hated was heavy metal, which to him was synonymous with evil. I knew this to be false. God was not as close-minded as my dad. He hears everything and everyone, and, since power ballads are awesome, I knew He must be a fan.

"He told me I don't have to follow all of the mission rules yet—they can change from mission president to mission president anyway. He just told me to be good and not do anything stupid, basically."

"All right."

"It's okay?"

"Go ahead."

I popped in my *Brock's Utah Trip 1* cassette and sat back. Track one: "Tonight, Tonight" by Smashing Pumpkins. To my ears, the song was a thing of rare beauty, an aural feast that could be forever dined upon for helping after helping of inspiration and uplift. It featured lots of dad-friendly orchestration and a haunting lyric that meant . . . something I had never quite been able to parse.

> *Time is never time at all/*
> *You can never ever leave without leaving a piece of youth/*
> *And our lives are forever changed/*
> *We will never be the same/*
> *The more you change the less you feel*

"How can you listen to that?" Dad said after only a couple of verses.

"What are you talking about?"

"Turn it off. I'm not listening to that."

"Dad, just give it a chance."

"I did. I don't like it."

"How can you say that? This is a great song." I was a little offended and more than a little disappointed. I had taken great pains to create a mix both Dad and I could enjoy. Like any good mix, I led with my best stuff. If he didn't like the Pumpkins, then what were we supposed to listen to?

"That's not a song, son. That's noise."

"What's wrong with it?"

"Listen to it. You call that music? He sounds like he's whining. This is whining with accompaniment. Did you bring anything good?"

"Seriously?" I got angry. Why was that? It was just a stupid song, but I wanted Dad to like it. I didn't know why, but that was important to me. "You really think it sucks that bad?"

"You honestly don't?"

I didn't, but I turned it off anyway.

We arrived in Provo during what turned out to be the worst blizzard of the year. Our Volvo skated around the city streets, nearly missing street lamps, parked cars, and mailboxes. We should have gotten chains for the tires, but he was convinced he could navigate without them. Only the grace of God explains why we didn't hit anybody.

The next morning, we got up early to trek up the hill to Salt Lake City. The temple in Salt Lake is one of the more beautiful temples in the world, and Dad wanted to take me through it now that I could go in. There wouldn't be another chance for us to do so for another couple of years. I was against it simply because the roads on the hill toward the city were just as icy as the ones in Provo, and the traffic twice as fast. We had to get out and push a few times and stay in the right lane the whole way up, but we made it.

Of course, we had the same problem going back down after we were done. This was a particular problem because it was now late morning on January 31, 1996. I was supposed to report to the Missionary Training Center at noon. Instead, I was late by a couple of hours. Luckily, the orientations were done in shifts according to last names. We joined up with N–Z and no one was the wiser.

Walking the halls of the MTC in my heeled dress shoes with Dad next to me in his tennis shoes only made our height difference that much more obvious. He was bigger than me by about eighty pounds, but when we stood side-by-side I had at least a couple of inches on him up and down. I hated that. It was only when across the room from each other I could pretend he was just as large as he'd always been. When I was seven years old, I made a bet with him that one day I'd be taller. He bet against me and ten years later paid out the hundred dollars. I would have gladly lost that one. I preferred the version of Dad on the other side of the room.

I was the first Heasley to ever serve a mission. I felt the weight of that, but I didn't mind it. It was an honor, and, in a way, a culmination of the work Dad started long ago when he tossed out his booze and cigarettes. We didn't talk about it, but the glow on his face as we walked through the building spoke volumes.

We entered the orientation room together, knowing that after the presentation we'd be leaving separately. The speakers talked a little about the strict, work-hard life at the MTC, but more about the sacrifice families make when they send their children away to serve the Lord and the blessings that come from that sacrifice. The longer they spoke—the more my official entrance was delayed—the more nervous I got. Once Dad walked away, I'd be alone. For two years.

When it was over, everyone in the room stood up and all the parents made their way for the west doors while the missionaries went out the east doors. Dad and I shared a hug.

"Goodbye, son," he said. "I love you."

"I love you too, Dad," I said as I watched him turn to walk out. "See you in a couple of years."

It was the last time I saw him alive.

IV

THE GHOST

22

SPEAKING IN TONGUES

It's easy to go crazy at the Missionary Training Center. For the duration of my stay, I was one in a district of twelve missionaries who all needed to learn Spanish and how to share our faith without sounding like idiots. "District" was really just a fancy term for "class." Other classes learned Russian, Portuguese, German, Italian, and so on. The lucky ones didn't have to learn any language at all. They stayed for only three weeks, after which they went to serve in places such as Alabama or Ohio or the United Kingdom. Everyone in my district stayed for nine. For nine weeks, I slept in the same dorm with these strangers, attended the same classes, and ate at the same times. During our last few weeks, we all went a little mad together.

The MTC campus, located a stone's throw from Brigham Young University, serves to accommodate hundreds of missionaries, both men and women. Our movements were restricted not only by the severe winter weather but also by the perimeter of strict obedience surrounding the entire facility. Conscience was our guard tower and the threat of being sent home dishonorably the rifle to keep us constantly in line; a prison of our own making by virtue of the choice we'd made to be there.

Our first names were stripped from us, replaced by a title: Elder. I was Elder Heasley. Others were Elder Smith, Elder Elwood, Elder Henderson, and so on. The appellation made little sense. The title denoted our office in the priesthood, not our maturity, our ages still pointing correctly toward a fascination with girls' bodies and bad odors. The few female missionaries in the training center all went by "Sister," which, appropriately, made them sound like nuns. Their habits were long dresses or skirts, while us Elders stuck to a besuited look with never-crisp white shirts. Fastened to our tops or adorning our lapels was an ever-present black name tag with our title, last name, and the Church logo. Despite being the size of a credit card, you could see it from a mile away.

We came from all over North America. We shared a sacred purpose and difficulty navigating the icy outdoor walkways between the dorms and classrooms in slick shoes. More than once, my California feet had a hard time keeping me vertical.

For the first six weeks, my district endured with gladness the constant underarm smell permeating every crevice and cranny of our dormitory, and the twelve-hour days of gospel and language study in our non-descript classroom. We sang together. Moved by the Spirit, we cried together. We learned about the importance of OYM (opening your mouth) in spreading the gospel to strangers on the street. We practiced lessons and asking bold "Will you?" questions to help people read our books and set dates to be baptized. We were groomed to want nothing more in the world than to go out and spread the Word and teach. We had a gift to share—the gospel of Christ, the best news anyone had ever heard.

But, in our final weeks, the closer we got to leaving and actually doing what we had only thus far practiced, the more we lost sight of it. The random shouting and spontaneous singing of Beatles songs began at week seven. The throwing of our bodies against the drab brown walls of the cafeteria for the pure pleasure of some other sensation besides our thirty-seventh bowl of Cap'n Crunch rumbling in our stomachs began at week eight. At week nine, our eyes lost focus and the newer missionaries just beginning their own internment gazed upon on us in horror as the spiritually emaciated versions of their future selves.

It was the sameness that did me in. Same walls. Same books. Same lessons. Same people.

I got along with the other Elders in my district, but I never felt like one of them. Most of them hailed from nearby, in the holy and wholesome state of Utah (little known fact: Utah's border is outlined entirely by a white picket fence). My tales of the dangers of California and its armed robberies and low-flying helicopters at 1:00 AM made me exotic and different. I was one of only a few dozen Mormons at my high school, not thousands. No, I didn't call soda, "pop."

I'd idolized missionaries my entire life. They were spiritual giants who, on the day they put on that black name tag and clad their feet in spit-polished shoes, attained a gravitas and understanding that surpassed even the wisest of men. Now, on the inside of the great, 50,000-strong, worldwide missionary machine, I found this to only sometimes be true. Elders were as likely to bear an honest, powerful witness of Christ in the morning as they were to burst into the bathroom unannounced at night to take pictures of each other on the can. (This was supposed to be riotously funny. I was less than amused.)

I knew Elders out in the field couldn't be that immature. Elders in the field didn't dissolve into giggle fits when Elder Carnahan let one rip for the seventh time since lunch. Elders in the field didn't speak in cartoon voices and burp Pearl Jam songs into the night. Elders in the field weren't little boys; they were wholly dedicated to the work and to the people they served and to God. That's what the training center was for. To beat that out of us.

The craziest thing of all was that the other Elders in my district didn't realize learning Spanish was a fool's errand. We were handicapping ourselves and being made to look like fools by learning that turgid, clumsy language, and no amount of practice rolling our double "r's" would change that. Day-after-day, they all absent-mindedly repeated their *vocabulario* and counted north of *diez* in utter denial of the fact that God had put up a wall between us and our ability to share the good news. Even after nine weeks of intense study, none of us were fluent. Not one.

Least of all me.

As my flight out of the blizzard and into the desert neared, a feeling of dreadful anticipation took over. In Arizona, I would be expected to speak Spanish and no one would care how difficult it was for me to learn it or how maybe the prophet got the call wrong this time. All they'd care about would be whether or not I could speak the language. And when I couldn't? Blank stares. Mockery. They'd toss me in a ring with a hungry bull and watch happily as I got gored. My future in Arizona—despite a lifetime of preparation as a missionary—was a damned one.

By the end of my stay in the MTC, I envied and admired my new, intermittently and unashamedly flatulent friends. While they conjugated verbs seemingly with ease, happily ignorant of how white their speech sounded, I could only spit out the Spanish language equivalent of a five-year-old's testimony.

A five-year-old with a speech impediment.

* * *

My first day in the field was the beginning of a long joke that only got less funny as time wore on. Ostensibly, being a missionary was the best time of my life. But only ASU students on a bender have the time of their lives in Arizona. The Grand Canyon State is where the sun burns so hot God altered the very landscape to serve as a warning to all that absolutely, under no circumstances, should anyone ever attempt to live there. Grass, trees, and rivers—all good things necessary for life and its continuance—have been replaced by rocks, weeds, and dried, cracked beds of red earth. Prickly cacti—those frozen green men with arms reaching to the heavens for a relief that never, ever comes—dotted the roadside all the way from the Phoenix airport to my first assignment in nearby Mesa. Their spiny thorns jutting out at every angle were a clear signal to get out and stay away. And yet no one listened. I didn't listen. At first.

In 1996, Phoenix had only recently established itself as a burgeoning, sprawling metropolis. The outlying cities such as Tempe, Mesa, Gilbert, and Chandler with their wide rivers of gray pavement and sun-bleached edifices growing on either side of them, so completely bled into one another it was now impossible to tell when you were going from one to the other. Construction was on the rise, and the migrant workers from northern Mexico lived mostly within the multi-city boundaries. Out of the 230 missionaries in the Arizona Tempe Mission, I was one of only twelve Elders assigned to teach them. I, by some improbability that only either God or the devil could have enabled, was a specialist in a thing I did not know, living in a place I did not want to inhabit.

Nobody told me missionary work is equal parts hard manual labor. I knew it primarily as a spiritual calling, but we didn't just teach people the gospel; we helped them in their gardens and moved furniture, unloaded rocks, and painted their houses. We were there to serve, in whatever capacity we could. And when we weren't serving? That was for biking to and from the service. Twenty miles or more a day. In the Arizona heat. With a tie on.

Never did that hanging, strangling piece of cloth make less sense.

At the end of the first week, I peeled a horrific mask of skin off my freckled face. "At least it's a dry heat," some people would say. *Screw you*, I would think back. A lot of water and a lot more sunscreen were my only survival tools—once I got less stupid and stubborn about using them. Tanning was out; my skin only knew how to achieve deeper shades of pink. I ended every day of those first weeks feeling like I'd been drop-kicked straight into the bowels of hell.

One man I encountered in downtown Mesa confirmed this. I was a "greenie," a new missionary who thought he knew better. I didn't think my Peruvian trainer, Elder Gatica, was older and wiser and more experienced. He was jaded, tired, and stuck in his ways. Sure, he was fluent in three languages and knew the lessons so well he had little need of me, but he was three months away from the end of his mission and had lost touch with the real reason we endured the long days and inconvenient weather. When we grabbed a hot dog from a roadside vendor one afternoon and a man of questionable appearance sat at the only table with spare seats, Elder Gatica motioned me to come sit on the curb with him. I dug in and sat right down next to the man. Missionaries don't judge, after all. Elder Gatica reluctantly followed suit.

The man looked to be in his mid-thirties. Glistening, bald head. Wraparound sunglasses. Sharp nose. He was hunched over, quiet, munching on a hot dog it didn't look like he particularly enjoyed. I had only gotten in a few quick bites of my own dog before he, without even turning to look at me, asked the question.

"So, who's Joseph Smith?"

I had only been in the field for three weeks, and already I knew no one liked to talk about Joseph Smith. I got excited. This was why you don't judge people by their appearance.

Elder Gatica grabbed his hot dog, got up, and walked away. *Burn out.*

I turned to face the potentially newest member of the kingdom of God on earth next to me and said, "Joseph Smith was a prophet of God in our day, just like the prophets of old—of the Bible."

The man didn't move. He appeared to be staring ahead, but his mirrored sunglasses made it impossible to see his eyes. I continued: "So . . . have you heard of Joseph Smith?" I didn't know what else to say.

"Yeah," the man said. "I think I seen him."

Joseph Smith died in 1844.

"O-oh," I said. "You have?"

"Yeah, I'm a sentinel."

"A sentinel? What's a sentinel?"

"A sentinel guards the gates of hell." He paused, allowing his statement to sink in, then asked, "Do you believe in angels?"

"Yes," I said. "We believe in angels."

"What about demons? You believe in those?"

"Yes, we believe demons exist."

"Well, I'm a demon," he (it?) said, finally turning his face toward me. "I'm a demon that guards the gates of hell."

"Oh. Huh."

"That's right. I'm the worst demon you ever seen."

He was also, to my knowledge, the only demon I had ever seen. I decided to let that point go and instead said to him, "Okay, well, we've got places to be. You have a nice day."

I got up and left with the wise and experienced Elder Gatica. So he knew better. So what. At least I finally got to talk to somebody in blessed, beautiful English.

* * *

It surprised me how quickly the fatigue and the fast, constant pace—even under that unconscionable, hot yellow blister in the sky—became routine. My body was young and strong enough to adapt to just about any condition, which I never knew it could do.

My brain gave me slightly more trouble. My aptitude for adapting my thoughts into a foreign tongue increased not at all as my mission went on. That wasn't how it was supposed to go. I was supposed to be supported by God in my efforts to learn a new language. My brain was supposed to be able to make the connections and the words flow. Instead, I felt very alone.

The more I tried to learn it, the more nonsensical and frustrating Spanish became. No one, not even Elder Gatica, could explain to me why in the world it mattered if a noun was a boy or a girl. The logic of the language (irregular verbs? don't even start) was beyond me. I was told over and over again in the MTC that Spanish was the easiest of the foreign-speaking missions. What I wanted to know was, what difference does it make if a rock weighs one ton or two if you can't lift either one?

Rarely has a language been butchered as mercilessly as it was during those early springtime days of my mission. That was the real joke, on the unsuspecting Spanish speakers of Arizona. Why I had been called to teach in Spanish and not, say, Russian, was completely obvious to me. There are no nicer or more generous people on the face of the earth than Latinos. They didn't mock me at all. They smiled with pity in their hearts.

The longer I stayed in the field—the more I stumbled my way through rote greetings and clumsily expressed my faith in God—the more impossible serving an honest, useful mission seemed. I wasn't serving a mission at all. I was enduring a two-year replay of my most hated class in high school. Only now there were real, eternal consequences to getting bad grades. What if I put the accent on the wrong syllable and somebody thought they were supposed to, I don't know, fornicate or something instead of getting baptized? You don't mess around with people's salvation like that.

My only contact with my family during this time was in the form of letters and scheduled phone calls. We were "allowed" (only in the sense that, as volunteers, this was a restriction we had agreed to) three calls a year, one each on Mother's Day, Father's Day, and Christmas.

The Mother's Day phone call with my parents came at exactly the wrong moment. Instead of the mature, valiant young man she was expecting, the voice Mom heard on the other end of the line was that of the saddest of all sacks.

ME: I think I should just come home.
MOM: Don't say that, Brock.
ME: I'm just . . . I'm wasting everyone's time out here.

Oh, and Happy Mother's Day! Great job on me!

MOM: Don't say that. You know that's not true.
ME: You don't know that. Which one of us is here to see? You're spending a lot of money to have me out here and—
MOM: Don't worry about the money.
ME: No, I do worry about the money.

It wasn't hard to read between the lines of Mom's letters. She wrote now and again about Dad working late into the night because he, all of the sudden, had less help at the Reedley store and needed to pay off some debts. I was able to work out that Dad's business partner had made some bad deals and left him high and dry when they didn't work out. Dad was draining finances from every corner just to keep up with creditors.

ME: You can't just brush that aside. If I'm wasting everyone's time out here, then I'm also wasting your money.
MOM: I'm gonna put your father on the phone.

Dad came on the line, and I got him up to speed on my plan to disappoint him in a way neither of us thought possible. It was the only way to minimize the fiscal and spiritual damage I was responsible for.

DAD: Don't worry about the money.
ME: Okay, fine. But do you hear what I'm saying? Did Mom tell you? I don't want this to be true—I really don't—but I honestly hate this language. I hate it so much. The people—the people are great, don't get me wrong. They've been extremely nice and patient with me and I—that doesn't matter anymore. We're all suffering together over here because I can't conjugate verbs. That's what it's come down to. The other day, Elder Gatica—frustrated, unfairly-saddled-with-me-at-the-end-of-his-mission Elder Gatica—sent me on a team-up with an English Elder into a neighborhood all the missionaries call—and I'm not making this up—Little Mexico. People let me in out of pity. They're too nice here. One woman nursed her baby through my entire lesson, topless. I didn't even have enough vocabulary to ask her to cover up.
DAD: Does that happen a lot?
ME: Just the once so far.

Dad was silent. I don't know what I expected unloading on Dad like that, but silence seemed about right. He had no frame of reference for my problem, and there wasn't a whole lot he could do for me from California and we both knew it.

DAD: Son, I never served a mission so I can't say as I exactly know what you're going through here. I've never learned another language, neither. But, if I had to guess at what your problem is, I'd say you've got a bad attitude. Coming home isn't going to solve that. There is a time for you to come home, and that's about twenty months from now. Let me ask you something. Have you prayed about this?

ME: Yeah. Basically.

DAD: Okay, and?

ME: And what? And nothing. Clearly, nothing.

DAD: What do you think about that?

ME: I-I think I should go home.

DAD: *Sigh.* Okay. All right. How can I put this delicately? No one wants to see you here, son.

Ouch.

DAD: You go home now and it would not be with honor. This is your time right now. Your only time for this. You are in the place the Lord and I and your mother want you to be. Where we know you should be. And where you know you should be.

ME: I guess.

I more than guessed. It was just easier and more comforting to be angry and pretend coming home and ditching my missionary responsibilities was an option. Which it never was. I was just as stubborn about my commitment to the mission as I was to this idea that I couldn't learn Spanish and never would. That was the real problem: I was stuck. Dad knew better. He knew I couldn't remain in that limbo of resentful ambivalence for very long.

And he knew how to pull me out of it. After the call, he bought me a set of Spanish language tapes he'd seen advertised on TV and shipped them over. If nothing else was working, then they couldn't possibly hurt. They cost a hundred dollars.

When they arrived and I pulled them out for the first time, I felt a kind of self-loathing wash over me like a cleansing bath. I had saved a little money on my own to pay for some of the mission, but Mom and Dad refused to let me contribute it. They insisted I'd need that money more after the mission, so they would foot the entire $10,000-bill themselves. Now, I had added to that another $100. That fact hit me hard. As a person who came into contact with native speakers every day, I was in a better position than most to learn a new tongue and now I was going to resort to, what, the couch potato's language learning weapon of choice? I decided I'd be damned if I wasn't gonna make it work.

I was a missionary called by God to serve in Arizona in the Spanish language. Yep, I was in the hottest, driest, most boring state in the Union and saddled with an unfair speech handicap. So what? So *what?* If I truly believed my calling was from God, then mine was not to reason why.

So why had I been spending so much time trying to reason why not? God was on my side. There was no reason why not. There was only me impeding myself. I'd been stubbornly refusing His help with my indifference and insistence on clinging to a finite idea of what I was capable of. How tedious and ungrateful I'd become.

What shocked me was how little time it actually took to get comfortable with Spanish once I finally got over myself and just put in the humility and sincere—not token—prayer necessary. I dove into the language tapes like a man possessed, dedicating a full hour each day to the endless repetition of phrases and the refinement of pronunciation. It worked.

Two months after the Mother's Day phone call, I became a senior companion for the first time and was assigned to partner with a missionary with less field experience—and less facility with the language—than me. I was by no means fluent in my speech, but I could form relationships and teach and ask women to be not so much topless.

Stupidly, I'd have refused the tapes if Dad had given me a choice.

23

THE SECOND TIME

It was Saturday, November 23, 1996. My new companion, Elder Vaughn, and I came home early. I was now in Gilbert, a town with a tiny Spanish-speaking population whose doors we'd already knocked twice over. It was dark out, and preaching and teaching opportunities after 7:00 PM were, honestly, pretty non-existent without an appointment. We had simply run out of things to do.

Not that we needed much of an excuse to get off the road. Vaughn was a glutton for bicycle accidents. He'd had no less than seven face-to-pavement mishaps in the six weeks we'd been together, bringing his total to forty for the eleven months of his mission he'd served so far. This was an unprecedented number and, I was convinced, entirely and psychologically self-inflicted. The less time we spent outdoors, the better it was for the sidewalks and the safety of the people of Gilbert.

Just after 7:30 PM, we entered the upstairs apartment we shared with two other Elders, rolling our bikes to the spot of tile where it didn't matter as much how freshly oiled the gears were. We had the distinction of living in the largest apartment in the entire Arizona Tempe Mission, and it had the vaulted ceilings and balcony to prove it. Tired and worn out even at the end of this short day, we tossed our backpacks full of helpful pamphlets (Do *you* believe in God? So do we!) and Libros de Mormón under the kitchen bar, near the answering machine. I noticed the light was blinking. I pressed the button.

Beep.

It was President Hedrick, the closest thing I had to a boss while out on the mission. It was his job to take care of, assign, instruct, and put the fear of God into the Elders and Sisters in his charge. He excelled at his job.

As soon as I heard his voice—before I even knew the content of his message—all I could think was *how does he know? How does he know we came home early?* I thought of my mission president as a great man, a spiritual and wise man, but this was amazing. Any justification I had for leaving potential converts out in the wind seemed very, very weak indeed in that moment.

> **PRESIDENT HEDRICK:** Hello, Elders. I hope you've had a wonderful evening. Elder Heasley, would you call me right away, please? It's very important. Thank you.

Okay, I was convinced. He really did know. I reminded myself that the great thing about the gospel of Christ is that you can always say you're sorry and do better the next day. The thought did not offer much comfort in the moment. I told myself to suck it up and I gave President Hedrick a call.

> **ME:** President? This is Elder Heasley. I was, uh, just returning your call?
> **PRESIDENT HEDRICK:** Hello, Elder Heasley. How are you doing this evening?
> **ME:** Good. I'm doing—doing great, President. How about you?
> **PRESIDENT HEDRICK:** Fine, fine. Sister Hedrick and I are doing fine. How's Elder Vaughn?
> **ME:** Well, he's alive.
> **PRESIDENT HEDRICK:** Huh hah. That's good to hear. Elder Heasley, I got a call from your grandfather not too long ago. You have a family emergency he needs to speak with you about. You should call him right away.

Grandpa and Grandma Heasley lived about thirty minutes away in Fountain Hills—one more reason I desperately did not want to serve my mission in Arizona. I had been to so precious few other places besides California, and I'd been to this particular part of Arizona most of all. Because Grandpa and Grandma were members of the Church but hadn't actually seen the inside of one in quite some time, President Hedrick allowed me to visit with them on occasion. I, in turn, allowed them to buy me lots of groceries and take me out to dinner. This made them very happy and the other Elders I lived with very fat. Logically, with Grandpa calling, it would have made sense to assume there was something wrong with Grandma. Life had taught me to think of Dad first.

> **ME:** Okay. Is there anything you can tell me? What happened?
> **PRESIDENT HEDRICK:** I think it would be best if you asked your grandfather about that. Now, I need to speak to Elder Vaughn, briefly, and then I want you to call him.

I handed the phone off to Vaughn. I couldn't imagine what any of this had to do with him unless sacrificing someone to oncoming traffic was going to fix whatever was wrong. Vaughn was from the Deep South. I heard a lot of 'yessirs' and 'no sirs' before he finally hung up.

"What was that all about?" I asked. "What did he want with you?"

"He . . . " Uh oh. This wasn't going to be good. Vaughn was a stutterer, but he was taking his time with this one. "He said that you were about to get some really bad news and that I needed to be here for you in case you needed someone to lean on."

"Did he say what that news was?"

"No."

I started to get excited. My mind was brought back to that moment nearly eight years earlier at the hospital when I happily ate an entire bag of M&M's (by myself!) while waiting to see Dad before his surgery. This felt similar. Something important had happened, and I was headed straight for it. Whether it was tragic or not (okay, so it was going to be tragic), it would be important. Worth remembering. It was a selfish thought (after all, I knew *I* was okay), but I couldn't help it—I was looking forward to whatever came next, no matter how terrible.

The quiet-as-a-whisper part of me that was older scolded the little boy inside me jumping up and down. I shushed him quickly and moved over to the living room to sit down on the beat-up, secondhand couch. I called Grandpa, fingers trembling mostly in anticipation as they dialed the number.

The tremor in Grandpa's voice told the story before his words got the chance. He had been crying.

This was new. As reality grabbed hold and started gently shoving my head into the wake-up wall, I attempted to think of things Grandpa could say that wouldn't be so bad. That wouldn't be one of a dozen end-of-the-world scenarios that flitted through my brain. Nothing came to mind that still involved him crying.

Still, I imagined. I tried to live in that brief sliver of time before knowing, in that space between my asking what was wrong and Grandpa telling me. Where anything could be the matter. Whatever the news was, it was still possible he was overreacting. It was definitely possible.

Maybe Mom let my comic book subscriptions lapse, I thought.

GRANDPA: Brock . . .

Or Logan borrowed some of my CDs and scratched them.

GRANDPA: . . . your dad . . .

Dad. Dad let algae build up in the pool and the tile would need to be replaced. That's it.

GRANDPA: . . has been shot,

. . .

GRANDPA: again.

. . .

24

FAITHLESS PRAYERS

Again?

No. Perhaps I had misheard or Grandpa had been given bad information. Or it was an accident or it wasn't as bad as last time or it was—*Dad is dead*—worse?

My nose was running. Two seconds had passed and I was already crying. My head convulsed and any part of my face that could emit fluid, did. Like a stream—no, a waterfall. It was wet and gross and sticky and I couldn't stop it.

He's gone. Who said that? No one had said that.

I shook hard, knocking my knees against the small coffee table in front of me. I was glad to already be sitting. I might've fallen over otherwise.

As I dripped onto the phone's receiver, I couldn't help but be fascinated by my own grief, as though I wasn't the one experiencing it at all and was instead merely peering curiously at the human mess in the living room. Like Elder Vaughn was doing. Like the other Elders we lived with would soon. I tightened my grip on the phone and tried in vain to hunch down further into myself to block Vaughn's view and spare us both the humiliation.

Dad is dead. Stop it.

My physical response was instinctual, but I didn't agree with it. I'd faced Dad being shot once before, and this wasn't how I reacted to tragedy. I did not cry and I certainly did not weep. I reacted to bad news by looking within for some sign of assurance or comfort that comes from without. I reacted calmly, with a hopeful heart and patience.

But what assurances can you have when your father is dead?

I already knew, didn't I? In almost the same instant Grandpa told me Dad had been shot, I knew it was fatal. I knew it like I knew nearly eight years prior that Dad would be fine—with a certainty that trumped every other thought in my head. The message then was clear: *your father will be all right.* And I could *feel* that, then. And he was. But this time:

He's dead.

Where was my measure of comfort? Why did I not feel that peace—that assurance that God was in charge and would make things right? Instead, I was swallowed up in my hopeless knowledge and left to powerlessly protest my fear and despair and anguish. God was nowhere. He did not accompany me this time.

While Grandpa waited for me to say something, my mind screamed. I begged God that it might not be true. I pleaded with Him to visit me and release me from my cynical conviction and prove me wrong with His warmth. Instead, I was cold.

Elder Vaughn made no motions to leave the room. He alone was witness to my ugly, ugly display. I wiped what I could from underneath my chin, but it kept pouring out. I needed to concentrate. Five seconds had passed since I'd been told Dad had been shot and there was a question I needed to ask. To be sure. To hope.

> **ME:** Is h-he okay?
> **GRANDPA:** Oh, I don't know, son. I just talked to your mother a little while ago and that's all she knew. We know your dad was shot earlier this evening by two men, but we don't know any more than that.

But I did.

I pushed all thoughts of Dad dying out of my head and focused on what Grandpa had just said: "We don't know." I lied to myself and asserted that it was possible things were going to be okay. Not knowing is half full of that kind of comforting possibility. There was nothing good that could come from sitting and blubbering like an idiot. That wouldn't help anyone, least of all me.

ME: Should I call Mom? When are we going to know more?
GRANDPA: I don't know. Your mother said that she'd call you as soon as she can with an update. For now, we all have to just wait. There's nothing we can do right now except maybe pray.
ME: Okay.

I hung up the phone and took Grandpa's advice. I prayed my father would be restored to health. I prayed the doctors who were working on him would be guided through their life-saving measures. I prayed my mom and brothers would be all right and that Dad would not suffer too much pain. I prayed for those things because I didn't know what else to pray for, and I thought praying would make the crying stop. My whine turned into a sniffle and I welcomed the small relief.

" . . . your dad was shot . . . we don't know any more than that."

The more I got away from my conversation with Grandpa, the more likely it seemed that I had panicked in the moment and assumed the worst. My negative, entirely unhelpful thoughts were most likely those of an attention-whoring jerk who needed a slap in the face.

That was the alternative, desperate hope—that I was so vain and loved the attention heaped upon the family members of victims of tragedy so much I would seize any opportunity to have it. I certainly had Vaughn's attention. I prayed that I might be so ridiculous.

My prayers were entirely faithless.

Elder Vaughn milled about behind me. I gave him nothing but my back as I bent low over the coffee table, hands clutched together and pulled in close. I wouldn't move from the living room and I wouldn't stop praying. Not until I knew more. I supported my weight on my elbows, resting them on the Church magazines and books we never bothered to put away properly.

As I whispered my prayer, the tears would not stay out of my mouth. I spit, doing my best to keep that awful, salty taste out. I heard the front door to our apartment open as our roommates, Elders Suggs and Weldon, came in. Vaughn quietly pulled them aside to explain what was going on and why there was a watery mess on the living room floor. They did their best to move through the apartment without bothering me. They took off their ties and set their packs down just as they did every night. That seemed wrong, somehow, but I couldn't figure out why. I felt stupid and frustrated and angry at all of them. They didn't even know my dad.

Forty minutes after talking to Grandpa, the phone finally rang again. I got up off my knees as quickly as I could and sat down on the couch.

I pushed the call button on the phone.

ME: Hello, missionaries. This is Elder Heasley speaking.
MOM: Brock? This is your mother.

She didn't sound like I thought she would. It had been many months since we'd last spoken, but even in the best of times her voice was always a bit shaky. It wasn't shaky now. Whatever she was going to tell me, she'd either had some time to work through it already or it wasn't all that bad.

ME: Mom, what's going on? Is Dad okay?
MOM: Brock, your father died.

My eyes swelled. Through ever narrowing slits I could barely make out the three figures lingering awkwardly across the room, watching me. I ran my fingers through my hair and grabbed the back of my head. My hand slid to the front of my face, and my fingers stuttered and danced and pushed the reddened skin around my eyes. My left leg wobbled and I couldn't tell—was I even breathing, or was I just breathing really hard? I didn't care. Physical composure became a secondary concern, and my awareness of anyone else in the room with me fell away.

MOM: Brock? Are you there?
ME: I'm fine. Fine. What—Mom, what happened? Grandpa said he was shot again.
MOM: Yes, that's all we really know. It was at the Shop.
ME: The Shop. Then what was he—at the time what was he—
MOM: Brock, we just don't know anything for sure right now.

Mom knew a lot more than she was saying. She had been on the phone with Dad when he was killed.

25

WORSE THAN DEATH

The shop was closed. Dad had been at the Trap and Skeet Club for most of the day shooting with some buddies and was just dropping by to help his assistant manager shut things down. He'd already taken several guns out of the glass displays to go into their cases to be carried to the safe. Just like before.

He called Mom to let her know he'd be a little late getting home. Their talk was light and fun. There was a sweetness to Dad's voice that Mom hadn't heard in a while. They spoke of positive things. The debts were nearly paid off, and Dad's physical health was on the rise, for once. A few months earlier, he'd had a hip replaced. He talked about how nice it was to be able to run again (even just a little) and how much he looked forward to having the second hip put in next year.

Mom heard it through the phone. A loud, sudden sound in the background.

"What was that, Bill?"

"Jill," Dad said without hesitation. "Call the cops." And then he hung up.

Mom hung up her phone, picked it back up again, and called 911 immediately, but it was already too late.

The two men came in fast. They trained their guns on Dad first, but this time he managed to get his weapon up and pop off a few rounds before the shooters took him down. Two bullets in the chest, one in the stomach. Dad's assistant manager was in the back, but by the time he came out the shooters had already taken what they came for and left.

It was done. Dad's biggest fear did not come to pass and he went quickly.

I wouldn't find out these details until much later.

* * *

> **Me:** Mom, are you okay? What about Logan, McKay, and Tyler?
> **MOM:** They're fine. Fine. I mean, they will be. They're doing as well as can be expected under the circumstances. I don't know that it's completely hit them what's happened yet.

Mom's calm freaked me out. Perhaps she spoke more for herself than for my brothers.

> **ME:** What about you?
> **MOM:** There's lots of people here. My sisters are here. The Garvins next door and the Milligans. The bishop and his wife.
> **ME:** The Milligans? Why are the Milligans there?
> **MOM:** They're here for me and for your brothers.
> **ME:** You don't even know them that well.
> **MOM:** We see them all the time, you remember.
> **ME:** No, Mom, they never—when I was there they—
> **MOM:** Just a minute!
> **ME:** Who was that?
> **MOM:** No one. Just some people in the kitchen.
> **ME:** What's going to happen now? Are you guys going to be okay?
> **MOM:** We will, yes. Eventually, of course. What about you, Brock? Are you okay?
> **ME:** I'm, uh, I don't know.
> **MOM:** I'm so sorry, Brock.
> **ME:** I'll be fine. Is there anything I can do for you?
> **MOM:** I want you to come home.
> **ME:** Okay. Okay, but I-I don't know if I . . .
> **MOM:** The funeral will be next week. We need you to be here.

ME: I honestly don't know if that's a good idea, or if I'm even allowed to do that.
MOM: Of course you are, Brock. Your father just died! They're not going to say you can't go to his funeral. Surely it will be all right if you come home for a little while.
ME: I mean, that—that makes sense, but I don't know. I don't know.
MOM: Will you ask President Hedrick about it?
ME: Yeah, I guess I could.

This was Mom, arguing for exceptions as though what she wanted was not only paramount, but wholly righteous. There was so much power in her want that it could overcome any obstacle and bypass any roadblock. If fifty women had to wait outside in the cold for the JC Penney to open on the day of a Christmas sale, she'd be the one woman inside warming up and promising not to touch anything.

MOM: I want you here.
ME: I know.
MOM: Good. No, that's—Brock? Brock, I've got to go. Someone needs my help in the kitchen. I'm going to call you back a little later, all right? We'll try to get a flight figured out.
ME: O-Okay. We'll see, Mom. We'll see.
MOM: Brock, I'm so sorry. I hate that you are alone right now with this.
ME: It's okay. I'm worried about you guys.
MOM: I've already called the Hedricks and asked them to come be with you.
ME: Mom, no, I don't need them to do that. I don't want to bother them. I can—
MOM: They told me they were already on their way. Yes, I'll show you in just a second. I've got to go, okay?
ME: Bye. I love you, Mom.
MOM: I love you, too.

I pushed the button on the phone to disconnect it and looked down. For a long while, I just stared at myself. I was sick of wearing my clothes and wanted them off. Especially the tie and white shirt.

Without a word, I got up and walked straight past my roommates and into the back bedroom I shared with Elder Vaughn. At the foot of my bed was the door to our closet. I stood in front of it, squaring my feet until I had them perfectly positioned, toes at a right angle to the closet threshold. The precision of the move pleased me.

I looked down again at my shirt and tie ensemble. My name tag was attached to my left breast pocket, dragging it down with its weight. *Elder Heasley*, it read. *La Iglesia de Jesucristo de los Santos de los Ultimos Dias.* There wasn't one day in the past ten months that I had walked out the door without it, but in that moment it didn't belong.

Without thinking, I removed the badge, unbuttoned my collar and turned it up, and slid my tie over my head.

I was careful as always not to undo the knot that held the loop in place and gently placed my tie on the rack alongside the others with their loops still intact. There was a comfort just in looking at them. I hated retying ties. They didn't change unless I said they could.

I felt a surge of powerful energy rush into my head. My heart swelled and beat with a ferocity that threatened to knock me out. I turned my gaze toward the blandness of the carpet at my feet and let it swallow the surface of my attention with its inconsequence. Around me was a void. Everything happening was in my mind.

Thoughts fell in, piled one on top of another without order or priority. Dad. Where was he and what was he doing? He was finally seeing it, the life after next. What did it look like? What did he look like now? The form of his spirit couldn't possibly look like the broken, middle-aged man that he was. Did he have to wear a toga? Who was there to greet him? I was a little jealous. His long-held dream of discovering the secrets of what comes next was finally fulfilled.

I thought about the length of the new now. Nineteen years old seemed too young to have a dead dad. My life without him would likely be longer than the life I had with him. Would he fade away from memory the further into its distance he went? Of course he would. I suddenly wondered if Dad had any moles. It had already been too long since I'd last seen him, and I couldn't remember. Already, I was starting to forget.

I panicked. Was this supposed to happen? Was this when Dad was supposed to die? I reached out for some understanding of how it could be that while I was riding a bike out in the Arizona desert Dad was being shot to death in Fresno. How did this fit? It was incongruous.

Impossible. I rejected the newly revealed events of the past five minutes on principle.

Had I not been praying? Wasn't I serving a full-time mission? Blessings were supposed to come along with that. Was my sacrifice not acceptable? I had heard so many people in church speak time and again about how having their son or daughter in the mission field brought them blessings of prosperity and increased spiritual growth and health. And safety.

Liars. Did my service, then, mean nothing to God? It was supposed to mean that my father wasn't dead.

But I knew—and I had known for fifty minutes. I knew that Dad was dead. The ten months that had gone by since I had last seen him? They were never going to end.

I collapsed my face into my chest and wept again. I thought of my brothers. They were all younger than me. Tyler was almost eleven. Five, ten years from now, what would he remember? As the youngest, what did he even have to remember? Dad took me out on his motorcycle when I was four. He got rid of it when I was five. Tyler didn't even have the motorcycle.

What about Mom? I ached for her. It was hard to imagine her life without Dad. Whatever strength she had always came from him. She hadn't held a job since before I was born, and the thought of her running the Shop was laughable. I knew the calm, rational person I heard on the phone was a hostess, not a grieving widow.

I thought about the two men that had caused all this.

There were two men that did this. Two greedy men who pulled triggers and sprayed bullets and watched with probable glee as Dad fell to the ground a second time. His blood pooled while they collected his guns. Then they ran away, leaving behind a mess that would not be cleaned up for years, if ever.

This wasn't a natural disaster. There was a responsible party. Did they—for even a *second*—give any thought to my father other than what they wanted from him? He was my dad. A husband, a son, a brother, an employer, a friend. Did they stop to imagine the impact of the loss of such a man? Or had they ripped him away from this world without even bothering?

Every thought and feeling I had, I put toward the two men. The killers. I allowed myself the delicious luxury of anger toward two people whose names I did not know and whose appearances were a mystery to me.

In that moment, I made them monstrously foreign. They weren't human. They were faceless agents of a change I did not want. They deserved my scorn, my hatred, and whatever foul epithets I could conjure. It didn't matter that I didn't swear. The badge was already off, and this was an exception. This was what the family of the murdered was supposed to do. Cuss up a storm. Get mad.

With eyes shut tight, I balled my left hand into a fist and slammed it into the frame of my closet.

Wham!

"Those *jerks!*"

It was all I could think to say. I imagined that somewhere, somehow the killers heard my insult. Even through the tears, I smiled faintly in recognition of the absurdity of the notion. Not only was my communication, at best, psychic in nature, but my insult was embarrassingly pathetic. I'd used stronger language taking out the trash.

I raised my head up and looked into the closet and saw the clothes and the shoes and the spare bicycle parts. I stopped crying. I didn't have it in me anymore. I allowed myself one, sweet, ridiculous moment of anger and then it just left. Like a passing car disappearing from view. I could feel the vacancy in my mind and soul and the swiftness of the transition startled me enough I wondered if it was even real.

My heart still thudded hard with grief, and the magnitude of my loss still threatened to tip me back into a state of despair. But now no hatred or anger grew out of it. Those coarser feelings had been taken from me—and that was a gift. A gift born of experience—of the first shooting; of long talks with Dad on the route; of bad, morbid jokes; and of ten months as a missionary with total, eschatological concentration.

People always wondered why Dad wasn't angrier toward the first shooters and how he could be so matter-of-fact about it all, but in that moment I think I finally understood. There were so many other, more important things to worry about. It didn't seem natural to hold onto bitterness and spend my energies on negative feelings that would only perpetuate the more I indulged them. The killers had enough power already. They had taken my father. They didn't get to have my mind and heart as well.

My body went limp, and I had to catch myself from falling. Something new was happening—something I'd been waiting for since the moment Grandpa first told me Dad had been shot. The warmth was back.

It spread from inside my chest outwards and enveloped me completely. I felt—of all things—a searing gratitude that burned away the last vestiges of destructive thoughts and feelings within me.

I thought about the killers again. They deserved my pity. They weren't faceless agents of change, they were people. Children of God.

One day, they would remember that. We were brothers. Before this world began, we stood up for what was right and followed Christ—together. At one time, we shared the same hopes and dreams. But, somewhere along the way, they took a different path that led them to the Shop that night. Their dream of taking Dad's guns away was a small one compared to the other, bigger dream tucked away inside of them. One day they would discover that their sin had eaten away at their hope and destroyed their dream.

That would be a very bad day indeed. What could be worse than to fall and know precisely how far—to look up from the bottom of a pit and see no one standing at the edge? To know that you'd leapt in and not been pushed? There was not a more miserable state I could imagine. Least of all death. The more I thought about it, the more it seemed like Dad had gotten the better end of the deal.

And yet that the killers had made a pit for themselves at all—even with a crime so terrible as murder—was a supposition on my part. God judged, not me. And God loved the killers and knew them, just as much as He knew and loved me. For that very fact alone, His judgment would have to be so utterly fair and just that my fist against the frame of the closet was as pointless and presumptive an act as I had ever committed. Trust in God's judgment was a special kind of relief, a mercy not only for the killers, but for me as well.

I felt free. I stood still and silent and allowed the great burden of judgment to lift off of me. My every muscle relaxed, save one. My heart pounded with love and sadness for the two most unlikely and unknown people in my world. I didn't think it possible, but I ached for my father's killers.

Even so, I couldn't deny what they had done. I stared downward again and shuddered, imagining Dad lying dead on the cold floor of the Shop. I knew exactly what that scene looked like and the image haunted me. But, I forgave. It was the only thing left to do. Whatever anger I had felt or might later feel, I made the decision to set aside all ill thoughts toward the men who killed my father and forgive them.

A feeling of peace unlike any I had ever known before washed over me. It cleansed me. I wept more, harder—now with thankfulness and gladness that such feelings were even possible and that I was lucky enough to have them.

It was a small, quiet moment. Anyone looking at me would only have seen a half-dressed missionary staring intently at the carpet at his feet, but so much more than that was happening. It was the most important moment of my life up to that point, and I knew it.

My mourning refocused into a different direction. I felt empathy not only for my father's killers, but most especially for all those who had not made a choice and yet had still been negatively impacted by the events of that night. Death had given one life conclusion, but it was hardly the end of all things.

I wiped my tears. There was work to be done.

26

TO THE LORD

The phone rang and I walked into the living room to answer it. No one else dared touch it that night. My roommates sat on the couch and in chairs, huddled together, doing their best to avoid looking at me directly. On the phone was Elder Roberts, our district leader and the keeper of all things statistical. He was only about a year older than the rest of us, but he was balding so much he was the only Elder in the Tempe Mission allowed to keep his head shaved bare. He wore it like a mantle.

I had lost track of time and forgotten all about our nightly report. Roberts called to ask about how many lessons we'd taught that day and how many hours we'd spent knocking doors. Usual stuff, but he wasn't going to get it from me that night. I couldn't remember anything that had happened earlier in the day.

> **ELDER ROBERTS:** What's goin' on, Heasley?
> **ME:** Well, my dad died.
> **ELDER ROBERTS:** Ha. Right. Seriously, how did you guys do today?
> **ME:** I am serious. He died today.
> **ELDER ROBERTS:** Today?
> **ME:** Yeah, couple hours ago. I just found out.
> **ELDER ROBERTS:** Put Suggs on the phone.

I just didn't have it in me to mince words. Roberts was, I knew, justified in his skepticism. His disbelief was one of the many consequences

I sometimes had to suffer for having a slightly morbid sense of humor. Claiming my dad had died when he had not was exactly the sort of stunt I would have pulled just to see if I could get away with it. I probably could have opened with something a little softer than "Well, my dad died," but it was the combination of cavalier and grave that hit my humor sweet spot. Even given the events of the night.

After Elder Suggs confirmed my father was indeed dead, Roberts asked to speak to me again and offered his condolences. He was the first.

> **ELDER ROBERTS:** My mom died two years ago. You know that?
> **ME:** No. Really? I'm sorry.
> **ELDER ROBERTS:** Don't apologize. Let me tell you something: I know how you feel right now. It's gonna suck for a while. It's gonna suck and you're gonna wanna cry and you should. You let it out and you let it do its thing.
> **ME:** Yeah, I was crying before. I think I'm done now.
> **ELDER ROBERTS:** Nah, you're not. I know where you're at. It's just starting.
> **ME:** What is?
> **ELDER ROBERTS:** Everything. Trust me. I know how you feel.

The more Roberts spoke, the angrier I got. *I know how you feel.* That didn't seem right to me. He was assuming identification with what I was going through because we shared a similar experience in which the details likely differed on more points than just gender. Grief is a unique experience with only a dead body in common. He couldn't possibly know what I was going through, so why minimize my experience by saying, essentially, "been there, done that?" It felt like such an odd, self-serving way to offer comfort, but I was so shocked by my almost violent internal reaction to his words I didn't say anything to call him out. Instead, I thanked him and hung up the phone. I didn't want to seem impolite.

President and Sister Hedrick arrived shortly thereafter. Unsurprisingly, they dressed in their Sunday best—leaving me feeling slightly silly in my t-Shirt and slacks ensemble. President Hedrick reminded me of Dad in a lot of ways. He was close to Dad's age, stocky, imposing, and warm (once you got to know him). Sister Hedrick radiated class and a youthful energy her years did not indicate, a combination I found odd yet approachable. For us Elders and sisters in the Arizona Tempe Mission, they were the closest things we had to parents while out in the field. Once they were in our apartment, I was instantly glad Mom had called them.

After exchanging brief pleasantries with the other Elders (who stood at attention in outfits even more dressed down than my own), President and Sister Hedrick moved with me into our living room to sit down.

"Elder Heasley," President Hedrick began. "How're you holding up?"

"I'm fine, President. I really am."

"Of course you are." President Hedrick had a way of addressing his missionaries that made us feel like we were capable of handling anything, no matter how unknown or how far below our shallow depth of experience. It was in his tone. When I was around him, I believed in the absolute strength of the best parts of myself. The other parts—the temptations and the laziness and the reluctance—seemed so easily circumvented, even insignificant. As tedious and depressing as missionary work often was, his was a welcome voice to have in my head reminding me that, yes, knocking on those thousands of doors only to have them slammed in our faces was not for nothing.

"How's your mother?" he asked.

"I think she's good. She's in shock, but she has a lot of support back home."

"Lots of people at the house?"

"Yeah."

"Isn't the Church wonderful?"

"Elder Heasley," Sister Hedrick interjected. "If there's anything President Hedrick and I can do for you or your family, that is what we are here for."

Well, actually . . . I was going to say, but President Hedrick beat me to it. "When's the funeral?" he asked.

"Later next week. Maybe Wednesday? Thursday is Thanksgiving"—*holy crud Thursday is Thanksgiving*—"but Friday seems too late. I don't really know."

"I know your mom wants you home."

"She does."

"Elder Heasley, you have a decision to make. You're not the first Elder or Sister to lose a family member while out in the field. There are many in this mission right now that have had to deal with that. Brothers that have passed away. Sisters, grandparents . . . even parents. Usually, they want to go home to be with their families. In most cases, we discourage this and they don't go."

"I understand." And I did. Life was always going to go on without me back home. That was the reality I had accepted, but it was easy to forget. Our focus was total while in the field. It had to be. The entire point of the two years was to serve others. Casting off the usual concerns—even family—was the most efficient way to do that. It wasn't a cruelty, it was a help. It was why we served somewhere other than where we lived, and the farther away the better. It was all about the mission for two years and we did not, under any circumstances, go home. Even if we couldn't speak Spanish. That was the commitment. "But . . . " *But.* "People do go home."

"Yes," President Hedrick said. "They do. Now and again we have Elders and Sisters returning home for medical, sometimes personal, reasons. But make no mistake—this is very difficult. When they come back—*if* they come back—they are usually not the same missionaries they once were. They slide easily into old routines back home, and a lot of the discipline they've worked so hard to achieve here falls away there."

"That's not what I want."

"That doesn't surprise me. You know, Elder Heasley, as well as I do that your commitment to be here isn't to me or your companion or even to the people of Arizona. It's to the Lord."

"Yes."

"However, yours is an extreme circumstance. Your father's death was unexpected, violent, and sudden—and you are the oldest of his sons. I'm sure your mother and your brothers could use your strength right now."

"Yes, I know they could."

"I'm not going to tell you not to go home. This is entirely your decision, and we will support whatever you decide. But—and I have to tell you this—I have grave reservations about you going home. What I have said tonight is true. It will be very hard for you to come back here, and it may take many months for you to get back to normal, if you ever do."

"I understand that, President. I've thought hard about this, and I share your concerns and I already know what I want to do. I want—"

"No." He cut me off so sharply I thought I had done something wrong. I suppose, in his mind, I did. "I want you to sleep on this. Don't make any decisions right now."

"But I already know what I want to do. I'm not going to change my mind in the morning."

"We'll see. Get some sleep tonight. If you need anything—anything at all—feel free to give Sister Hedrick and I a call. Otherwise, call me first thing in the morning with your decision. We'll work it all out then."

We stood up, he gave me a hug, and then he gathered all my roommates to lay their hands on me and give me a blessing of comfort. It was now well past our mission-mandated bedtime of 10:30. The Hedricks left quickly afterward. I was left to sleep (as much as I could) and decide if I'd be going home.

But I already knew what I was going to do.

27

BEING A HUMAN BEING

When I woke up the next morning, my resolve was as firm as it had been the night before. For months and months now I had been out there every day, strapping on my tie and helmet, biking my way through the hot oven air Arizonians called the outdoors, dodging their occasional thrown beer bottles and ducking the rocks they aimed at my head—and I was at my very best despite all of that. Because I had something with me that silenced all attacks. I brought redemption. I brought eternity. I brought purpose and peace to gang bangers, alcoholics, housewives, deadbeats, delinquents, migrant workers, businessmen, students, and children alike. I wheeled through the city as one who was just one step removed from this reality, seeing everything more clearly from a higher vantage point. I saw the temporary and the unimportant littering the world like small, shiny stones to be stumbled upon and tripped over. My task was to guide my brothers and sisters away from those enticing pebbles and into true, real happiness. My charge was to participate in the enlightening of the world. I couldn't imagine a greater work, and there was no greater feeling than performing it. I was on the Lord's errand. I was a missionary.

I had it easy.

Total immersion in the mission life made it hard to view Dad's death as anything besides a temporary inconvenience to communication. There were those who mourned more deeply and did not have the benefit of daily humiliation for the sake of Christ to lift them up. That meant my principal concern had to be how Dad's death affected them. I got out of bed and went into the kitchen to make the call.

> **PRESIDENT HEDRICK:** Elder Heasley, how are we doing this morning?
> **ME:** Good, President, good. Better than good. President, I think I should go home.

It would be a sabbatical, of sorts, but only in appearance. I had no desire to rest or set aside my charge. I had a job to do, and I wanted to work.

> **PRESIDENT HEDRICK:** Good. What's the plan?
> **ME:** I already talked to my mom, and she was up all night looking at flights. The earliest she found is out of Phoenix at 2 PM today.
> **PRESIDENT HEDRICK:** When would that put you back in Fresno?
> **ME:** This afternoon. Yeah. Yeah, wow, that's soon. I just realized how soon that is. My only problem is getting to the airport.
> **PRESIDENT HEDRICK:** Sister Hedrick and I can take care of that if you can find your way to us in Tempe. Is there a local member you can call on for that?
> **ME:** I think so. It's Sunday. Everyone should be home.
> **PRESIDENT HEDRICK:** Right, that's true. How's your mother doing this morning?
> **ME:** She's okay, I think. She still hasn't slept. It's hard to tell from here.
> **PRESIDENT HEDRICK:** And now you're going there.
> **ME:** Yes, that's right.
> **PRESIDENT HEDRICK:** Do you have a return ticket or are you going to wait and see?
> **ME:** I'll be back on Friday.
> **PRESIDENT HEDRICK:** You don't have to decide that right now.
> **ME:** I already did. It's done.
> **PRESIDENT HEDRICK:** Of course it is.

The tricky thing was finding someone to take to me to the airport who wouldn't make a big deal out of my awful, terrible, tragic, worst ever news. I knew right away it was going to be seen as a hard thing that Dad had died while I was on the mission. Granted, sympathies were going to be acute no matter what just because of the violence of it all, but most would see the fact that I was on my mission as a real next-level tragedy.

I was uncomfortable with the thought of undue attention, so I called Sister Reynolds, the local bishop's wife, who I knew kept things on an even keel. Some mistook her icy blue eyes and constant, still demeanor for coldness, but I knew she was warmer than that. She had taken a liking to me and was more than happy to help out. We scheduled my departure for noon without too much fuss.

With my plans set, I had a new problem. I had five hours to kill and nothing to kill it with. Dad had died less than twenty-four hours ago. No one would have blamed me if I had chosen to simply sit down and wail. That was far and away the most unappealing option available, so what else was there to do? Sleep? Play cards? Phase 10 and Uno were fun and good for wasting time, but I didn't want to have to answer for that later.

That's terrible.
I know. While I was on my mission.
I can't imagine.
I know.
Surely they let you return home the next day.
I don't know if "let" is the right way to put it, but yeah, I flew home the next afternoon.
Wow. I bet you couldn't even sleep that night. What did you do in the morning?
I played cards.
What.
Not face cards. Don't worry. It wasn't poker or anything.
But you played . . . cards?
Yeah. Phase 10. Uno. You know, the usual.
But your father had just died.
I didn't kill him.
You're a horrible human being.
I might be.

Was it any less horrible to jump on our bikes and go to our regular Sunday meetings? I hoped not because it was the only thing that made sense to me. There was no one in Arizona to mourn with nor—so long as what had happened was kept quiet—anyone who expected me to be in mourning. My grandparents were already on a flight out. I wanted to keep busy, and missionaries keep busy by doing missionary work. It was sensible. Inarguably righteous. *What better time to just get out and work than this?* Yeah. Yeah, I was really feeling it.

Besides, work would help me ignore that other nagging feeling I had—that feeling of shame. Shame because of that damnable excitement I never seemed to be able to set aside.

I *was* going home after all—after ten months of being away. The circumstances of my return weren't exactly ideal, but it was still a return. That, in and of itself, was thrilling. I was going home and I would wear my missionary badge and everyone would look and they would see me and think me awesome.

Another in a long line of vain, awful thoughts. I needed to leave the apartment if for nothing else than to get away from it.

Horrible. Just horrible.
I know.

"Elder Vaughn," I said. "Get dressed. We're leaving."

"Wh-what? Uh . . . are you sure you don't want to just stay here?" Every step outside was a risk of fatal proportions for Elder Vaughn. Staying indoors was his only insurance. It's entirely possible his hesitation was also out of concern for my well-being, but I was now a man on a mission. Well, *more* of a mission.

"No. I'm going crazy just sitting here. We have a meeting this morning at the church, don't we?"

"Yeah . . . " Vaughn sighed. Dressed only in his sweat shorts and undershirt, he had made it clear into which direction he thought our morning was going and had gotten out of bed only to eat breakfast.

"Then let's go."

Once a month we had an early-morning meeting to coordinate our missionary efforts with the local church members. On that Sunday, it was a welcome bit of regular business that didn't know my father had died. More importantly, it wasn't knocking on doors.

We got dressed, said a prayer together, and exited the apartment, clipping the cuffs of our slacks to our ankles to keep them away from the greasy gears on our bicycles. Once downstairs, I sat on my bike for a brief moment in the parking lot and took in the fact that neither nature nor the cracked, heat-abused handiwork of man acknowledged what had happened last night. The world still spun. I put on my helmet and took off after Elder Vaughn as he veered too far to the right through the gate and left the relative safety of our apartment complex.

The sky was a slightly overcast, early morning red. We took the two-mile journey to the chapel slowly, a gentle breeze at our backs. Vaughn wore his long trench coat and rode hands free, shivering and hugging himself tightly just as he always did when the thermostat dipped below 85 degrees. He proclaimed his hometown in Corpus Christi, Texas, was much, much hotter than Arizona and that his body just couldn't get used to the cooler temperatures.

I gave him the space he needed (to inevitably crash) and hung back several dozen feet as we made our way through the quiet streets. Gilbert skewed wealthy, but we passed by a couple of the poorer Latino neighborhoods along the way. Crowing roosters sounded our familiar arrival as we waved to the kids running barefoot down the alleyways and across dusty yards to catch up to us. The ones we knew called out "*¡Misioneros!*" and chased us with great big smiles on their faces before giving up and waving goodbye as we rode out of sight. Because construction shut down on Sundays, their fathers and uncles and grandfathers sat on their porches, talking and laughing together. Wives and aunts and grandmothers hung up clothes, tended to their babies, and gabbed.

Most of the Hispanics we taught our lessons to hailed from northern Mexico, where opportunities and decent jobs were few. They'd come to Arizona looking for a better life for their families. Even in their current poverty, they had found exactly that. Each was suffering in their own way—whether it was from being far from the families they left behind or from the constant fear of deportation—but their community was tight knit, hopeful, and, for the most part, they buoyed each other up. They were strong. I felt lucky to be part of their world, if only for a little while.

That was when I realized the first of my two errors: First, I had called a Mormon housewife and told her everything about last night. I could depend on Sister Reynolds to not freak out, but I hadn't said anything about keeping quiet. It was likely that within the hour every member of the Church in the state of Arizona (and, possibly, some of the lower and hotter parts of California) would know all about "that Elder whose father got killed." There was no safety in going to the coordination meeting. I would be met only with sad looks and awe at my situation.

Sure enough, by the time we reached the chapel, the attendees were well aware of my specialness. They looked at me like they would a particularly lovable animal at the zoo, with equal parts fascination and pity. Except for one woman. She alone endured the entire meeting completely unaware of the human tragedy and triumph on display simultaneously before her. How she escaped the net remains a mystery to this day, but her tears upon finding out were all the more effusive for it. "Oh you poor dear! You poor, poor thing. Wh-what are you doing here? This meeting? You came for this meeting? Your poor mother. Oh my . . . oh my goodness. Are you all right? How is your *mother?*"

And that was when she hugged me. Illegally. In addition to every other normal form of socialization a nineteen-year-old male might otherwise enjoy, missionaries are not allowed to give or receive hugs from the opposite sex. All members of the Church know this, and still this woman did what she did.

She was not the last. I did a lot of illegal hugging over the next few weeks.

My second error was thinking that going to the meeting would remain a purely noble effort. The guilt of attention gained weighed on me as the renewal of the long-forgotten feeling of a woman pressed up against me registered in the most narcissistic, puerile recesses of my brain. My conscience, ever my most unwanted and most attended to companion, wagged its accusatory little mind finger at me and asked, *Are you really giving your father's death the weight it deserves if you're going to feel such things and think such thoughts?*

Yes.

Are you sure?

Of course not.

I could have stayed in the apartment with Elder Vaughn and played cards. No one would have ever really known. Instead, what did I do? I went out. Toward other people. I was now that Elder with the dead dad who was so *strong*, so *committed* to the work, that he attended his Sunday morning meeting anyway! It was as if I was screaming at people to mythologize me. To stand there and receive that illegal hug was to feed my vanity and to regard myself as large. I wondered in shamed silence if a conscious act that makes for a good story could ever be completely noble.

After letting me go, the sobbing woman dabbed her eyes and wiped her tears on behalf of my tragedy. I responded in kind by setting aside my obscene elation and casting my eyes downward. I spoke quietly and I moved slowly. Just like the day at school after Dad's first shooting, this was the part I had to play. That was what I had gotten myself into.

This time, I was glad for it. I decided it was not a lie to receive those who would grieve with me and to respond with equal tenderness and solemnity. It actually felt good to do that. Even if I felt slightly more energized than sober, Dad *was* gone. He was not coming back in this life. Whatever understanding I had of the necessity and nature of death, I could mourn the separation. And whatever other hidden and licentious desires I felt, I could choose to be better than them.

28

IN THE ABSENCE OF KNEELING DRAGONS

From the moment an Elder enters the field, there is very little he looks forward to more than the day he returns home. Only hearing the words "Yes, I would like to be baptized" ranks higher. And when the long-awaited day finally does arrive, there are certain expectations that Elder has for the rock star moment when he steps off the plane.

Banners reading "WELCOME HOME" and "WELCOME BACK, ELDER ___" are certainly staples. So are hand clapping, back slapping, and the grateful tears of mothers and aunts. Preferably, small children will surround him with small gifts and trinkets, gazing upward with wonder and awe as they imagine the day when they too might put on the shiny, black tag with their own name on it. There should also be an attractive young woman there ready to size up the progress the Elder has made toward matching her maturity level. She will not find him lacking, and they will obviously marry three weeks later. Party poppers and air horns are a must. As are trumpets. Something needs to sound his arrival, certainly. Video cameras will record his triumphant airport entry from every angle for the sake of posterity, and a celebratory raffle for a fancy red sports car will be held (which he will win, obviously). And dragons. Kneeling dragons on either side will attend his coming.

That's the best case scenario, and it usually happens after twenty-four months of blood, sweat, and bittersweet tears. When your father dies ten months into the mission, you get your Uncle Richard, his daughter Natalie, and your brother Logan. And nary a banner in sight.

Logan and I hugged first. I asked him how he was doing, and he responded with a quiet "okay." Wiry, athletic, and now just a hair taller than me, he stayed mostly silent as we walked to the baggage claim. It was just as well. My cousin Natalie was a chatterbox and went on and on about how many people—and how much food—was at the house.

As we drove the five miles from the airport in Fresno to our home in Clovis, my gaze was fixed out the window. I expected to be warmed by the familiar sights of home and was instead thrown by how quickly the landscape had changed in my absence. The long, straight streets and criss-crossing telephone wires hanging overhead were as I remembered them, but they were now flanked by new stoplights and stores that had gone out of business and been replaced. Vinyl signs bragged of new restaurants and office complexes coming soon. Even some of the long forgotten empty lots and overgrown fields dotting Fresno were cleared of brush.

I couldn't help but appreciate the desert of Arizona more by comparison. Cacti, at the very least, made things interesting. And red dirt was far prettier than brown dirt. Fresno was so spare and devoid of color—and so unlike the green pastures and orchards in the surrounding rural farmlands of the Central Valley. Only sometimes did those farmlands leak into the city to give it character and warmth, sheep and cows and horses grazing just one block over from the Clovis mall or near a school. My hometown came up short in a way it never had before. Ten months was a lot longer than it seemed.

We arrived at the house, and I got out of the car, shaking with anticipation as I made my way up the walkway to the porch and into my father's house. Crossing the threshold was like stepping out of a dream and back into reality. All of the warnings from President Hedrick suddenly made a whole lot of sense. The mission faded back into my mind, made hazy by the sudden return of the forgotten familiar. The squeak of my shoes on the entryway tiles. The banged-up oak hutch against the wall where I always put my keys. The light switch around which my mother would soon paste up an altar of Christmas cards.

I caught myself. *This is temporary.* My name tag stared up at me, reminding me and bringing me back from the brink of total immersion. "Elder Heasley," it said. Five days. That was all I had given myself, and it had already been decided. *In five days, this will be the dream again.*

I was not allowed to dwell on such thoughts. As soon as Mom spotted me, my time—and body—were no longer my own.

"Oh Brock, oh Brock, oh Brock. You're home." Her voice cracked as she rushed toward me, held on tight, and wept. She repeated my name over and over again, like a mantra, as though my being there was something she had to convince herself of.

The house had an unfamiliar, tense feeling about it, as if the air had been sucked out hours ago and everyone had forgotten to breathe since. Just past my mother's mess of dark hair I could see the approximately 523 people (give or take) who had descended on our living room like miners during a gold strike, each of them greedily occupying what precious real estate they could find. Some stood, others, if they were lucky, sat on chairs both dining and spare—whatever could be found in the garage and in the rooms throughout the house. There were people in the kitchen, of course, and those sitting on the floor. In the pole position on the couch next to the empty space from where Mom had just gotten up were the Milligans. I wanted to punch them.

Why were the Milligans even there? I could see my aunts and my mom's parents and dad's parents (Grandma Heasley didn't look so good) and close neighbors around the perimeter of the room. And it was the Milligans who rated the spot on the couch. They were acquaintances, at best, and yet Mom had suggested they were—or had become—much more than that. Another change. Was I honestly supposed to go along with this and welcome these almost complete strangers into the beginning hours of our new, very much unwanted life? Intruders, all of them.

Mom held me tight. Everyone else alternately stared and shifted their eyes away from us. Did no one understand that the last thing she needed right now was to make sure everyone was comfortable and knew where the bowls were in the kitchen? The presence of so many was such a ridiculous burden to place on a new widow. Help was one thing, the population equivalent of Rhode Island quite another. This wasn't a party. This wasn't the time for the gossips and the reflected glory hounds to bask in the immediacy of our circumstance. This was a time for regrouping and comfort. The Milligans and everyone like them could just get out.

Mom held onto me for far longer than a normal embrace. Her calm and mantra-free demeanor on the phone hadn't prepared me for this close, in-my-face reality. How could this be her state? She was so utterly relieved by my presence, and it reminded me of the solace I sought while in my own shattered state the night before. Now, those same desperate feelings threatened to rise up once again. I forced myself to choke them down.

I wanted to offer up some positive words of encouragement, but I couldn't think of any and Mom didn't ask. She needed to weep. And she needed to weep on my shoulder. That was all.

"W-will you go talk to your brothers?" she asked.

"Are you sure you don't want me to stay out here with you?" I said.

"No, no. Go talk to them first. They need to see you."

"How are they?"

"Well . . . " Mom hesitated. "They're not doing great."

She described to me the scene from yesterday: It wasn't too long after hanging up with the 911 dispatch that she got a call to go to the hospital right away. All they would tell her was that Dad had been injured, but not by what and not how. Mom's sister Robin and her husband, Dave, escorted her and my brothers to the emergency room. As soon as they arrived they were ushered into a private room. It was small, softly lit, and, to Mom, ominously familiar. While they waited for a doctor to come talk to them, she steeled herself. My brothers had no past associations to draw upon and talked and laughed as though nothing in the world was wrong. When the doctor finally came in, he told them flatly they'd "lost Bill." The light mood in the room crumbled. Mom collapsed as Aunt Robin held her tight. Logan, rendered numb by the news, sat quietly and stared straight ahead.

"But McKay and Tyler, they just couldn't process it," Mom told me. "They cried, of course, and then started screaming. Over and over again, *I want my dad! Where's my daddy? Where's my daddy!? I want my dad!* I couldn't . . . Dave told me later it was the most awful thing he'd ever seen."

"Mom, I'm so sorry,"

"Please," she begged me. "Go talk to them."

"All right. You're gonna be okay out here?"

"Yes. Go."

I backed away from her and the full-court press in the living room, and went down the hall to McKay and Tyler's room. I wasn't entirely sure what I was going to say, but whatever it was, I very much wanted to say it. I entered to see them sitting silently on their beds in front of the giant world map wallpaper. They looked as though they'd been talking before I came in, but I didn't hear any of it. McKay was much taller than

I remembered, and both of them much older than I was expecting. These guys weren't my little kid brothers. They already looked like young men.

"Hey, guys," I said quietly.

"Hey," they said back, almost in unison.

They were no longer wailing, but they weren't exactly okay. I wondered how I might have comprehended it eight years earlier if Dad had died then—back when I was the same age as Tyler. They did not have the same luxury I had—the luxury of possibility. All they had was a long-suspected eventuality that had finally come to pass. What was okay about that?

Both of them accepted Dad's death and that he wasn't coming home, but the magnitude of those facts and how massively their lives would change as a result was beyond them. It was as though a great weight hovered above and all they could perceive was the shadow. I knew that weight wasn't going to stay up there forever. Eventually, it would have to come down.

As we talked, it was tough to know if anything I said had any impact. McKay had earned the nickname "space cadet" because of the faraway look in his eyes and his tendency to forget the point of the sentence you were speaking by the time you reached the end of it. Tyler, though younger, was more thoughtful—too thoughtful, at times—and given to stresses and neuroses that ranked far beyond his actual age. Eventually, they loosened up and started talking.

"Mr. David came by this morning," Tyler said.

"Mr. David? Isn't he McKay's teacher?" Mr. David was also Logan's sixth-grade teacher. He was an enthusiastic, caring man who spent more time than he needed to after school, helping kids who were falling behind. He thought well of our family and was held in high esteem by all of us.

"Yeah," McKay confirmed. "He talked to us about . . . about stuff and life and stuff."

"What did he say?"

"He said our lives are gonna suck now," Tyler said.

McKay explained that Mr. David told them that when he was a young boy his own dad had died. He told them all about how horrible and hard his life was afterward. He talked about how many milestones and events were coming up that our dad would miss out on and how that's just the way it is. He assured them he'd be there for them for whatever they needed. All they had to do was call.

Mom was quick with the damage control after Mr. David left and explained he had only shared his perspective and that their lives wouldn't be like that, but it was obvious McKay and Tyler were still a little shaken up by what he'd said.

"Listen, guys," I said. "Do you think Dad was scared of dying?"

They both shook their heads no.

"No, he absolutely wasn't. You know what was scary to Dad?

They both shook their heads no.

"It was only ever one thing—whether or not we were okay. Dad knew this moment in all our lives was coming, and he made plans for it and for us and we're gonna figure out what those plans were."

And we did. In the garage was an iron safe with a collection of gold coins and the paperwork for the life insurance policies Dad had taken out on himself. They would supplement the money Mom would get from Social Security, ensuring I could stay on my mission and that my brothers could also go on theirs when the time came. The mortgage was taken care of as well. When Dad took out a loan for the house in Clovis, it was a Cal Vet loan through Veteran's Administration. A premium attached to the loan Dad opted to pay for stipulated that, in the event of his death, the house would be considered paid for in full. And now it was.

"But," I said. "None of that matters, right?"

"W-what do you mean?" Tyler said.

"I mean, you don't care about that stuff. You just want Dad back, right?"

"Yeah," McKay said.

"I do, too. But, I don't think my life sucks all of the sudden, and I don't think yours does either. Dad dying doesn't create suckiness."

"But he's gone!" Tyler looked like he was going to start crying again. Did I make things worse?

"Yeah, you're right. He is gone. He's gonna miss out on stuff, and I don't think you're ever going to stop missing him. But c'mon, you know better than to think he's actually gone. He still exists. You just can't see him right now. One day, though, you will. And in the meantime? It's not going to be all bad, I promise you. Because you guys know better and you're about to learn something most people never figure out."

"What's that?" McKay asked.

"That 'okay' isn't something defined by how things actually are or what's happening. 'Okay' is something that we—that *you*—control. Yeah, we all want Dad back and this is not really the best of circumstances for us to be seeing each other again, but it's not the circumstance that matters. What matters is what we do with it, not what it does to us. Right?"

They nodded yes. I congratulated myself silently for not sounding like a complete moron.

We said a prayer together, and they clung to me tightly before I headed out to my own room. I had never thought much before about my responsibilities as a big brother. I'd always spent much more time selfishly lamenting the fact I didn't have one of my own to teach me stuff like how to ask out a girl or how to make bombs out of household items. Now, I felt a strong, familial pull toward McKay and Tyler that gave me pause. I wanted to protect them and teach them and stay in California for them, which surprised me. Had I given my fidelity to the cause of missionary work a little too much credit?

If you think about it, technically—given the situation and all—staying in California was not a wrong choice.

29

THE SHOULDERS

I entered my bedroom, breathed deeply, and took in the familiar smell of pencil shavings and old, yellowing paper. For a moment I just stood there, mind reeling. It was still hard to believe I was actually home. Thanks to mission rules about staying in the same place as your companion at all times, this was my first minute alone outside of restroom visits in ten months. I was both relieved and unsettled by the simple sensation of being in a space otherwise unoccupied.

The room had hardly changed in my absence. Drawings of comic book heroes and villains still lined the walls. The bed, smaller and lower to the ground than I remembered it, was made—clear evidence the door had been opened at least once since I'd left. The twelve-inch black and white TV Mom and Dad gave me for my sixteenth birthday stood waiting on the corner of my small entertainment center (it would have to wait a little longer). And there was my drawing desk and my chair with the wheels. Right where I'd left them.

I set my small suitcase on the bed and Mom poked her head in.

"Are you settling in okay?"

"Yeah, just let me change real fast and I'll—"

"I'm just so glad you're back." Mom looked at me with eyes still red from our encounter in the entryway.

"Yeah. Me too."

"How did it go with McKay and Tyler? How do they seem to you?"

I told her I wasn't sure how our talk had gone but that they at least seemed in better spirits now. She breathed a sigh of relief, and I asked her about Logan. "The moment we got back from the airport, he just disappeared."

"Logan . . . Logan I know nothing about," she said. "He spends all his time in his room with his friends. Did you talk at all in the car?"

"No. Not really. Have you been able to do anything besides hold court?"

"It hasn't been like that. Everyone has been very nice."

"There's so many people out there."

Mom paused for a second. "Sister Caniff told me she knows just how I feel."

"I hate it when people say that."

"She said her mother had an entire litter of kittens just last week that all died. She was devastated."

"That was not said," I said, horrified. "That did not happen." Mom's nod and slightly amused smile told me that, sadly, yes, it had. "Who? Who was devastated? Her or her mother?"

"Her mother, I think."

"Oh, so she knows *exactly* how you feel."

"People get nervous. They don't always know the right thing to say." Mom liked giving people the benefit of the doubt, sometimes refusing to see the obvious if it could be unpleasant to do so. She tried to change the subject. "Everyone wants to see you. You'll come back out when you're done?"

"Yeah," I said. With great reluctance. "Mom, why are they still here?"

"What do you mean? They're here for us."

"Not dead kitten lady. You're allowed to tell people to go home. They have their own homes."

"Keep your voice down!" Mom's patented angry whisper jumped out for just a second. "I want them here, Brock. It's comforting and I don't want to be alone right now. Do you know that the last time your dad was shot some of our neighbors marveled—*marveled*—at the support we got from our family and from the Church? They couldn't believe it. The meals, the visits, the babysitting, whatever we needed, there was always somebody to help. We're lucky to have that. Most people don't."

"I'm not saying that's bad. What's bad—what I don't like—are the attention hounds. You can't tell me there aren't some of those out there, sniffing about."

"I'm grateful for the support. I don't care *why* they're here."

"Or even what they say?"

"*Especially* what they say. It's just nice to know that they care, on whatever level they can manage."

Maybe. I thought Mom a little too charitable. If she found comfort in laying her head on the many shoulders waiting to be cried upon, then I supposed that was her business, but they would be waiting a long, long time for mine.

With that thought steeling me, I emerged. Once I was spotted, person after person shook my hand and told me how sorry they were about Dad and how glad they were I could be home to help Mom. "She really needs it," they would say. "I know," I would tell them, and then they'd tell me the proverb about the silver lining on the other side's grass where everything happens for a reason. Some were family and some close friends. Those that weren't were just shoulders to me. To my surprise, I was attracted to them. Being pitied was frustratingly pleasurable. In that way, I disappointed myself. I really wanted to move past such petty enjoyments after the incident at the coordination meeting in Arizona.

My interactions with the Shoulders were mostly brief and uniformly awkward. Inevitably, once the condolences and empty-headed platitudes were out of the way, the conversation would go quiet. And in that silence they would inevitably ask, "How are *you* doing?" As if they honestly wanted to know. But they didn't, not really. They wanted a brave face and a reassurance that everything was okay and that life would go on. Anything less than that, I knew, was a serious breach of decorum. So, it fell to *me* to make *them* feel better, as if handling any delicate emotions I might have would be too much.

"I'm doing just fine," I would say. "We all are."

"Are you sure? When I think about what you all must be going through . . . " (And then they would tear up.)

"No, no. It's great. We're great." (And I'd pat them on the back and give them a tissue. Maybe some water.)

By the time I'd dropped my mollification bombs all around the room, Sister Milligan was chomping at the bit. She called out my name and beckoned me over to the couch where she'd somehow managed to once more capture the attention of my mother. I thought about pretending I didn't hear her, but when she called out for me again I decided that would be a cruelty to anyone within earshot of her louder-than-necessary, cat screech of a voice. I turned around to see her long neck extended upward like a periscope trying to spot me amongst the assembled. "Coming!" I said. I moved through the crowd to the couch and sat down next to Mom, who looked like a scared rabbit.

"Oh, Brock. So good, so *good* to see you," Sister Milligan said excitedly. She and Mom were about the same age, but she looked much older. "I was just telling your mother to look on the bright side!"

"Oh?" I said. "What bright side is that?" I wanted to know as much out of morbid curiosity as a need to be polite.

"I was just saying that the bright side is that your mom has never been a single mother before. This will be like a new adventure for her!"

A couple of years earlier, I might have sarcastically responded with, "But not exactly 'Choose Your Own,' right?" Instead, I excused myself to go talk to the Shoulders who weren't insane. All of the sudden, the rest of them didn't seem so bad. Mom, to her credit, took Sister Milligan's latest bon mot in stride and made sure she had helped herself to some food.

I noticed something missing in Mom's eyes. She was genuine in her grief and made no attempt to either play it up or dismiss it, but there was a strength there, in her interactions with the Shoulders. In her smiling and in her laughing. I thought of that night in the hospital nearly eight years earlier when she held me tight and sobbed at the thought of Dad leaving us. On that night, she was scared. But that fear was gone from her eyes now. She was not that frightened, timid person who once put her head on *my* shoulder.

That thing Mom had been dreading since before I was born had finally happened. Bill, her husband—her *world*—was gone. Yes, she was distraught and in mourning and concerned about her sons, but she wasn't falling apart. Nothing she said or did suggested she was worried at all about what came next. She had passed through the worst thing imaginable already. This was Mom on the other side of fear.

30

SPEAKER FOR THE DEAD

As a missionary, I often knocked on doors for hours for the chance—the smallest, slightest *chance*—to talk to just one person. I understood why those doors often didn't open. I shared a bond with the people hiding behind the curtains and telling their kids to stay low and quiet that was completely unknown to them, but very real for me: neither of us wanted me on their porch. I didn't enjoy interrupting meals or telenovelas any more than they liked seeing me standing there in the white shirt and tie, eagerly hoping for a few minutes of their time. Yes, I wanted to talk and teach, but not to anyone who didn't want to listen. So, when Mom asked me Sunday night if I would like to speak at Dad's funeral and to the hundreds of people who would be there, I responded with a resounding *Yes!*

In my head. I didn't want to sound too eager given the somber reason for the opportunity.

What I said out loud was, "Me?"

"Yes," Mom said. "Don't you think that would be nice? I think that would be nice."

It was a safe bet the funeral would be covered by the local media and half of the people there would not be members of the Church. I couldn't imagine *not* speaking at the funeral. A more captive audience I'd never find. Any other path led to regret.

The Shoulders had gone home. My first day back in California was almost over, and Mom, Uncle Richard, and I sat at the kitchen table together to talk about the next few days. Mom left most of the decisions to me. I don't know if it was the name tag or that I was not a gooey mess in a house of gooey messes, but she seemed to think me perfectly capable of handling all the necessaries. The idea I speak at the funeral was one of her lone contributions to our plans.

"Richard is giving the eulogy, and Bishop Pauline will be giving the gospel talk."

"What else is there to say?" I asked.

"I don't know," she admitted. "You'll think of something. You always give such good talks."

"Yes," I said. "I'm amazing."

Uncle Richard laughed. "You knew your dad, Brock. What did he believe in? What would he want you to say?"

Ah. *What would Dad want?* We thought we knew, the three of us. It was something we asked and answered with confidence several times that night. Dad wouldn't want a sad, depressing funeral. A patriot, Dad would want the military involved despite the fact he hated his time in the service. He would want this hymn sung and these people as pallbearers and that person to say a prayer and that other person to feel like they were included. Maybe that guy could, I dunno, usher at the door?

It helped that Dad was dead and couldn't argue with us. We, the living, were so sure about the identity and personality of our newly dead and gone, deciding what his responses would be to a life now going on without him. Who would challenge us, the ones who knew and loved him best? No one, not even him. This was the neat and tidy version of Dad, the one who did everything we told him to and behaved precisely as we had come to expect. It wasn't the Dad any of us knew, but it was the only one we had left.

"All right," I said. "I'll do it."

After all of our talks about the gospel and his death and what came after, who was more qualified? According to Mom and Uncle Richard, no one. I knew only one thing for sure: the talk would somehow involve words.

* * *

The next day's errands gave me the perfect excuse to procrastinate. There was a gravesite to select and a funeral home to visit and an obituary to write and many more decisions still to be made. My guide through it all was Uncle Richard. Outside of our home, as a full-fledged, temporarily displaced missionary, I still needed to be accompanied by an adult male who could serve as a companion while I was away from Elder Vaughn. It saved me from asking for the help I so desperately needed. Tall, commanding, and at ease with every person he met, my mother's oldest brother probably could have done it all without me. Instead, he was my chauffeur around town and stood behind me as I made the key decisions.

Our first stop was Red Bank Cemetery, far outside of the Clovis city limits. Tall trees stood at attention on the main drive up through the middle of the property and along the outer perimeter, but otherwise the grounds were bare and open. On a good (smog free) day, there was a clear view of the nearby Sierra Nevada Mountains and, unlike the more populous cemeteries in town, this one was always quiet. I chose an untouched spot without many other graves around it, which was easy enough to do.

Afterward, we went back into the city to the Smithson Funeral Home. It truly looked like a "home," complete with a well-manicured lawn and an interior layout suggesting less a business and more a converted mini-mansion. The director, a short, greasy little man too old for the brown hair he sported on his head and above his lip, wore a smile that never cracked. He greeted us at the door and took us through a series of tight corridors and narrow doors—the kind you usually only see in older homes—to a large, well-lit back room with two rows of caskets on either side. All of them were open. It wasn't actually the barracks of a vampire army, it just looked like one.

The creepy and quiet showroom for the final vehicles of the dead came complete with a pushy salesman. As the director highlighted the features of each casket—solid mahogany casing, almond interior, ebony finish, head panel designs adorned with praying hands or doves flying or some other art the earthworms could admire—Uncle Richard and I walked down the aisle, noting the price tags as we went, each one more shockingly expensive than the last. I couldn't understand why the dead needed an elaborate coffin in the first place. What good did gold trim ever do for those who couldn't open their eyes to admire it?

The director was a seemingly nice enough man, but he had his agenda. The people he led into this room were grieving—at their most vulnerable and most willing to move through a sale as quickly as possible. How else could he charge thousands of dollars for a box—a box!—and get away with it?

Thankfully, I knew exactly what I wanted, and the thicker the director laid it on, the more sure I became. Down at the end of the rows, away from the others and painted the most offensively unattractive pale blue the world had ever seen, was the cheapest casket available. A pine box for my father. You could light a match under it and watch it burn.

"A-are you positively sure that's the one you want?" The director went into a flop sweat.

"Yes, of course." I said. "It doesn't really matter, does it?"

"It, ah, matters more than you think. But if that's the—if you want that one then I suppose it's, ah, up to you. It's not the one I'd choose for my father, certainly."

What would Dad want? I figured Dad saw death as such a temporary thing he'd be upset if we spent a lot of money on something that was just going to get buried in the ground anyway. Dirt could be shoveled onto blue wood just as well as gold trim.

The matter settled, we moved into the director's office to discuss our ideas for the funeral and transportation and the graveside service. His people would take care of everything, including setting up chairs and shuttling the body in and out of the church. The funeral would be simple and short. Hymns, prayers, an a capella rendition of "True to the Faith" by a group of Logan's friends, and a few talks (including mine about . . . something super special). Afterward, we'd convoy over to the cemetery and be met there by volunteer Army veterans for the 21-gun salute.

Was I *sure* I wanted the pale blue one?

Absolutely.

* * *

Since I had never before been entrusted with anyone's legacy in print and microfilm, I pulled the last few days of newspapers from Mom's recycling bin to get some idea of what obituaries were supposed to look like. It was my last task that Monday evening, and it had to be done immediately to make the next day's paper. I didn't trust anyone else to do it properly.

Most of the obituaries I read were little more than a cold list of accomplishments and a note about the time and place for the funeral. There was no sense of who the person was or what all those accomplishments added up to. That didn't seem right. If they didn't result in a human being worth describing in even the broadest of details, what possible meaning did any of the plaudits and degrees have?

My word count was limited by our budget. I packed in as much as I could:

William Maurice Heasley

A loving husband and father, Bill died on November 23, 1996 a happy man. Bill spent much of his life in the service of others; in particular his family and including his country through a 3-year service in the army. He is also a faithful member of the Church of Jesus Christ of Latter-Day Saints and served in many capacities in the church. Exhibiting a Christ-like love toward those he came in contact with, Bill Heasley was an example to all of humility and firmness. He instilled a kind of hope in others that continues even after his death. We know that we will see him again one day and he is dearly missed.

I had perfectly codified my father into one paragraph. The changing tense precise and each adjective chosen for maximum impact and information. It was succinct, and I was quite pleased with it.

No doubt Dad, who was not around to tell me differently, would have thought it the greatest obituary ever written.

* * *

The Shoulders returned on Tuesday, which was motivation enough to stop procrastinating and just write my talk for the funeral already. I had been so sure when I took on the assignment that I would think of something vital to share, but trying to represent Dad's worldview and take on faith turned out to be harder than I thought. I knew Dad had faith, but I still couldn't grasp *how*. I dug around the house, looking for notes, books, pieces of mail, anything Dad had put his hands on for some sort of clue or inspiration.

I found a copy of an audio tape I had received from my family back in March while I was still at the Missionary Training Center. Dad's hip was replaced in February, just after our trip to Utah together. At the time of the recording, he had just gotten home from the hospital.

> **DAD:** Hello, son . . . I'm sitting here on the throne—the easy chair here. Just got through cleaning myself up and I'm doing pretty well. Doing my exercises. I've been walking down to the end of the block and back, so I think I'm doing well.

The tape was front loaded with Dad's 911 call, and I had shared it with the other Elders in my MTC district because by then they'd heard the story and were curious. Their jaws dropped appropriately, which never stopped being a thrill. Most of the rest of the sixty-minute tape was filled with news, greetings, and personal messages. Mostly from Mom. According to her, the big news around the house was Dad's newfound ability to cluck like a chicken. She insisted I hear it, but Dad was a bit more reluctant about sharing.

> **MOM:** Do the chicken thing.
> **DAD:** Huh?
> **MOM:** Do it. Do the chicken.
> **DAD:** Well, why can't I just take him out and let him listen to Daisy, our pet chicken?
> **MOM:** All right, go ahead.
> **DAD:** Nah, I'm just kidding, we don't have a pet chicken Daisy.
> **MOM:** [Bursts out laughing] What, did you think he was gonna believe you? I can barely put up with the cat.
> **DAD:** Well, you never know what the boys will bring home from school.
> **MOM:** McKay wants a rat.
> **DAD:** A rat? Your mother says McKay wants a rat for his birthday.
> **MOM:** Next week.
> **DAD:** Um, I don't think he's going to get it.
> **MOM:** No.

I hadn't listened to the tape since Utah. It was the last record of his voice I had.

> **DAD:** Well, I don't know much else to say. I miss ya. Um, I guess I'll sign off by doing my one lone impression of the farm animal. I don't know if this is something you really wanna hear, but I guess this is my one claim to fame.
>
> Oh yeah, I guess Mom is sending you the 911 tape. It had been some time since I heard it, so . . . it's funny how

> you remember things a little differently over the years. But, of course once I heard it again it brings it all back. That was definitely an eventful evening. So, I guess I shouldn't say I hope you enjoy it [chuckles]. But, uh, it is quite unique I suppose. Well, I think your Mom's got more to say. Surprise, surprise. So, here it goes.
>
> [Dad imitates a chicken. Very and creepily well.]
>
> I love you, son. Talk to you later. Buh-bye.

Dad's segment of the recording stopped, replaced by an empty hiss. With eyes beginning to water, I stared at the tape player in disbelief. Was that all there was? Was this the last record of him I had?

> *You hadn't seen him in ten months. And then he was gone.*
> Yup.
> *Do you remember the last thing he said to you?*
> He told me no one wanted to see me and that I shouldn't come home.
> *Oh.*
> Yeah. But, he meant it in a good way.
> *Of course. What about the time before that?*
> He clucked like a chicken.
> *Seriously? Last thing he said?*
> That time, yeah.

For the first time since the night he died, I felt the sting of Dad's absence. I hadn't stopped missing him since he'd gone, exactly, but I hadn't experienced it this acutely, not even when Mom sobbed all over me Sunday afternoon. I felt a kind of aching despair, worn out and hollow, and I knew that space would never be filled again.

The reality of speaking at my own father's funeral came into focus. What if, instead of having nothing to say, I got up and couldn't speak? I was proud of the fact I hadn't cried since the night Dad died, and the last thing I wanted to do was put myself in a position where I could potentially break my manly streak. I was at risk of making the funeral into the kind of spectacle it was not intended to be.

The tape clicked and a high-pitched rub out sound transitioned the audio to something new. The background hiss resumed, and Dad's voice came back on.

> **DAD:** Brock, it's me again. I felt that after I ended I, well—prompted by the Spirit if you will—that I should make a comment about the 911 tape that you and your companions have listened to.
>
> Um, I just—it was as you know, son, a life-altering experience. It was an experience that changed my entire life and I believe that—ultimately—that it will be for my good. And there's been a variety of other things that have happened since then that, uh, I guess don't happen to too many people, but they seem to be things that the Lord has seen fit to throw my way to strengthen me. I believe they have, although I think for a period of time there I wasn't really aware or could really accept that fact.

"Your father always said he never got any answers to prayers."

"What?"

Mom poked her head into my bedroom to see how my talk was coming. Her words confused me. I had seen Dad pray, but had we ever had a discussion about it? I couldn't remember. There was that night in my bedroom when I vomited words and feelings and Dad thought I was crazy and needed therapy. He said he never got an answer about the Church being true, but I hadn't thought he was talking about prayer in general. That seemed like a declaration I would have remembered.

"He just didn't feel like Heavenly Father answered him," Mom explained. "He used to say it all the time."

"Even after the shooting—the first one?"

"Yes."

"How could he even think that? Of course he got answers."

"Well, I know that and you know that, but your father didn't think so."

"That doesn't make any sense."

"No, it doesn't. That was your father."

"But that doesn't make any sense."

"He was a contradiction," Mom admitted. "I could never figure him out. Believe me, I tried."

I felt my funeral talk and my perception of Dad collapse under the weight of Mom's words. I couldn't accept any of it.

"But," I said, "we would talk all the time about life after death and the gospel and all that. It wasn't some abstract thing to him. He believed in it. He knew there was something next, and he looked forward to it. We talked about that. All the time. I can remember being six and talking about it on the route."

"Well, hold on," Mom said, her hand up. "I didn't say he didn't have any faith at all."

> **DAD:** But I knew when all this was happening—at the time the shooting was going on—I never did lose consciousness. There was a time when I felt, well, this might be the end of my life. And as you heard on the tape I felt that could be so and tried to say goodbye, but it wasn't too much longer after that that I felt, well, y'know, I'm gonna get through this.
>
> And then after the surgeries and getting out of the hospital and being able to revisit the scene and so on and so forth—and then later on finding out that even though they only hit me thirteen times I was actually shot at thirty-five times and basically every one of them were from point blank range, no more than eight feet away—so you can see that a miracle was in its work there that I was only hit that many times.
>
> And as I've stated many times after going back into my shop and seeing where the bullet holes were, that right where I was standing—cuz I can remember everything, every second of it as if it happened yesterday—there should have been bullets that had gone through my chest or my head. Just like the three bullets they tried to put in the back of my head when I was sitting on the ground—and these are armor-piercing bullets, some of them—and the second wooden door, a one-inch wooden door

> stopped the bullets, which they shoulda' never done. So, there was a lot of things going on and I really do feel that somebody was looking after me. It wasn't my time to go, but for whatever reason the Lord allowed this to happen.

"So . . ." I said to Mom. "He did have faith. I didn't imagine that."

"No," she said. "That was the thing that used to make me so mad. Your father never doubted for a minute."

To a lot of people, Dad was the guy who—when he was able to attend church—never wore a tie because of his thick, nearly non-existent neck. Business concerns kept him away from Sunday services with enough frequency that people noticed. They thought of Dad as a store owner or a bait distributor or a gun salesman or that guy with the Swiss cheese legs. But to me there was more to him than guns and worms and the ultimate how-I-got-these-scars story. The concerns of this life sometimes demanded more of his time than he would have liked, but his chief interests lay in the next world. He was very up front about that.

Or was Dad confused? He believed in a God that never answered his prayers and allowed him to be shot nearly to death—only to actually die later when it happened again. Was that madness? Was there any sense in that?

"Okay, right," I said. "Right. So, if he didn't believe in prayer then how . . . ?"

"He believed in prayer as much as he did anything else," Mom said. "He just didn't think he got answers to *his* prayers. For whatever reason, he just didn't see it."

"So he had faith, just not a lot of it."

Mom looked displeased. "I don't think that's fair."

"Well, that's why he worked on Sundays, isn't it?"

For years, working on Sundays was a matter of no small disagreement between Dad and me, though he was mostly unaware of this. Sunday, as the designated day of rest, was a day to refrain from working and from doing things that would cause others to work—things like buying groceries and eating out.

It wasn't until I was several hundreds of miles away and had nine months of pious living behind me that I worked up enough righteous fury to tell Dad that he broke the fourth of the Ten Commandments each and every Sunday by selling his guns and his beer. He did this either in person (missing church in the process) or by not closing the Shop so his employees could go home and be with their families. It bothered me that it was on this gravy train of disobedience that a roof was over our heads and a pool in our backyard. I explained to Dad that greater blessings awaited him if only he'd do the right thing. Dad wrote me back two weeks later. It was our last communication.

"Your father told you why he worked on Sundays," Mom said. "He talked with his bishop about it years ago and was told that if the only way to support his family and keep his business going was to work on Sundays, that was between him and the Lord. Your father prayed about it and felt good about staying open on Sundays. And that was that." Her face couldn't help but sadly register the many discussions they'd no doubt had on the subject.

"He prayed about it," I said.

"Yes," Mom said.

"And he felt good about it."

"Yes."

"And he never received answers to prayers."

"Exactly."

> **DAD:** And, like a lot of things in life, I think, the shooting was to eventually get me into a more humble position—which it certainly has. Of course I do hope that He doesn't have any more experiences like this in store for me. I think I've had my quota for this life anyway. I hope so. It was one of those, hopefully, once in a lifetime experiences that most people don't ever go through.
>
> But it was a character-building experience, I believe. One that someday I think I will probably know all of the ramifications as to why and so on, but I know at least part of it was to prepare me for—for whatever He may have in mind.
>
> So I don't have any feelings of "why me?" or any feelings of, well, that was a terrible thing to be allowed to happen to me. Or anything like that. I don't blame the Lord for allowing it; I thank Him for allowing me to get through it and giving me the strength to do so. Because

it was something I don't believe I could have done without some help.

So anyway, that's all I really had to say about it. I guess your mom wants to take up the rest of the time here so I'll sign off again. And so, uh, I love you and look forward to hearing from you again, son. Buh-bye.

31

THE EYES OF A DEAD MAN

The local media had been on the story of Dad's death since the weekend, asking us for interviews and access to the funeral. Memory of our appearance on *Rescue 911*, which ended its run as a television program just two months prior, still lingered. Our priorities differed slightly from theirs, so we didn't allow the new crews inside the church building. They set themselves up outside, cameras trained on our entrances and exits like macabre Rodeo Drive paparazzi.

I walked into the makeshift viewing room at the church early Wednesday morning to see not the pale, blue wooden angular casket I had picked out, but a beautiful, brushed metal gray coffin with gold trim, a rounded top, and a sturdy frame impervious to matches. I was told that, for some reason, the funeral director decided a free upgrade was necessary. We guessed it had something to do with the cameras, but it was a nice gesture nonetheless.

Normally, the viewing room was used as a meeting place for the women's organization in the ward, the Relief Society. Every burnt gold colored chair was cushioned in maroon, and long white linens draped over the windows ran nearly the entire height of the walls leading to the vaulted ceiling. Flowers of many colors with names I did not know sat on tables and in pots on the floor. Dad's coffin took up the length of the head of the room next to the upright piano, warmly lit and cold to the touch.

It was also open.

It was the first time I'd been with Dad in the flesh since January, when we said our goodbyes and see-ya-laters at the Missionary Training Center. I stood in front of his body more out of curiosity than a need to see it. It wasn't the first dead body I'd ever seen, but it was the first one I could stare at for however long I wished without fear of anybody bothering me to move along.

He looked older than I remembered. His skin was thin and stretched and powdery in texture. His face was puffy, like they'd stuffed cotton balls into his mouth (maybe they did). At the same time, paradoxically, he looked hollowed out. His eyes, closed and unnatural looking, were set so far back into their sockets they seemed to be sinking into his skull. Had they been sewn shut? It was hard to not think about how frightening it would be should they suddenly flutter open. That wouldn't happen without some manual stimulation, possibly scissors. I imagined Zombie Dad anyway.

I could see it. He'd shock us all, open his eyes, sit up, and walk right out of the church on his two stiff legs and one new hip. Being a zombie, his first thought would be for brains to satiate his incredible hunger after being dead and without food for four days. He'd ignore us, his family, out of residual affection, but even that would fade over time and we would ultimately admit he would have to be stopped. The police would be ill-equipped and useless when it came to handling the reanimated corpse insomuch as battling the walking dead was not covered by their Academy training. Desperate, the mayor would go to the airwaves to make a public plea to the only ones who could save us in this dark hour—the men who had proven once already they could do the deed and had the skills necessary. In the time of the city's greatest need, only my father's killers would be able to save us all from the rotting, shuffling plague his body had become. Armed with shotguns, hacksaws, and a pardon from the governor, they would go forward and restore peace to the community in the brutal manner to which they were accustomed, allowing us to finally resume our mourning.

I stifled a laugh, then turned away from Dad and winced, ashamed of myself for such a dark, ridiculous thought.

Although I could have, I did not dare touch him. I knew he would be cold. He looked so white and so fragile, like chalk. I was afraid he might fall apart in my hands.

McKay and Tyler came up and stood beside me. They stared at Dad, expressionless. I gave them brief hugs before they shuffled off silently to sit on the front row of chairs next to Mom and wait to be ushered into the chapel. They'd spent most of the past couple of days more or less happily playing the Super Nintendo a neighbor lent them. The time between Dad's death and the funeral now seemed a cruelty. They were right back to how I'd found them on Sunday.

The viewing room filled up slowly in the hour leading up to the funeral. All were quiet and respectful. Even Sister Milligan. Many had a story about Dad to tell and bent whichever of my family's ears they could grab. Everyone dressed in their Sunday best except for those I didn't know very well. It was easy to tell who knew Dad from the Shop and who knew him from church.

Mom surrounded herself with her sisters, constantly blocked from my view by the parade of Shoulders moving through the room and lending words of support. In that moment, I was grateful for them. Logan stayed huddled with his friends on the margins of the room. Grandma and Grandpa Heasley stayed near the back, teary and comforted by the old California friends they'd left behind after moving to Arizona.

"Your dad ever tell you 'bout the time he fought off those drunks bare-knuckled?"

I turned around.

"I'm sorry?" I didn't recognize the man, but I had seen him before. He looked like a lot of Dad's buddies from the gun club and shop—big guy, flannel shirt, unruly brown hair, tattoos, questionable facial hair, and rough around the edges. He surprised me by coming up from behind. "Uh, no. No, he didn't."

"He didn't? Well, let me tell you, your dad, he didn't have no fear whatsoever. This was back when he was the manager at Blackbeard's. He told you about working there, right?"

"I remember," I said. "He helped build part of the pirate mini golf course."

"Right, yeah! Yeah, I worked on that, too."

"He used to take me there after hours to help him empty the arcade of quarters."

"Oh, then you must be his oldest, right? Logan?"

"Brock. Well, Elder Heas—Brock." Hearing my first name again—much less using it—was something I just couldn't get used to.

"Yeah, that's right, Brock. So anyways, there was a bunch of us working there this one night and there were these guys that were getting really rowdy in the parking lot. They were drunk as skunks and making all kinds of noise. Beer bottles smashed on the ground, that sort of thing. Real rowdy-like. Your dad—he was manager at the time—he decides he was gonna ask them to leave. He got a few of us to come over with him and we grabbed us some golf clubs to defend ourselves—show 'em we meant business. But Bill, we asked him if he wanted one and he said no. He went over there with nothin'. He took point and just bareknuckled it right up to those guys like it was nothin'."

"No way," I said. How had I never heard this story before?

"Yeah, yeah. So, Bill, he asks the guy who was the loudest for him and his buddies to leave. He was real nice about it. Guy wouldn't budge. He—bottle swingin'—he got real testy and asked Bill who he was to be tellin' them where to go. He gets right in your dad's face—like this close, closer than how I am with you now—but Bill, he wasn't gonna back down an inch.

"So your dad, he squares up and gets ready like he's gonna box the guy. Bill wasn't real tall or anything, but, y'know, his arms were built like tree trunks or somethin'. And this guy, I don't think he thought Bill was serious cuz he took a swing at him and then it was on. They traded a few blows and got into a fight while the rest of us just watched. Honestly, it wasn't much of a scuffle because pretty soon the drunk just figured it wasn't worth it anymore and they all left.

"But I'll never forget that—your dad goin' into that fight bareknuckled. He had no fear—just no fear at all!"

No one had anything unkind to say about Dad. Over and over again I heard fantastic stories about how he was helpful and friendly, tough and generous. It wasn't always the smart move—people betrayed him or took advantage more than once—but he gave freely of his time and even his money if need be.

I both did and didn't see Dad in their effusion of praise. No one talked about how easily he got frustrated or what a taskmaster he could be as a boss or the occasional coarse language that crossed his lips. His (freakishly white and disturbingly still) dead body was nearby. No one wanted to say such things. You'd think, from standing in that room, that Dad was a saint who did nothing but good in the world, making it all the more evil that he had been taken out of it.

It was his funeral—his one day to be perfect.

* * *

Everyone stood in reverence as my family walked into the chapel, sitting down only after we did. We sat on the front most pew, our backs to the congregation while we faced Dad's (now closed) casket. We were so close we could reach out and touch it. The large chapel was quiet save the echo of Bishop Pauline's voice as he thanked everyone for coming and outlined the program. I was announced as one of the last speakers. I had plenty of time to sit and worry and scold myself for attempting to speak at my father's funeral in the first place.

After Uncle Richard gave the eulogy and Logan's friends sang their song, everyone waited. The silence that filled the room spoke my name. I jumped up from the bench and bounded up the stairs to the wooden podium as it lowered to meet my relatively depressed height. What I hoped look like enthusiasm was more a product of fear and a desire to get it over with as quickly as possible. Only an empty stomach prevented me from throwing up.

The vinyl curtains in the back that served as a partition between the expansive gymnasium and the chapel had been opened to accommodate the large crowd, something I only discovered as I faced them for the first time and adjusted the microphone to my level. Many, many stares crowded the combined mega-chapel.

I lowered my head and gripped the sides of the podium to steady myself. I focused my eyes on the shapes in the grain of the wood and asked myself how tiny and diseased my brain must be to have ever thought this a good idea. Far more people had shown up than anyone anticipated. (Later, the estimate would reach seven hundred.) And there I was in all my stupid, cherub-faced glory. In that moment, I was grateful for the suit, tie, and name tag asserting in a way I could not that the nineteen-year-old man/boy standing at the head of the congregation actually had any business speaking on something other than the relative merits of Weezer's latest album.

I raised my head.

"This is not my father," I said, pointing at the coffin directly in front of me. "He is not there."

I saw my family from a new vantage point. Just on the other side of Dad's casket, opposite from me and directly below. They cried softly. I raised my gaze immediately, lifting my chin high to block them from my view. My speech stumbled and my tongue tied itself up somewhere deep inside my throat. I forgot, entirely, what I was supposed to say. I could feel the base of my eyes swell up, and those in the front rows of the pews grew foggy. I swallowed, begging back the tears with a silent prayer and an ever-tightening grip on the podium. I was committed enough to keep going, but I never dared to look down at my family again.

I choked out the next sentence. "A dead body is dead because it houses nothing." And then the next. "Earlier, I got a chance to look at this one, and I didn't see my father for one very good reason—it isn't him." I kept going. "He, now as a spirit, is somewhere else, incomplete and waiting. His body has been marked 'Return to Sender,' and soon enough it will be shipped off and put back into the dust where it came from, only to come back at a later date in proper working order and with the right parts."

The night before, when I couldn't put it off any longer, I settled on talking about the Resurrection—the idea that both body and spirit will be together again in their perfect form at some point after death. Christ was the first to undergo the process, and now because of Him we would, too. This was Dad's hope, the thing about post-death life that excited him most. I could feel that excitement in me now.

"Often were the times Dad and I would talk of the next life, and even his own death, but there was no significance to any of it without the Resurrection. Dad's hope, particularly after the first shooting in 1989, was for the time when his body would once again work as it should, without a limp and loose bullets and artificial hips. Perhaps he'd even lose some of the french fry weight." Scattered laughter. "He was broken and his belief—his faith—was that he would be fixed."

I kept going, barely even stopping to think about what I was actually saying. I talked about the eternal nature of the soul and the hope we have in Christ for eternal life with God. This wasn't an abstract. This was something happening now, with my father only the latest person to take the next step on that journey. I talked about the possibility of an eternal family and that in the same way the spirit and body would be restored to each other, so too could our relationships with our loved ones. My parents were still married, and in whatever society that exists after this life, we would still be the family we always had been. Dad's passing was an entirely temporary condition. Sad, difficult, and significant—but temporary.

I grew more comfortable and confident as I went on. There was something else being said outside of the scope of my words alone. There was an electricity in the room, a current running out from me and connecting with everyone present. I could see the honesty of our intimate, shared moment in their faces, and feel it in their rapt attentions. It was a communication beyond words; it was spirit speaking to spirit. I could say anything I wanted and it would barely register. What was being felt was greater.

I spoke more in terms of my father's faith instead of my own. I worked from little more than an outline and some of the things I said and recalled over the course of my talk surprised me. As hard to understand as Dad's approach to faith was for me, I couldn't deny that his footing was sure. Dad's faith was practical, matter-of-fact, and, frustratingly, oddly stronger for it. He did not doubt. He did not waver. He believed, unceasingly.

I continued. "Dad never experienced psychological trauma after the shooting in '89. That bothered a lot of people—people Dad had no patience for. He acknowledged the awful things that happened to him as bad, but he did not let them stay that way after the fact. Trials and tragedies built him up and shaped him. They increased his patience and faith.

"I hope you understand that I am not saying my father was perfect. Besides my mother, I may know that better than anyone. He and I disagreed often and didn't always understand each other. But I can tell you that all his hopes, all his understanding of how to conduct himself in this life—whatever his shortcomings—came from his faith. That's who he was. He was what he believed in. His imperfections were who he was when he wasn't being himself."

I kept going. I was off outline now. I had no idea what I was going to say next anymore, and what I said next was exactly what I was supposed to say.

"Dad knew exactly how he wanted to live his life and who kept it going. He spoke of his gratitude and recognized God's hand when it was obvious to him. When it wasn't, he said so. What he did not concern himself with—what was of very little consequence to him—was the now. He didn't need God to manifest Himself here when he'd see Him just as well in the next life. He did not need present evidence of what he, in all confidence, knew was coming just up the road. Dad's faith was firmly in the future, for a life decidedly beyond the current one. He required nothing of now because, to him, everything was already past.

"If it is often only after the fact that we see things clearly, then how lives the man for whom death is an imminent and ever-present reality? My father wasn't perfect in his faith, but he moved on from his trials and challenges with lessons learned and forgave easily. He saw so clearly in the moment, almost as though he was outside of it. He didn't let cynicism, hatred, victimization, and fear rule over him. He was not surrounded by a perimeter of self-righteous narcissism that held forth against empathy and understanding, justifying a desire for vengeance no one would have questioned. His vision was clearer than that. Dad, whatever his failings, did his best to let his more forward-looking perspective and faith guide him when the limited present could not. He favored his limitless future and defined his life backwards from there."

I stopped, concluded in the name of Jesus Christ, and returned to sit back down with my family. I shook so badly the entire pew vibrated.

32

GROUNDED

BLAM! BLAM! BLAM!

The seven rifles fired three times each, and half the crowd put fingers in their ears. There was something disconcerting and wrong about shots being fired at Dad's graveside service. Are microscopes ever set up so those mourning can see the cancer cells up close? Does a parade of buses go by in honor of the dearly departed struck down in the crosswalk? Should a knife-thrower be hired to entertain the loved ones of those who are stabbed? Still, I had to admit, the 21-gun salute was pretty cool.

Everyone gathered at the cemetery stood in a slight stair-step pattern. Setting the grave on a bit of an incline sloping away from the Sierra Nevada Mountains in the distance made it easier to enjoy the skyline with a full 360-degree view of the cemetery and everything else in the surrounding countryside. It made me feel small, and I liked that. It helped me think of Dad.

I felt only slight stirrings of emotion as we carried the coffin from the hearse to the four-walled hole. With the vessel for Dad's body closed and my talk still present in my mind, it was hard to think of the body as having much current significance. Dad wasn't in there and hadn't been for a while. My chief concern was to not drop my end of the coffin as we walked it over. The sucker was heavy.

The military veterans presented an American flag to Mom and a prayer was offered to dedicate the grave, but very little was said otherwise. All were quiet until they were thanked for coming and dismissed.

We headed back to our cars, whispers floating between us. For some, it was one last opportunity to extend their condolences. I had been avoiding her all day, but now Sister Milligan finally caught up to me.

"You are *wearing* that suit!"

"Yes," I agreed. "Yes, I am. These are my clothes." This was basic stranger conversation. Statements of facts spoken as revelation in lieu of anything substantial to say.

"Being a missionary suits you, Brock. I was telling your mom that just a minute ago. I enjoyed your talk very much. You looked real good up there. Quite dashing."

I had never been very good at cluing into this sort of thing, but I was fairly certain Sister Milligan was flirting with me. I tried to back away and join up with people who understood the significance of the name tag and age differences, but I was trapped. I thanked her for the compliment.

"You've been such a strength to your mom this week. Horrible, horrible that this happened to you all. But, you know, bad things happen to good people."

"Yeah," I said. "And sometimes they happen twice."

Sister Milligan looked at me for a second. First with confusion, then shock. Then she burst out laughing. I couldn't help myself and started laughing too. Those nearby looked at us in bewilderment. I realized who I was sharing a laugh with and laughed even harder.

Life, which had stopped so suddenly when Dad died, was about to resume. All was back to normal and yet not at all. Not ever again. Those who hadn't had a chance yet came up to say "hi" and "welcome home" and ask, as most everyone did, "When are you heading back to Arizona?" Friday morning. Two days. Behind us, Dad was lowered into the ground.

After we left, a temporary concrete marker was put in place to mark the grave with the simple inscription, "W. Heasley." It would be a couple years more before the full metal plaque was laid down with the quote selected by my mother:

> Tell my wife that I love her.
> Tell my boys to be good.

* * *

Several messages on the answering machine from the local media welcomed us home after the family luncheon at the church. One station in particular didn't want to focus on the great story that was the symmetry between Dad's death and the shooting years earlier. *ABC 30 Magazine* was a new show with a recurring segment highlighting heroes in the community. They thought Dad would be perfect for it.

That very night, the news crew descended on the house to set up their lights and cameras. It felt familiar to have them there, even comfortable. Dad had been shot, so of course the living room should be turned into a set for television. All that was missing was a bucket of fried chicken. Grandma and Grandpa Heasley and Dad's brother, Jim, all agreed to be interviewed. Mom declined. They wanted to interview me as well, but they had one request.

"Do you think you could take off the name tag?"

"What? Why?" I was surprised. It didn't occur to me that my name tag would be a problem. If anything, shouldn't it be helpful? They could save whole minutes in post-production by not applying the footer graphic with my name.

The reporter, pretty and tiny with hair sculpted by hairspray into a hardened block, shifted uncomfortably. "It's just that . . . " *I* was uncomfortable for her. "If you wear the tag then it becomes a thing."

"Okay," I said. Unhelpfully.

"It would just be a lot easier if we didn't have to explain it."

What was there to explain? The tag had my last name on top, and below that was the Church's Spanish logo, *La Iglesia de Jesucristo de los Santos de los Ultimos Dias.* Hispanics made up a large majority in the Central Valley. Besides, it wasn't like people didn't know what a clean-cut kid in a suit, tie, and name tag meant anyway. Missionaries had been annoying people on Saturday mornings with their incessant knocking for too many years now for that to be the case. All I was missing was the bike.

I thought about it and hesitated. That was fear. Fear that I'd make the reporter even more uncomfortable with a refusal. Fear that keeping the name tag on was a deal breaker and they'd ask me to step away from the camera's glare. But also, I was afraid of doing the right thing for the wrong reasons. I liked being thought of as strong and dedicated. That was vanity. Would keeping the name tag on be no better than showing up to a Sunday morning meeting the night after your father was killed?

I set the fear and myself aside. I was tired of these thoughts. This was a chance to shine but not with my light. How was my duty here any different than in the mission field back in Arizona, or at the funeral in front of all those people? It wasn't.

"No," I said. "I think I'll keep the tag on. Is that okay?"

"Sure."

The segment highlighted Dad's military past, of course, and how well liked he was by the residents in the rural neighborhoods near the Shop. Mention was made of his positive and forgiving spirit, and a particular focus was put on Dad's newest employee, a young kid about my age who had stolen from him a few months earlier. That was news to me, but it didn't surprise me that Dad would reach out and try to help someone like that after they'd wronged him. He'd done it plenty of times before.

Sure enough, some voiceover explaining my dress and appearance was added to the segment to explain I was on a mission "for the Church of Latter-Day Saints." In one of the two bits from me they used, I talked about how Dad loved games, particularly Monopoly, and that I never beat him. Which was true.

In the second bit I said, "The thing . . . that makes his death easier to bear is that I know I'm going to see him again."

And that was true as well.

* * *

The next day, Thursday, *finally* was Thanksgiving. What missionary gets to say they had Thanksgiving dinner at home? None. That's how many.

I slept in, a luxury I had not been afforded in many months. When I awoke and emerged from my room, it was to a house entirely different from the one I'd been living in the past several days. The Shoulders were absent, all of them gone to conduct their own holiday celebrations. For the first time, I saw Mom alone.

She sat sideways on the couch, legs lifted to rest on the cushions, looking at old home movies for glimpses of Dad. He was quick on the scene when the first home video camcorders went on sale in the early 1980s, but back then the setups were so complicated and the camera so bulky, he didn't trust anyone else to do the filming. Any footage of him was usually by way of small cameos (thanks to the tripod) that occurred with roughly the same frequency as Sasquatch sightings.

"Brock," Mom said without looking at me as I groggily stumbled my way through the living room. "Do you remember this?" On screen was the first Christmas after Tyler was born, back in the old Buckingham house. Dad had us all gathered together with him on the couch and led us in a chorus of "Merry Christmas" to some unseen party. Presumably ourselves in the future.

"Yeah, that was the year I swore up and down that one of my boxes under the tree was the Transformers set with all the jet robots."

They were called Aerialbots, and they combined to form the giant robot Superion. I didn't mention the names to her because Mom didn't care and because I didn't want my clear memory of the single greatest disappointment of my present-opening career to suggest I was still bitter about getting knock-off Legos that year instead. Because that wasn't true. At all.

"Oh? I'm sure your father wanted to get that for you, but we just couldn't afford it back then."

"I didn't know that." Of course. Mom and Dad would rather I think they hated me than suggest we might be poor.

"There's a lot of things we didn't tell you like that. But, you're older now."

"Yeah."

Mom watched the home videos, color commentating and shouting anecdotes to me while I poured cereal in the kitchen. Most of her Thanksgiving day was spent like that, not doing anything in particular. The funeral behind them and their concentration fully back on Super Nintendo games, McKay and Tyler stayed otherwise occupied and kept their minds off the events of the past week as much as possible. Logan, as usual, did his own thing in his room. No one really knew what. Dad's absence filled the house.

Mom tried to do things to be useful and made several trips to the kitchen to demonstrate this, but inevitably she headed back out to the living room to watch the home movies again and again after accomplishing not much of anything. The time the Shoulders spent in the kitchen now paid huge dividends. Food made in our home and brought in from outside was stacked high both in the fridge and on the counters and kitchen table. I scolded myself a bit. Not all of the Shoulders heard about Dad's death from the news. Probably not even most of them. They attended to McKay and Tyler when Mom couldn't. They stayed with Mom and made sure she wasn't alone during the worst of it all. Maybe I didn't need to participate in group mourning, but that made me either weird or in a different place emotionally, not the Shoulders unwelcome.

It was because of them that Thanksgiving was exclusively a day of relaxation and eating heartily and constantly. There were casseroles without name and seemingly without number. There were green Jell-O salads, yams, French bread already buttered, and more cookies and pies than could possibly be eaten (not that we didn't try very, very hard). Mom had very little to attend to. After five days of constant activity and attention, she did not know what to do with herself and nothing was required of her. It was a blessing.

Both sets of grandparents and several aunts and uncles returned for Thanksgiving dinner. They kept things light and respectful and were mindful of Mom's state of mind. It was a good meal and a good time to be with family. Although he didn't pick it, there really wasn't a better week for Dad to die.

I sat at the table with all the other grown-ups, talking and laughing and remembering. I ate more than my fair share of pumpkin pie because it was my favorite and, thanks again to the Shoulders, we had more than a lot of it. I held court and told stories from my short, momentarily interrupted tenure as a missionary. The man I met while buying a hot dog who claimed to be a demon from hell. The time Elder Gatica tricked me into knocking on doors in a Spanish neighborhood without him. The beautiful night just a few months earlier when, for some inexplicable reason, I spoke perfect Spanish to a family I was desperate to teach with precision.

I was, honestly, quite bored. These were stories that were supposed to be told at a much later date. With nothing to do or take care of, my presence served very little purpose other than to entertain. My legs twitched and begged to get out from under the table and onto a bike. Every minute I spent sitting and eating and talking and not doing anything of any particular import was pure torture. When the conversation moved to the living room and everyone's efforts toward action served only to communicate the score on the television or to get into a comfortable position for a nap, I thought seriously about asking Uncle Richard to drive me down to South Fresno to go knock on some doors. It was exciting seeing everyone again, but they could nurse their food babies without me.

Any thought I'd had about staying home beyond Thanksgiving disappeared at about 4:00 PM when I asked Mom what else was going on that day and she said "nothing." I was in the wrong place. By the time Friday morning rolled around and it was time to leave, I felt like an intruder in my own house.

During my little sabbatical, I'd found peace in a nightmare. I'd seen and felt and experienced the power of the principles and ideas and faith I'd been teaching firsthand. All along I'd had this precious stone to share, and now, finally, I could fully behold its shine and its glow. That was amazing, a gift to be prized above all else, and an impetus for returning to the mission and using what I had learned in service to God. To finish the work.

33

LIFE AFTER DEATH

There wasn't much ceremony in my exit from California. McKay and Tyler stayed in their room, leaving only Logan and Mom to see me off at the curb in front of the house. Mom gave me a long hug, just as she did ten months ago before I left for the MTC with Dad.

"We'll be fine," she said. "I don't want you worrying."

"I'll be back in fourteen months," I said. "And we'll talk in a month, on Christmas."

"I want you to call me when you get there."

In my mind, I sighed. "I can't do that. You know I can't do that. If it's important to you, I'll ask somebody to give you a call to let you know I made it."

"Ask him if you can call."

"Who?"

"President Hedrick."

I thought she was kidding at first, but one look at her face and I knew she wasn't. Mom couldn't see any reason an exception couldn't be made for her. Always for her. As if there hadn't been enough exceptions made already. I decided not to argue with her.

I tossed my carry-on into the backseat of the car. Logan leaned in for a hug, saying only, "See ya," before going back into the house. I got into the car on the passenger side, and Mom motioned at me to roll down the window. She gave me one more insistent embrace before allowing the window back up and me to speed away out of her life once more. I turned to my driver and said, "Let's go, Tom."

Tom Mariner attended Dad's funeral. I was honestly surprised. We'd spoken very little since going our separate ways, and not at all since high school ended. None of that mattered now. When he overheard that no one was exactly sure how I'd be getting to the airport on Friday, he volunteered immediately. I returned the favor by giving him an exclusive first look at my new missionary super zeal. By the time I'd boarded the plane, Tom had shared his feelings on God, heard the first of the missionary discussions, and committed to read a few highlighted passages of the Book of Mormon I gave him. He was cordial about it, but I could tell I'd freaked him out a little. That didn't stop me from doing the same thing with the woman next to me on the flight from Fresno to Phoenix.

As we flew over the state border, a beautiful red landscape emerged, meeting up with the blue and purple sky. I reentered the dream completely at peace. My family remained very much on my mind, but I couldn't doubt I was heading in the right direction.

Once back in Arizona, one of the first things I did before we'd even left the terminal was tell President and Sister Hedrick all about my new, full tilt, no-one-is-safe proselytizing attitude and the battle with the news reporter over my name tag. I got big smiles and a hearty "Good job!" I grinned and, as they power walked ahead of me to baggage claim, I felt that never-ceasing twinge of shame. I reminded myself their approving reaction wasn't the only reason I'd done it, and made a mental note to not be quite so vocally pleased with myself in the future.

During the car ride back to Gilbert, just to be able to say I'd done it, I asked President Hedrick if it would be all right to call California.

Mom won again.

"Of course," he said. "You should talk to your mother whenever she needs it."

"Whenever? Like, today?"

"And tomorrow, if need be."

Had Mom called him while I was in the air? What voodoo was at work here? A bigger breach of mission rules I could scarcely imagine as nothing distracts a missionary so much as voices from home. Letters are a different animal—there's a distance with letters—but with a voice comes intimacy and immediacy. I got smart and kept such thoughts to myself, choosing instead to make a simple inquiry for clarification.

"How often?"

"Don't ask me that, Elder Heasley," President Hedrick said. "And I won't have to tell you. That's between you and your mother."

This was the second time now President Hedrick had taken a basic law of missionary life, set it aside, and refused to tell me what to do. I did my best not to abuse the privilege. For the next two months, Mom and I talked nearly every day. After that, it was once a week, sometimes less, and it stayed that way for the rest of the mission. I felt a little guilty each time.

It wasn't until we arrived at the apartment in Gilbert and I was greeted by a harried, grateful Elder Vaughn that Arizona stopped being the dream and my brief time in California turned into one. Everything in the apartment was exactly as before, as though I'd never left at all. Pamphlets and books all over the coffee table. Dishes I'd left in the sink still needing to be done. Vaughn nursing bruises from a bike accident just a couple days prior.

As soon as I was unpacked, Vaughn cited my trauma and suggested we stay home. I picked up my pack with books and pamphlets. We left immediately. Later that night, we ate dinner at the home of a generous church member, and I recounted for the first of many times my extraordinary time away from the mission. For me, for the next fourteen months, that was the big change: I had a new story to tell. Dad had been mostly gone from my day-to-day life for a while now. I imagined that back in Clovis, with all the commotion and attention inevitably fading away, my family was having a much different experience.

I was lucky enough to have an impetus and a mechanism by which to move forward. President Hedrick later remarked that the visit home hadn't affected me like he thought it would. If anything, I worked more diligently than ever, spurred on by what I'd gained after Dad left—peace and understanding. It was a gift. I wanted to share it with everyone.

Later that Friday night, Elder Vaughn and I returned home, called Elder Roberts, and reported our stats for the day. We ate a light snack and said our nightly joint prayer with Elders Suggs and Weldon. Then, each of us retired to our rooms. My first night back, and already it felt like I hadn't left at all. I reached into my suitcase, pulled out four comic books, and settled into bed. After a quick explanation to Vaughn, I opened the first comic and began to read.

I brought the comics back with me from California at the request of a friend. Two days earlier, after the funeral and after the news crew had left, he stopped by the house and insisted I take them.

"Brother Jennings!" I said, grabbing his hand. "Hey, how're you doing?"

"Good, Brock," he said. "How's your family?"

"They're doing—y'know, they're all right."

Brother Jennings was fifteen years older than me, a veteran, and a family man. We shared a love for comic books and superheroes. He got a big kick out of introducing me to the characters from his favorite era of comics publication, the golden age of the 1940s. His favorite was Billy Batson, the boy who could turn into the adult superhero Captain Marvel by uttering the magic word *SHAZAM!*

"That was a great talk you gave this morning," he said. "One of the best I've ever heard at a funeral. Or ever, really. I saw a lot of people in tears."

"Yeah, the church isn't usually so dusty," I said. You'd think I had given the Gettysburg Address of funeral talks. When I returned from my mission (again and permanently this time) a year and a half later, there were still people who wanted to talk to me about it. Before Brother Jennings had arrived, I was actually listening to an audio recording, just to hear what the fuss was all about. My stumbling speech in the beginning and some unnecessary, overly dramatic flourishes made it obvious I'd received some invisible help no tape could ever record. "But thanks," I continued. "I appreciate that. I don't think I had much to do with it, but I thank you. What's up?"

"I just . . . this is going to sound funny. You've heard of *Kingdom Come*?" I had. Anyone reading comics at the time had. It came out during the summer of 1996 while I was still in Mesa, but I'd been anticipating it for at least a year before that. Instead of the usual pen and ink, four-color serial drama, *Kingdom Come* was a beautifully painted, four-part miniseries about the complicated, difficult future of the DC superheroes. I had, of course, entirely missed out. Brother Jennings told me he bought two copies each of all four issues. "One for me, and one for you. I was going to give them to you when you got off your mission, but I just . . . well, here."

He reached into a small paper bag and pulled out the comics.

"Uh, thanks," I said.

"I know that it's against the rules for you to read comic books—"

"It is, yeah."

"—but, truly, I felt like you should get these now. I know it sounds weird. Call it the Spirit inspiring me if you want. I mean, look at this. It's beautiful."

I flipped through some of the pages. The art by painter Alex Ross was a step above the work he'd done on the *Marvels* series a couple years prior. The beautiful, detailed books were filled with page after page of gorgeous, iconic images. They had a raw power and depth of realism that even the few good superhero movies had been unable to capture. I salivated like a thirsty man too long deprived of sweet water.

"It's a really, really good story," Brother Jennings said. "It's about how Superman grows frustrated with the world and turns his back on it, only to return years later. He knows he's needed because there's no one else strong enough to do what needs to be done, but his time away has made him cynical. He makes a lot of mistakes when he gets back and, in some ways, makes things worse—but he ultimately figures it all out and does the right thing. I know you're gonna like it and I just, like I said, I feel like it could . . . help you? Maybe. I just really, really felt like I needed to give them to you now."

"Wow, thanks." How was I supposed to argue with that? "Seriously, thank you so much. I'll—I guess I'll make an exception."

"And wait until you see what they did with Captain Marvel. I don't want to ruin it for you. It was like, yeah, somebody finally used him right. He and Superman fight a bit, but in the end he does what Superman can't do. It's awesome."

"I'll definitely read them."

And I did. And he was right, the story and the books were exciting. That first night back in Arizona, I read the first book. Most of it concerned the younger generation of superheroes and how they'd lost their way. When I got to the last page and the big reveal of an older Superman back in action and ready to set things right, I wanted to cheer. *Kingdom Come* was the one contraband item I kept with me during the rest of my mission. I tried, but I never could quite manage to feel guilty about that.

As I turned out the lights, ready for the first real rest I'd had in a week, my mind stayed active. I wanted the feeling of that Thanksgiving week—that clarity—to last as long as possible. Over and over again I rolled over the events since last Saturday night in my mind, trying to process and remember everything I could. I thought about what I'd said at the funeral. Did I get it right? Did I represent Dad fairly? Did he approve?

Did it matter if he didn't?

There was one haunting moment, just before the funeral on Wednesday, I kept coming back to.

Stake President Tanner, a tall, thin, older man who made no unnecessary movements and used no uncalculated words, presided over the many congregations in the Clovis area. He invited myself, Mom, and my brothers into his office on the other side of the church, away from all the activities of preparation for the funeral. We entered the office quietly. He motioned for us to sit in the chairs that lined one of the walls, opting to not seat himself behind his large desk and choosing instead to move a folding chair out in front of it to sit directly across from us without any barrier. We respected him a great deal. If I had ever known anyone I considered a spiritual giant before President Hedrick, it was him.

He expressed his condolences, of course, prayed with us, and gave Mom a blessing. Before we walked back out the door, he paused for a moment, stopped us, and gathered his thoughts. He said he had one last thing to share and he wasn't sure how to go about it. He paused again, then began:

"My hope is that you will not be offended by what I am about to say next and that you will receive it with the spirit with which it is intended. I know that feelings are delicate right now, and it is not my desire to tread upon them."

"Oh," Mom said, slightly taken aback. We all were suddenly curious. "Of-of course."

"But, I have a distinct impression, and I feel that I must share it with you. There are so many things in this life we would rather not happen. But they do and we endure and if we are paying very close attention we might find that even the horrible things have something to offer. My feeling is this: my feeling is that Bill—your father—he needed to die in order for the boys to become the men they need to be."

Not knowing what to say, we received President Tanner's words in silence and proceeded out the door of his office to go join everyone else in the viewing room. I was with him up until the last part. I could not imagine how Dad's death was in any way necessary.

I wrestled with his statement that Friday night as I lay in my bed wide awake, staring at the ceiling, and for some time afterward.

It would be many years before I fully understood what he meant.

EPILOGUE

It is one thing to move past grief. It is quite another to live with loss. It's like a tick under the sleeve. It nibbles and bites imperceptibly, but you know it's there. It's always there.

I cried on my wedding day. I'd love to say my wife was so stunningly beautiful in her gown (which she was) that I couldn't help myself, but my tears were not those of joy. Instead, I was a mess because of Dad. We lit a candle in his honor (her idea) as a way to make him part of our special day, but it wasn't good enough. I wanted him there. Our backs mercifully to the audience, I managed to mutter, "I miss him so much," and my bride held my hand tight and everyone waited. "I know," she said. And I got why she said that and I knew she was doing her best to sympathize. But she didn't know. Both of her parents were there.

Mom sat next to her new husband. That was okay with me in a way that Dad not being there was not. I knew Mom couldn't stay a grieving widow forever, and I didn't want her to. It helped that he was a good man—a former cop—and the only kind of father-in-law my wife would ever know. In this life.

The candle glowed brightly. Logan, just weeks away from completing his mission, was still in the Philippines. McKay and Tyler served admirably as part of the wedding party. One hundred and fifty family and friends surrounded us, but one more would have been nice.

I wiped my tears and we turned around. The somber mood was interrupted by a loud *RIIIIIIP,* and I looked down to see where the sound came from. Under my feet was the hem of my new wife's dress, now with a big, fat, fraying hole in it. Scattered laughter rose up from the front rows. The pretty lady holding my hand looked up at me with initial horror and disbelief. Her beautiful, perfect white dress was no longer that. I apologized with my eyes, but she turned her face into a smile and laughed. "What are you gonna do?" she said quietly.

What are you gonna do? That's the question. That's always the question.

It's not an easy one to answer. Grief is such a swift punch in the gut. It takes us a little while to catch our breath and realize we can stand up again if we try. But loss is different. Loss remains and endures. It circles us. Hangs around and slaps us in the face when we least expect it. It can make life look like a series of calendar reminders. There's always some holiday or some anniversary coming up to force us to recall what's been lost.

I wish Dad had been around to see my brothers go off on their own missions and to see us all marry our wives. I think he would have liked them, and I know my wife would have loved him. I'm gonna go out on a limb and say that seeing Mom remarry wasn't something he would have wanted to be around for, but I'm pretty sure his threats of haunting her if she did so after he died were a joke.

I wish he had been there for the birth of my three daughters and for the day we found out one of them has special needs. Every time I've been knocked down, I've wished he was there to help me back up. It's not the most rational thought, I know. Dad threw his hands up at me as often as he was able to get through to me, but he's gone now. It's hard not to romanticize. It's the express privilege of those left behind to do so.

I wish Dad had been around for the TV show *Lost*. I think he really would have dug it. Sometimes, I think about the world that went on without him and what he would have made of it. I wonder if he'd have sold targets with Osama Bin Laden's face on them at the Shop. Probably. He did that with Saddam.

But . . . *What are you gonna do?*

About a year after the wedding, I took a college class on juvenile delinquency and crime, one of the more obscure classes that met the general ed. requirements. One day, we broke off into groups to discuss the effects crime has on its victims and the retribution so many of them seek. One woman, quite vocal, proudly proclaimed that if anyone killed—or even hurt—her brother or sister, she'd do whatever she could to see them pay.

She'd beat the hell out of them. Kill them? Sure. If someone touched her little sister, she wouldn't even hesitate. The others in our group nodded in agreement. I sat silently, waiting for my chance to speak. When it finally came, I tried to tread lightly.

"I think that's a trap. I don't think it's healthy for the victims to go after the person who's done them wrong. Honestly, that attitude really bothers me."

Angry Girl looked at me skeptically. "You don't think that would make you feel better? You don't think they should be punished?"

"Punished, sure. But not to make me feel better. Revenge, vengeance—all of that, it doesn't help. It makes your heart hard. People who cry for blood, they're giving what the criminals did even greater reach. They're extending their power. Why would I want to do that?"

"Oh, come on," Angry Girl said. "If someone killed someone you love, you'd be glad to see them dead. Their 'power' or whatever would be done. Over."

"No, honestly, that wouldn't make me happy at all. It wouldn't help me move on from what happened. That can only happen with forgiveness. Opposite of vengeance."

Angry Girl looked at me like I was self-righteous idiot. The rest of our group looked uncomfortable. "That's real easy for you to say," she said. "Until someone you love has been murdered, you don't know how you would react."

I couldn't help it. I smiled.

I told Angry Girl about Dad and how he died. I told her about his suspiciously peaceful attitude toward death and the first shooting—*yes, there were two shootings*. I talked about how my mission and my relationship with God enabled me to look at things like anger and vengeance in a different way. I told her I knew it was weird and not normal, but my circumstances had given me a different perspective and I'm grateful for that. I don't think I changed her mind or anything, but she didn't have much to say after that.

Even now, all these years later, when I think about Dad's killers and what they took from me and my family, I don't think badly of them. I don't think of them much at all. I didn't go to their trial because I couldn't see the point, and I couldn't fathom taking pleasure in their sentencing and suffering. I have sometimes fantasized about visiting them in prison. I'd like to let them know, *Hey, I'm okay.*

It was pretty awful what you did, I would say. *But me and my family are doing all right now. Even better; I've learned a lot. I reach out and empathize with others, and I look to God in a way I never would have otherwise. I don't want to say "thank you" or anything, but good things have come out of that particular bit of violence and death, and I can't deny that.*

Death and dying and injury and loss are not necessarily cheery subjects. But, I think death is glorious. I think suffering is glorious.

Not that I enjoy either one. They're heartbreaking. But, they work. If we let them, they can do wonderful things. Dad's death, like every death, was a gift. It served as his jumping off point, but also as a clear line from which I could jump forward. It crystallized my perceptions and made my reflections more acute and my paths straighter.

Of course, given the choice, I'd have Dad back in a second. Given the reality I have instead, I laugh and I smile. I find the good.

There's a lot of it.

ACKNOWLEDGMENTS

This book is, ostensibly, my work, but also the result of the kindness, effort, and faith of so many other people.

To those who read early versions of this, the first book I ever tried to write, and did not tell me to stick to grocery lists, I thank you: Natalie Rozier, Kasie West, Jared West, Ryan Hull, Amber Irwin, Judy Ryan, Kathryn Ryan, Travis Ryan, Pete Maskovich, Lynn Campbell, Chip Skelton, and others I don't mean to forget but probably did because I am fallible.

Thank you also to all those who read these chapters after I had given up on any hope of publication, encouraging me to give it one more try.

A big thank you to Angela Johnson, Wesley Wheeler, Kimiko Hammari, Heather Holm, and everyone at Cedar Fort Publishing for having the guts to put out a story like this with excitement and without reservation.

To Bonnie Solow, who saw something in me and in this book when no one else did and took it to the top of the New York skyscrapers, thank you for your counsel, your direction, and your faith. You have no idea what your mentorship meant to me and how much I still draw upon the insights you gave me and the lessons you taught me.

Thank you, Mom, for having the courage and generosity to tell me to write this story the way I remember it and to not worry about anything else, and then heartily approving it once you read it. Thank you as well for your example of strength and faith.

To my wife, Erin: this book just would not exist without your encouragement and endurance of the many long hours I sunk into it. When I could no longer believe in myself and my abilities, you did. And here we are. You were right, okay? You were right.

To my Father in Heaven, I give all thanks. I never fancied myself a writer until that night many years ago when you set me on the path to tell this specific story above all. Thank you for the inspiration and the guidance without which not a word of this book would be possible. I can only hope the result is satisfactory.

And to my earthly father who is gone from this world and now in a far grander one…

How could I ever forget you?

ABOUT THE AUTHOR

Brock Heasley is a writer, filmmaker, and artist. From 1996 through 1998, he served as a Spanish-speaking missionary for The Church of Jesus Chris of Latter-day Saints. (But he speaks terrible Spanish now. Really, it's embarrassing.)

A graduate from California State University, Fresno with a degree in graphic design, Brock is a former art director, the writer and illustrator of the YA novel *Paper Bag Mask* (which reached the top of Amazon's Young Adult Fiction New Release chart in the first week of publication), and the creator and writer of the comic *The SuperFogeys*. His writing has appeared in the *Independent Journal Review* and at ForEveryMom.com.

Brock is also a filmmaker. His debut short film, *The Shift*, earned him an Outstanding Filmmaker of the Year Award from the Hollywood Dreamz International Film Festival and is streamed on VidAngel. Brock's second short film, *The Two Hundred Fifth*, made its world premiere at the renowned Fantasia International Film Festival in Montreal.

Brock lives with his wife, three daughters, three dogs, and one cat in California. He didn't want a third dog, but his girls made a killer Power Point presentation and he didn't want to look like a jerk.